Sāṅkhya and Science

Sāṅkhya and Science

Applications of Vedic Philosophy to
Modern Science

Ashish Dalela

SHABDA
PRESS

Sāṅkhya and Science—Applications of Vedic Philosophy to Modern Science
by Ashish Dalela
www.ashishdalela.com

Published by Shabda Press
www.shabdapress.net
ISBN 978-81930523-0-3
v1.4 (07/2015)

*Dedicated to His Divine Grace A.C. Bhaktivedanta
Swami Prabhupāda, whose conviction that it was possible to
speak about mind, soul and God in a scientific manner changed
my outlook towards religion.*

The working senses are superior to dull matter; mind is higher than the senses; intelligence is higher than the mind; and he [the soul] is even higher than intelligence
—Bhagavad Gita (3.42)

Contents

List of Figures

Preface

The picture of reality in modern science contradicts the idea that we have minds which enjoy and choose. This contradiction creates a problem: Should we discard a science that gave us all the fancy technology or discard the idea that we 'enjoy' this technology? Most modern scientists believe that the current materialistic approach to matter has been so successful that it will eventually explain mind and consciousness. However, progress in this direction has been scant. While science has uncovered facts about the brain and biology, basic questions of meaning and choice remain elusive. In fact, these questions are so hard that a solution may eventually be impossible without discarding many fundamental assumptions in current science, and starting all over.

The thought of a reboot in science is scary, and most scientists entertain only incremental additions to current science. The incremental approach is further reinforced by the fact that attempts to explicitly add mind into science have not worked and they end up as pseudoscience, making no verifiable predictions or even theoretical revisions. Most scientists therefore view any alternative approach with suspicion.

But there are others who consider the problem of the mind serious enough to keep trying alternative approaches, no matter how different they might seem to current ideas and practices in science. As a reader of this book, it is possible that you belong to the latter group. This book presents an alternative approach to the study of matter based upon Vedic theories on matter. The Vedic approach is radically different from the approach taken in modern science vis-à-vis matter. While modern science attempts to derive consciousness from material objects, the Vedic philosophy describes the creation of objects from consciousness.

I came across Vedic philosophy about 20 years ago. At that time, I was quite surprised that philosophers who had no access to modern technology could have formed theories of material nature, and curious as to whether these theories would be of any relevance to modern science. It was likely, for instance, that there would be no empirical proof of these theories and we just might have to accept them based on faith. However, as I delved deeper into the fundamental assumptions underlying the modern and Vedic approaches to describing nature, it became clear to me that the Vedic approach can also be scientific in the modern sense of theory and experiment, although these two sciences had very different assumptions, theories and methods of doing experiments.

As I explored more, I found almost no serious scientific or philosophical study that connects the theories of material nature in Vedic philosophy to those in modern science, in a way that could shape the future development of modern science. Most of what I found was New Age books that lack the rigor and clarity which is necessary to actually do new science. These books might be useful for understanding alternative philosophical views of nature, but they are not adequate to solve scientific problems. This book tries to address that gap. It undertakes an analysis of the ideas in Vedic philosophy and what they mean for different fields of science, such as mathematics, physics, chemistry, biology, and neuroscience. The last chapter in this book discusses how these fields of science would change by the application of Vedic ideas.

Most of the discussion on Vedic philosophy currently happens in two broad contexts. First, there are the spiritualists who seek to understand Vedic theories and practices for spiritual gains; they delve into the mystical aspects of the philosophy and learn from spiritual masters the intricacies of what they consider to be the pursuit of truth, leading to the perfection of their lives. Second, there are the Indologists who analyze the historical evolution of Vedic ideas as part of Asian Studies departments in academic institutions; they view the ideas in Vedic texts to be of historical interest but not necessarily true. The spiritualists are generally unconcerned about what the academics write in their journals because for them spirituality is a living tradition to be learnt from an enlightened master and not from someone with an academic degree. The academics, similarly, are unconvinced that there is any truth to the Vedic texts. There is pity little being done today by way of connecting the theories in the Vedic texts to the developments in modern science. This book hopes to bridge that spiritual-academic divide.

The connection between Vedic ideas and science can happen only if one begins with the idea that there is indeed truth in the Vedic texts. To demonstrate that truth, it is imperative to connect the Vedic ideas to those in modern science as alternative tracks of scientific research. This is precisely the type of approach this book will undertake. To me, any alternative approach to the study of material nature is viable only if it can solve problems that modern science cannot. If Vedic philosophy describes nature in a different way, and these descriptions are true, then they must also be relevant to the solution of the currently unsolved problems in modern science. Specifically, I will not be discussing the historical evolution of Vedic ideas, who wrote what and when, whether Vedic ideas are ancient or recent, whether Vedic philosophers were natives of ancient India or whether they emigrated from elsewhere, etc.

My primary interest in this book is whether Vedic ideas are true, in the specific sense of modern scientific theory development and problem solving, because if they are true then it makes more sense to analyze the history of Vedic ideas as we would have a much clearer sense of importance attached to Vedic philosophy. If ideas in Vedic philosophy are not true, then studying the history of these ideas is only an academic curiosity, which may be interesting historically but not scientifically.

1

Introduction

Science can purify religion from error and superstition;
religion can purify science from idolatry and false absolutes.
Each can draw the other into a wider world, a world in which
both can flourish.

—Pope John Paul II

What Is Sāṅkhya?

Sāṅkhya is a Sanskrit word which means counting. Sāṅkhya is also a theory of nature, as it delineates a method for counting objects. To count objects, we must distinguish them from one another. Distinguishing involves the selection of concepts and categories in terms of which we will divide the world into distinct things. To enable the counting of objects, Sāṅkhya therefore presents a system of concepts and categories in terms of which we can divide the world into distinct things. Once the world has been divided, it can also be counted, and counting is a consequence of distinguishing. The system of categories and concepts described in Sāṅkhya forms an elaborate theory of material nature in Vedic philosophy. Vedic philosophy is somewhat unique (as compared to other traditional systems of thought that are generally called religious ideologies today) in the sense that it expends a tremendous amount of effort in detailing the nature of material reality. This reality is described as the concepts and categories that can and must be used for distinguishing. While other religious systems of thought focus almost exclusively on the nature of God, soul, afterlife and moral principles, Vedic thought also provides a very detailed picture of material nature.

1

The descriptions of material reality in Sāṅkhya are quite different from how matter is described in modern science. The contrast between Sāṅkhya and modern science presents interesting possibilities for a different understanding of material nature, and I will be discussing the philosophical differences between Sāṅkhya and modern science and the implications of these differences through the course of this book.

The basic idea behind Sāṅkhya philosophy is that prior to the creation of the universe, matter is undifferentiated—i.e. matter exists but is not individuated into objects. The process of creation differentiates primordial matter into objects—e.g., galaxies, planets, living beings and atoms. The system of categories and concepts described in Sāṅkhya represents the manner in which a primordial, undifferentiated matter is divided into individual objects. Ideally, the manner in which we divide the world into individual things should be just how the things exist in the world. Such an approach to dividing represents a *theory* of reality.

One important difference between Sāṅkhya and modern science is the types of things that they try to count. Modern science, for instance, only counts objects. In contrast, Sāṅkhya also counts different subjective aspects of the observers, such as senses, mind, intelligence, ego, consciousness and their experiences. The recognition of the subjective aspects of the observer as separate material categories irreducible to material objects represents a crucial point of difference between Sāṅkhya and modern science. This recognition leads to further differences in how material objects are described in the two views. In science, material objects are described independently of the existence of the observer (science believes that matter should be described as it exists even when no one observes it). In contrast, Sāṅkhya describes matter just as it is experienced by the observers. Thus, for instance, science describes matter in relation to other material objects such as a meter, clock, kilogram, etc. while Sāṅkhya describes matter in terms of how it is sensed, thought, judged, intended and enjoyed. This difference between Sāṅkhya and science results in radically different pictures of causality. While matter, in science, evolves due to mathematical laws regardless of any observer's choices, matter in Sāṅkhya is controlled by the observer's choices. In fact, the laws of nature in Sāṅkhya are laws of choices.

It is noteworthy that the subjective aspects of the observer mentioned above are also material, but of a different kind than the material objects current science studies. These are distinguished as subtle and gross matter, respectively. While modern science only acknowledges the existence of gross matter (that which can be seen, tasted, touched, smelt and heard), Sāṅkhya describes both subtle and gross matter (subtle matter comprises sensations, properties, conceptual objects, intentions and morals). Indeed, gross matter in Sāṅkhya is described in a way compatible with the existence of subtle matter. For instance, since the observer is capable of perceiving concepts in the world, material objects are described as symbols of meanings. Similarly, the intentionality of an object—e.g., that an object belongs to me—is an objective fact about that object, not merely a belief in my mind. Whether some action is morally right or wrong is an objective fact about that action, not just a socio-cultural opinion in our heads.

This point is crucial because it changes the theoretical approach to nature. Material objects in modern science are described in relation to other material objects. Material objects in Sāṅkhya are described in relation to the senses, mind, intellect, ego and consciousness of the observer. While modern science describes matter in terms of its physical properties such as mass, charge, momentum, energy, etc., Sāṅkhya describes matter in terms of its ability to encode sensations, properties, objects, intentions and morals, which are respectively perceived by the senses, mind, intelligence, ego and consciousness. Sāṅkhya therefore represents a radically different theory of nature, and its differences with modern science—and what these differences entail for modern science—constitute the main subject matter of this book.

Different theories of reality are different ways of dividing nature into distinct and countable parts. The results of such division may be true in some respect but they may fail to make some distinctions, and hence count fewer things than there really are. They may also assume distinctions that can never be made in reality, and hence count more things than actually exist. In other words, an erroneous theory of material nature will count either more or less objects than there really are. Such an erroneous theory of nature can be empirically falsified.

Sāṅkhya is a theory of nature that can be empirically tested. It draws some distinctions that are not well-known and obliterates other distinctions that are well-entrenched. For instance, Sāṅkhya distinguishes between various aspects of an observer's experience—namely senses, mind, intelligence, ego and consciousness which are generally lumped into a monolithic 'psyche' in Western philosophy. And Sāṅkhya does not distinguish between primary and secondary properties which is a foundational cornerstone of modern empiricism. Material objects, in this view, can be described in terms of the same words that we use to describe our experiences; for instance, apples can indeed be red.

By drawing more or less distinctions, nature is divided into greater or fewer parts and the number of distinctions that are employed in distinguishing things changes our theory of reality. Sāṅkhya impacts our view of reality by providing a different set of distinctions than are accepted in modern science. This difference is instructive and useful in many ways as we shall see in this book. A theory of nature fixes the properties *in terms of* which we will distinguish and count things. We need to fix the criteria by which something will be considered a single thing rather than an ensemble of things. We also need to fix the methods by which we will determine if two states in observation pertain to the same thing so that we can say that the *same* thing now has a new state. All these criteria constitute what we generally call a scientific theory in modern times. Such theories help us count, distinguish and identify objects. The term 'Sāṅkhya' is thus nearly synonymous with 'science'.

And yet, there are considerable differences in how the problem of counting things is approached in Sāṅkhya and in modern science. The key difference lies in what types of things we suppose can be counted. Should we count only atoms and subatomic particles, or also include everyday objects like tables and chairs? More importantly, does the list of countable things include sensations, concepts, theories, problems and ideologies? Indeed, how many types of countable things are there? Do all these things constitute *fundamental* types or are they derived from something more fundamental? As you can see, the problem of counting quickly leads to a debate about which types of things exist. How we decide what we are going to count changes how we approach methods of distinguishing. If, for example, we want to count concepts, then we must find a way of ordering them such they can be mapped to numbers. If, instead, we want to count physical objects, then we must find all the ways in which these objects can be distinguished by their properties.

The main difference between Sāṅkhya and modern science is that Sāṅkhya counts different *types* of things than modern science. While science counts physical states, Sāṅkhya counts sensations, properties, object concepts, intents and morals, in addition to physical states. Indeed, in Sāṅkhya, sensations, properties, object concepts, intents and morals are not reducible to physical states. This greatly increases the number of things to be counted. But, on the other hand, while we use different languages to describe matter and mind, Sāṅkhya describes matter in terms of the mind. This greatly reduces the total number of words required to describe reality.

The first order of business in Sāṅkhya is detailing out the types in terms of which everything else must be counted. The second problem in Sāṅkhya is how these fundamental types create other complex types through combination. Finally, Sāṅkhya speaks about how the different types of things are interconnected, and how numbers that distinguish objects are related to numbers that count sensations, properties, objects, intents and morals. By introducing different types of things to be counted, the problem of counting is defined as: (a) knowing the fundamental types, (b) knowing how these types create a variety of more complex types, and (c) knowing how various types are related.

Why Should We Study Sāṅkhya?

When people familiar with modern science will look at Sāṅkhya, they will most likely struggle with the typology. Why do we need so many types? Why can't we suppose that there is just one type of thing to be counted? This problem is so intuitive at the everyday level, and yet so hard in science, that I cannot do it justice in a few words here. But, in short, *if* there are indeed many types which we decide to count in terms of a fewer number of types, a few problems will most likely crop up.

First, the description will be indeterministic; there are more unique things to count, but we are counting them in terms of fewer unique ideas, and therefore many unique things must map to fewer unique ideas, thereby creating indeterminism. For instance, if we count cars, trucks and scooters using only two categories—say four-wheelers and two-wheelers—then both cars and trucks will be called four-wheelers thereby creating an indeterminism in the nature of four-wheelers.

Second, the description may be incomplete; in trying to reduce many unique things to fewer unique types of things, we will invariably miss out on adequately describing some unique features of things. For instance, if cars, trucks and scooters are called vehicles then some unique characteristics of these objects—such as the number of wheels they have—will be missing from the description, making it incomplete.

Third, we may end up in logical contradictions; for instance, the word 'car' can denote a concept (a general class of things) and a particular individual car (e.g., BMW). Unless we distinguish between the name and the type, applying attributes of the name—such as that a BMW has two front grilles—to the concept of the 'car' in general would imply that the meaning of the word 'car' is that it has two front grilles, which would contradict the definition of a car as provided by the other car vendors.

Indeterminism, incompleteness and paradoxes abound in modern science. The problems are also known to be fundamental, which means that a solution requires the addition or removal of some distinctions. There are at least two ways in which this shift can take place. First, we might say that we have been thinking of everything in terms of type X, but reality is of type Y which X imperfectly captures. Therefore, let's shift from X to Y. Second, we might say that X is real, but it insufficiently captures Y, so we need Y in addition to X. Regardless of which approach you think is better *a priori*, a study of Sāṅkhya illuminates this question. If you think the first approach is more conservative, and therefore better, the study of Sāṅkhya will help you see why there is more than one type of phenomena, although only one type of reality. If you already believe in the second approach, Sāṅkhya will help you see which types are fundamental and how they create complex types by combination.

Sāṅkhya is very relevant to modern science from the standpoint of the problems of indeterminism, incompleteness and logical contradiction that exist in nearly all fields of modern science. As described above, these problems can arise if the types (or categories) in terms of which science currently distinguishes things are different from the types in terms of which nature is actually differentiated. These problems can also arise if science lacks in some distinctions that exist in nature. The study of Sāṅkhya categories helps us understand how the problems of indeterminism, incompleteness and logical contradiction can be solved by incorporating a different set of categories and logical distinctions.

This book is written with the intention of describing how Sāṅkhya is relevant to the problems in modern science. People unfamiliar with Vedic philosophy, and more specifically Sāṅkhya, may find it a useful starting point, not only to be acquainted with a novel viewpoint but also to understand why, from that viewpoint, current science is inadequate. Scientists may find this book a useful description of alternatives to current approaches in science, and they could understand how the alternative approaches solve the problems that are unsolved in current science. My attempt at linking modern science and Sāṅkhya aims to show that Sāṅkhya is a system of knowledge that is relevant to contemporary problems, specifically as they appear in modern science. The study of Sāṅkhya illuminates these problems and shows a path forward. The last chapter in this book is devoted to connecting ideas in Sāṅkhya to those in modern science, not in the sense of seeing a "parallel" between the two, but as strategic alternative tracks for future scientific research.

Attempts to connect modern science and Eastern philosophy are not new. These attempts in the past have, however, not really worked because they only aimed to show some parallels between science and Eastern philosophy. Apart from reinterpreting the mathematics in science as entailing a philosophical outlook that is different from the widespread materialism of modern science, these approaches did not contribute anything substantial to science itself. Over time, parallelism becomes useless because we cannot extend the parallel to develop or identify new insights about the nature of reality. This book will steer clear of attempts to see parallels between Sāṅkhya and modern science. Sāṅkhya and modern science are chalk and cheese; there is very little if anything common in these two approaches as far as their *theories* are concerned. Nevertheless, they obviously deal with the same experience. I personally, therefore, find it interesting that the same experience is described in radically different ways in these two approaches. This difference can help us see why solving some unsolved problems in current science requires not just incremental adjustments to current ideas, but may warrant a radical shift from one type of ideology to another.

Which Sāṅkhya?

Most people who speak of Sāṅkhya philosophy today attribute it to an Indian philosopher called Ishwar Krishna, based on his work entitled *Sāṅkhya-karikā* from approximately 3rd century AD. This Sāṅkhya is similar in some respects to the more traditional Sāṅkhya described in the *Upanishads* and *Puranās*, and especially in the *Śrimad Bhāgavatām*. But the newer Sāṅkhya also neglects many aspects of the original Sāṅkhya such as the role of God, Time and *karma* in the creation. Indeed, the modern Sāṅkhya recognizes only two broad categories—the puruṣa and the prakṛti—or the observer and the observed (matter), while neglecting the causal role that our actions (*karma*), Time and God play in the universe. This approach, as we shall see later on, is incomplete because karma and Time play a very important role in the causal explanation of changes within the universe. Therefore, when I speak about Sāṅkhya in this book, I will be referring to the more traditional Sāṅkhya, especially as described by the sage Kapila in the *Śrimad Bhāgavatām*.

It is also important to briefly understand the relation between Vedic philosophy and Sāṅkhya. The Vedas present a system of knowledge (Veda means "to know") that spans many aspects of material and spiritual experiences. Some of the material aspects of the Vedas are actively practiced in many parts of the world today. Examples include *Ayurveda* as alternative medicine, *Vāstu-Shāstra* as architecture and interior design, *Ashtānga-Yoga* and *Prāṇayāma* as health and healing techniques, and *Hora-Shāstra* or astrology as predictive and life planning tools.

Those who have benefitted from these forms of knowledge in the past are often curious to understand the concepts underlying their practices. This is especially true of those who have benefitted from more than one of the above practices; they find that there are common themes and concepts used in all of them, reinforcing these themes and concepts from different perspectives. But, given that these ideas reappear in many different contexts, is there a systematic core set of ideas that underlie their diverse applications? Indeed, there is, and it is called *Sāṅkhya*. In a sense, Sāṅkhya pervades all of Vedic philosophy and touches upon every type of mystical and mundane activity. Sāṅkhya is a theory of material nature, but its descriptions can also help one understand the nature of mysticism. While Vedic philosophy deals with mystical and spiritual aspects, and by many counts mysticism is the primary aim of Vedic philosophy, in this book, by "Vedic philosophy" I mean the theory of matter that forms the foundation of its myriad practices.

What Does Sāṅkhya Mean for Science?

Sāṅkhya espouses a view of matter in which the properties of observers are represented or reflected into matter. Current science is based upon one such aspect of the observer—the ability to have sensations. The idea of physical properties in science is based upon a refinement of the idea of sensations, and every physical property must lead to sensations, for science to be empirical. Physical properties in Sāṅkhya are therefore objective representations of the sensations[1]. However, the properties of the observer do not end with sensation. Beyond sensations are properties in the mind, concepts in the intelligence, intentions in the ego, and morality in consciousness. In Sāṅkhya, the senses perceive sensations (e.g., yellow and red), the mind perceives properties (e.g., that yellow and red are of the type color), the intelligence combines properties and perceives objects (e.g., that the white thing in question is a white flag), the ego perceives intentions (e.g., a person who holds and waves a white flag in his hand desires peace) and consciousness perceives morals (e.g., peace is a morally good thing). Each of these perception faculties is also capable of creating the perceived objects. For instance, the senses can create sensations (e.g., during dreams), the mind can create properties (quite like modern science invents properties like mass and charge, which cannot be directly perceived; mass for instance depends on gravity which in turn depends on mass), the intelligence can create objects (e.g., by combing properties to create technological products), the ego can create intentions (e.g., a specific kind of use of the created product like a knife can be used to cut, scrape, pierce, etc.) and consciousness can create new types of morals (e.g., that a specific use of an object constitutes a morally right action). The sensual faculties in the observer are therefore both creators and consumers of meanings. Each such perceived type of meaning can be represented in matter, and through such representation the perceived meanings can be attributed back to reality. The representation of these meanings creates new properties in matter, which could potentially be described by newer scientific theories.

Like current science postulates physical properties corresponding to sensations which are perceived by the senses (eyes, nose, ear, skin and tongue), the Vedic tiered view of the observer indicates that there are additional properties in matter that correspond to the perceptive capabilities in the mind, intelligence, ego and consciousness. As modern science was developed based on sensations, future sciences can be developed based on mind, intelligence, ego and consciousness. Specifically, the science solely based on sensations is incomplete because the observer has additional properties that are reflected within matter.

However, before this broader approach to science can be understood, there is one fundamental issue whose solution is essential before we can talk of perceiving matter though mind, intelligence, ego and consciousness. The most basic problem in science is that science does not even accept that properties experienced by the senses are actually represented in matter. In science, matter is described in relation to material objects, not in relation to the observer's senses, because science hypothesizes that the properties in objects are different from how we perceive these objects. For instance, science postulates that matter has mass and charge, which appear to us as color and taste; therefore, mass and charge are real properties of matter, but color and taste are not. Of course, science maps the objective world to our world of experience through experiments. But this mapping of reality to experience pertains to a very small subset of experience—pointer movements or detector clicks—and through this mapping, science tries to prove that reality is mass and charge, and not color and taste. How mass and charge are experienced as color and taste requires another explanation, which now becomes a problem for the neurologist. Despite great successes in describing physical states in material objects, there is still no theory that explains how physical states lead to experiences in the observers.

A new interdisciplinary field of study—called cognitive science or consciousness studies—has recently emerged, which aims to bring together a wide array of scientific disciplines to explain how physical states lead to experience. In other words, whilst objects have so far been successfully described in relation to other objects, how these objects create experience must be explained in terms of physical theories. This approach to the study of the mind carries forward a very fundamental distinction between primary properties (like length, mass and charge) and secondary properties (like color, taste and smell) which was used by early empiricists to give a firm philosophical grounding to science.

The distinction arose because of the recognition that what we experience may not be reality (that we might be hallucinating) so there must be a difference between reality and the observer's experience. Empiricists now *chose* to describe matter in relation to other material objects, using primary rather than secondary properties. This approach to science took away the ability to say that *sometimes* our experiences do correspond to reality and what we experience may in fact be about reality. By insisting that length, mass and charge are real but color, taste and smell are not, every claim that applies our knowledge gained through senses back to reality becomes false. For instance, we cannot say that roses are red, the sunset is orange or apples are sweet. Rather, we must say that all matter is comprised of atoms and molecules, that have mass and charge, but they *appear* to us as color, taste or smell. The notion that roses are in fact red is today derided as *naïve* realism.

Once you decide that matter does not have color and taste, all successive notions of reality based upon the reality of sensations must also be discarded. For instance, imagine that someone in distress is waving a white flag. There are various ways in which this simple fact is described in ordinary language, all of which are falsified if sensations are not real. For instance, if the sensation of color is unreal this implies that the concept of white—which is a color—must also be unreal. If the concept of white is not real, then the idea that white denotes peace must also be unreal. The idea that there are real things called white flags must also be unreal because the flag is only a combination of sensations and concepts (the sensation of a cloth fluttering in the air and the concept of a country). Someone's intentions—e.g., that they want peace by waving a white flag—must be unreal because the concept of peace is already unreal. The idea that desire for peace is a morally good intention also becomes false because desiring itself is an illusion. The entire everyday linguistic edifice collapses, simply because we cannot assert that color and taste are real. How can science then explain experience if everything in experience is false? Science must conclude that all experience is an epiphenomenon of physical interactions. That we imagine we know the world as smell and taste but there is no such thing as smell and taste; that we imagine that we have choices and emotions, but these are simply not real. The task of explaining experience in terms of physical interactions in science must conclude that all experience is ultimately an illusion.

To avoid this conclusion, science needs a new view of reality. In this view, it should be possible to say that—at least sometimes—when I experience red, the experience is telling me something about the nature of reality. That my experiences of sight, taste, sound, touch and smell can, in principle, be accurate descriptions of nature. In other words, that nature can in principle be described in terms of smells, tastes and sights, rather than just in terms of mass, energy or charge. This in turn opens science to many levels of descriptions—sensual properties such as color, form, flavor, and odor, everyday concepts such as table, chair, car and house, intents such as how an observer interprets the world, and morals such as whether these interpretations are right or wrong. There can now be sciences that observe matter not just through senses, but also through mind, intelligence, ego and consciousness. If the observations of the senses produce illusions, then the experiences of mind, intelligence, ego and consciousness will also always be illusions. But if senses are sources of truth about reality then other experiences could also be real. The need for epistemology—the method by which we separate knowledge from illusions—still exists because even the mind or intelligence can come under illusions. However, illusions do not preclude the possibility that the perceptions of the senses or the mind are—at least sometimes—true and that nature can and should be always described in the *language* of perceptions. If the apple is green instead of red, we will still be using the language of perceptions, although a different part of the perceptual language (green vs. red). If, however, perceptions are always false then we must only describe matter in relation to other objects and not to the observers.

This view of the observer, described within Sāṅkhya, is different than the idea of the observer widely used in current science. In science, the observer's consciousness is the *phenomena* waiting to be explained in terms of physical or chemical properties in matter. In Sāṅkhya, matter is the phenomena waiting to be understood in terms of the observer's faculties. Everything that the observer experiences can be potentially real and the observer's experiences reflect his conscious abilities into matter. The study of senses, mind, intelligence, ego and consciousness is therefore the study of different properties that can exist in matter and matter can potentially be described just as the observer experiences it.

To see the relevance of this idea to science, think of how we describe everyday behaviors—such as a person's laughter—using concepts about their mental states. When we see someone laughing, we generally conclude that they are happy. We don't say that they just appear to be happy, while there is no such thing called happiness. Of course, the person may not truly be happy and they may be feigning a happy look. But, potentially, there is room for allowing the fact that when a person looks happy, they are in fact happy. In concluding that someone is happy, we rely on knowledge about their bodily states, not firsthand acquaintance with their personal experience of happiness. For us to know about their mental state of happiness, signs of happiness must be physically present in the body, and accesible through observation. But we explain the bodily signs of happiness by a theory of the mind. Everyday explanations of behavior use a theory about the mind—namely that people can be happy or sad, angry or motivated. This is important for science because it tells us that material phenomena can also be explained on the basis of ideas about the mind. It does not reduce the experience of happiness to matter, although it makes happiness a useful *concept* in terms of which to explain observations scientifically. If the concept is found useful in making predictions, then it is real. Such a successful theory would reinstate the idea that happiness is real.

Developments in neuroscience and biology have already shown that observer reports of mental experiences have empirically observable counterparts. Many scientists therefore conclude that the mind is reducible to matter, without in fact carrying out that reduction. It is more likely that the mind is distinct from the body, although states of mind are somehow represented in the body and can be used to explain the body. The main problem in allowing this view today is that the mind and the body are described using two different *languages*. The language of science and the language of experience have gone so far apart that this in turn has created the mind-body divide. If matter were described using the same words as experience, the interaction problem would not arise. Mind and body would now be two different *models* of the same language. This is already seen in everyday experiences where happiness is not identical with the bodily state but the same word—happiness—applies to both the mental experience and the physical state. An explanation of the bodily state now requires a theory of the mind. This theory of the mind is a useful view of the mind, but it is also a valuable scientific theory in terms of which phenomena in matter can be explained.

This is a radical conception about the mind and its relevance to science—not as a study of the mind, but as a study of matter itself. Everyday intuitions and scientific experiments both tell us that experiences have physical counterparts. Everything an observer experiences can be known by others through observation, although the experience and reality are different. In Sāṅkhya, the observer has many facets which are called senses, mind, intelligence, ego and consciousness. Senses perceive sight, taste, smell, sound and touch, and because knowledge from senses is potentially real, sight, taste, touch and smell are potentially real properties in matter. Similarly, because the mind experiences properties like color, form, size, distance, direction and luminosity (which are created by dividing sight), these properties are real. Since the intelligence combines concepts into objects, the objects are also real. Since the ego creates intentions, potentially intentionality is also real. Since consciousness experiences morals and happiness, potentially morals and happiness are also real.

Note that I'm not claiming that sensations, properties, objects, intentions and morals should be reduced to matter. I'm only claiming that it is possible to use the same *language* to describe experience and matter. This means that—(a) experiences are true, and (b) matter has properties that are known by experience. Concepts about matter can thus be drawn from how the observer perceives this matter. If senses, mind, intelligence, ego and consciousness generate different kinds of experiences, and these experiences can potentially be true, then there are additional properties in matter that can be useful in explaining observations. The predictive successes of theories that incorporate such new properties will make these properties real in a scientific sense.

In Sāṅkhya, consciousness and matter are distinct types of entities but they can hold the same *information*. Information exists in consciousness as experience and it exists in matter as objectified symbol-tokens of that conscious state. When consciousness knows material objects, it possesses information that earlier existed in matter. When consciousness creates material objects then matter possesses information that earlier existed in consciousness. The interaction between consciousness and matter is mediated by information which potentially straddles both subjective and objective worlds. A symbol can be experienced as meaning and it can be objectified as a token. For instance, the word 'tree' is a physical token with some shape and phonetic sound. But this token also represents the concept of a tree. The experience of the concept is different from the physical properties of the token itself, but the token denotes the concept. Matter can therefore be described in terms of meanings, although matter itself is not the experience of meanings. Experiences of meanings are created when matter is perceived by mind, intelligence, ego and consciousness just as sensations are produced when matter is perceived by the senses. Accordingly, the same material reality can be described in new ways, each time treating it as a token of some kind of meaning or sensation. This leads to a new approach to science, and consequently to new theories about matter.

Can Ancient Philosophy Be Useful in Science?

Most people today will be averse to the idea that there could be any scientific content in the Vedic texts written thousands of years ago. Science, in their view, is a recent phenomenon created after great struggle to understand nature based on reason instead of faith. To these skeptics, I can offer two thoughts. The first is that the Vedic 'science' is unlike anything that we consider science today; there is nothing called quantum theory, relativity, electromagnetism or gravity in the Vedas, and I'm not about to claim that Vedic seers had formulated these theories thousands of years ago, or envision parallels between these two worldviews. In fact, I believe that there are very few parallels between these two sciences, and even where the parallels exist, we need a deeper appreciation of the key concepts underlying Vedic science, to even recognize these parallels. Second, current science describes reality in terms of the properties of some standard objects, such as kilogram, clock and meter. Vedic science describes the same reality in terms of the perceptions of the observer. The goal in this book is to show that nature can be described in a different way, compatible with the existence of the mind, and that we are mistaken in believing that modern science is the only possible approach to studying nature. The Vedas describe nature in a radically different way, and constitute a different type of 'science'.

Unlike past attempts to connect science with mysticism that dwell on the similarity between the two, this book dwells on the differences between modern and Vedic science. The mystical aspects of Vedic philosophy are based on a profound understanding of the senses, mind, intelligence, ego and consciousness in the observer. These aspects cannot be understood in current science because matter is presently disconnected from the observer. The connection between science and mysticism has to begin with the idea that if matter were not disconnected from the observer, it would then be described in a different manner. It is impossible to build interactions between mind and matter when each of these is defined independently of the other. The description of matter compatible with the existence of the observer would lead to a new kind of science, with different predictions. When the new description of matter has been empirically ratified, there will be a justification for extending its understanding of matter into an understanding of the observer. At that point, it will be possible to understand mystical aspects of the observer based on the confirmation of new properties in material objects. For instance, whether intentions have real effects in nature can be confirmed only when intentions are seen as objective properties in nature. Likewise, whether some action has moral consequences can be understood only if the morality of that action can be objectively defined.

There is hence a real connection between science and mysticism although it is premature to talk about that connection based on the current material theories of nature. This book delineates a new view of matter, before connecting it to mysticism. In that specific sense, the book thus lies squarely in the science-and-mysticism genre although I do not intend to use the prestige of science to further a mystical philosophy. I intend to clarify the conceptual foundations in Vedic philosophy using which both its material and mystical ideas can be better understood by scientists and non-scientists alike. Those who already subscribe to the Vedic ideas will be able to see the scientific implications of their beliefs. Those who are not familiar with Vedic philosophy will at least find a systematic description of esoteric Vedic ideas which might hopefully bring them closer to taking up a serious study of these ideas in the future. The study of Vedic science is useful because it tells us that there is much more to matter than modern science currently would like to acknowledge. By developing insights about the observer, we can describe matter in a new way. Just as the sensual confirmation of current scientific theories makes us believe in the reality of physical properties, the usefulness of other aspects of the observer in forming theories of nature may convince us about other kinds of realities as well.

Can We Measure the Soul?

The conventional wisdom on the study of the observer is that if there were a scientific theory of the observer, its effects would only be known to a specific observer in a first-person manner. That doesn't work too well for science, because scientists would like to agree on the outcomes in a third-person manner. Scientists ask: If the soul exists, can you *show* it to me? Sāṅkhya makes it possible to 'show' the existence of the soul in the same way that current physics 'shows' the existence of electrons.

However, to understand how Sāṅkhya shows the existence of the soul, we must first understand how modern science shows the existence of electrons. Many commonplace descriptions of science miss the point about how scientific concepts are proved. Philosophers of science recognize the fact that scientific concepts are never experienced although they can be known. Scientific concepts—such as the electron—always remain theoretical constructs in science although scientific theories allow us to predict the effects of their existence on ordinary sensations (such as taste, smell, sound, touch and sight). The confirmation of these predictions therefore allows us to believe in the existence of the electron although the electron is never directly observed. In the same way, the existence of mind, intelligence, ego and consciousness can be *known* from the effects their existence has on sensible properties like taste, touch, smell, sight and sound. But mind, intelligence, ego and consciousness cannot be *experienced* by taste, touch, smell, sound and sight.

In Sāṅkhya, the senses experience the objects, the mind experiences the senses, the intellect experiences the mind, the ego experiences the intellect, the moral sense experiences the ego, and the consciousness experiences the moral sense. There isn't therefore a single 'sense'; there are many of them, which experience different 'objects.' This idea can be illustrated through an example as follows. The sense of seeing experiences forms such as square, circle, triangle etc., colors such as yellow, red, blue, etc., and directions such as up, down, before, after, etc. However, the sense of seeing itself does not experience form, color or direction; for this, the mind is necessary. The mind is said to 'control' the senses because it comprehends the senses as objects—the mind can see the senses as *properties* like sight, taste, smell, sound and touch, and their subdivisions such as color, form, size, luminosity, distance, etc.

However, the perception of properties itself does not suffice, because a combination of properties constitute an *object*. Objects are conceptual too; for instance, tables, chairs, computers and houses are conceptual objects; they combine a set of properties which are then refined through sensations. Objects are comprehended by the intelligence, quite like properties are comprehended by the mind and sensations by the five senses. An ordinary physical entity, however, can be interpreted as many different objects. For instance, a hammer can be interpreted as a tool or a weapon, depending upon the *intentions* of the user. Each object therefore becomes a different conceptual object in relation to a user, and this conceptual interpretation depends on the user's *intention*. The intentional relation to an object is comprehended by the sense called ego in Sāṅkhya and it represents the manner in which we desire to interpret the world for our purposes. These interpretations may be right or wrong, and that judgment is perceived by a moral sense called *mahattattva*. The object in each of these perceptions is the same; however, that object is perceived variously by the different kinds of senses.

The tiered view of reality in Sāṅkhya presents a theoretical problem: if the senses perceive objects, the mind perceives the senses, the intellect perceives the mind, the ego perceives the intellect and the moral sense perceives the ego, then when does this hierarchy of perception end? Is the observer an infinitely deep tiered entity? Or does this hierarchy ultimately end? The Sāṅkhya response to this problem is that the hierarchy ends in something that perceives itself: that entity is consciousness or the soul. The mystery of the observer can therefore never be solved in a scientific *theory* unless that theory postulates the soul because the theory—if it explains the senses, mind, intellect, ego and morality—would be infinitely incomplete without the idea of a soul.

The theory of the observer can only be completed with the postulate of a soul—i.e., an entity that perceives itself. Furthermore, such an entity cannot be materially conceived because all material entities—objects, senses, mind, intellect, ego and moral sense—can only perceive other material entities and not themselves. Therefore, when such a theory of an observer is formed, and the theory is empirically validated, the theory will also theoretically confirm the existence of the soul, quite like modern scientific theories confirm the existence of an electron, even though we can never observe the electron directly by the senses.

Willard Quine formulated a now famous view of the scientific theory called *underdetermination* in which science is a collection of concepts which touches the world of experience only at the periphery. The ideas at the core of the system are never empirically confirmed, although they are ratified by the empirical successes of the theory that uses them.

The idea of a soul is an idea that lies at the core of the Sāṅkhya system, while objects lie at the periphery. A complete theory requires the postulate of a soul, although the soul can never be seen, tasted, touched, smelt, or heard. However, this fact is not unique to the soul but applies even to the experiences of the other senses more subtle than the eye, ear, skin, tongue and nose. Quite like the soul, we also cannot see the mind, intellect, ego, or morality. However, they are *theoretical* necessities in a complete theory of the observer, if that theory has to explain the experiences of properties, objects, intents and morals. These are therefore farther from the periphery although not quite the core.

The existence of sweetness therefore does not tell us whether this pertains to smell or taste; the existence of roughness doesn't itself indicate whether it pertains to the quality of sound or the quality of touch. The study of *synesthetic* people—those who can see color while they hear sounds, or have tactile sensations when they hear sounds—confirms the idea that the world exists as properties such as roughness and sweetness, although these cannot be called sensations because roughness underdetermines touch versus sound, and sweetness underdetermines taste versus smell. The world of physical states too has to be defined differently—e.g., as roughness and sweetness—rather than as current physical states. These states become sensations when they come in contact with the senses, so a sense is necessary to make matter into a sensation, although the world is objectively sweet or rough. The sweetness or roughness prior to sensation is different from the experience of sensation, and sensation overcomes the underdetermination of sweetness or roughness creating the sensation of smell or touch.

Synesthetic individuals have a much more vivid experience of this phenomenon because they can perceive the same thing in more ways than one, although even others can understand why the same material state—if it exists as sweetness or roughness—could be perceived differently. Similarly, the properties like smell and touch underdetermine the conceptual object; for instance, the fact that something has a square form doesn't itself indicate that it is a table. The conceptual nature of the object—e.g., that it is a hammer—doesn't determine whether it is used as a tool or weapon. And the use of a weapon itself doesn't determine whether the act of using is morally right or wrong.

These common observations are important because they indicate why a theory that relies on physical states would be incomplete without the senses, the theory of senses would be incomplete without the mind, the theory of the mind would be incomplete without the intellect, the theory of intellect would be incomplete without the ego, the theory of ego would be incomplete without the moral sense, and the theory of the moral sense would be incomplete without a sense that perceives itself—i.e. consciousness.

The soul and consciousness are—in this view—one and the same. As a sense that perceives, it is called consciousness, and as the object that is perceived by this sense, the same thing is also called the soul.

The soul is theoretically necessary because otherwise the theory will involve an infinite regress of cascading senses, and can therefore never be conceived. The soul is empirically necessary because successive theories of objects, senses, mind, intellect, ego and moral sense would only predict the experiences to a greater and greater level of accuracy but never completely. Ultimately, the soul becomes necessary because there can be more than one morally correct choice and which alternative is selected cannot be explained except in reference to something that chooses due to its innate and non-material personality.

The effect of a soul can therefore be empirically measured through its choices—when the choices are morally correct. I have separately shown in the book *Moral Materialism* that morally incorrect choices are not caused by the soul, but enforced by a very subtle level of matter—called *māya*—which distorts the soul's free will into wrong choices; *māya* works deterministically under the control of time, and under its influence to the soul is forced to do things that are outside its control. True free will is therefore not seen in the majority of the actions perceivable in the material world; they can only be observed in those individuals who reject the effect of *māya* and act outside the control of time.

The short answer to the question: "Can you show me the soul?" is therefore that it is possible in Sāṅkhya philosophy to show the existence of the soul by forming a theory that predicts and explains the effects of the soul on ordinary sensations. However, this proof of the soul would only be measurable for those souls which are liberated from the effects of material conditioning. Furthermore, this confirmation of the soul would constitute the *knowledge* of the soul and not its *experience*. Similar to how we can presently know the electron but not experience it, the soul can only be known in the current state of perceptual development. By observing the person liberated from the influence of *māya* one can become theoretically convinced about the existence of the soul. The practical experience of the soul, however, requires perceptual development. The soul produces choices which are in turn magnified into morals, intentions, objects, properties and things. The effects of choices are therefore measurable in things, although not every soul and not every thing represents the actions of the soul. In Vedic philosophy, the distinction between knowledge and experience is called *jñāna* and *vijñāna*. The term *jñāna* represents theoretical conceptual knowledge of reality similar to how we currently conceive of the electrons or can theoretically describe the soul but we cannot directly perceive them. The term *vijñāna* on the other hand represents the direct experience of reality[2]. Of course, before we can experience subtle forms of reality, we must theoretically know about them. In that sense, *vijñāna* of subtle reality requires the prior development of *jñāna*. Sāṅkhya philosophy illustrates how modern science can provide a sensation-based empirical theory of the soul—i.e. *jñāna*—before we pursue the soul-experience or *vijñāna*.

Gross and Subtle Matter

Perhaps the easiest way to understand the difference between Sāṅkhya and modern science is that science recognizes only one type of matter while Sāṅkhya recognizes two kinds of matter—subtle and gross. The subtle matter in Sāṅkhya comprises the senses which produce and consume information while gross matter comprises the elements which constitute information. The senses of the observer are therefore senders and receivers of information and gross matter is the information transmitted. Information in gross matter appears as structure and function which is generally described as 'order'. The senses create and destroy this order. While the order is objective and empirical, it is not *objects*. Rather, objects are produced from the objective information. This order appears as *relations* between objects and these relations are expressed as space-time organization of the objects. Therefore, while current science treats the space-time locations and directions of objects as physical properties, Sāṅkhya treats these properties as information.

In modern science, the universe is *a priori* real objects which acquire different locations and instances in space-time due to the forces of nature. In Sāṅkhya, the objects are not *a priori* real—they are instead produced when information is added to space and time. Information is described differently in Sāṅkhya as compared to science. For instance, a single electron's spin can encode a single bit of information in current science and information is viewed as the states of all the individual objects. In Sāṅkhya, all information is defined through relations and distinctions, so at least two objects are needed to represent a binary distinction. The objects thus produced by the addition of information to space and time are not independent things, as in current science. They are rather symbols of information whose meaning is given through the relations between symbols. An ensemble of objects collectively becomes a representation of meaning, not individual objects independently.

Thus, in modern science, objects are the primary reality and information is the epiphenomena of their states. In Sāṅkhya, information is the primary reality and objects are epiphenomena of its expression into space-time (the expression produces objects). Therefore, the causality in Sāṅkhya is not based on the physical properties of independent objects. It is rather based on the laws of information combining and the consequences of this combination. This description of nature is also objective and empirical but it has very different conceptual foundations.

Now, some readers may be wondering what value this new type of description brings when science is already quite successful in describing nature. The short answer to this question is that while science has been successful in describing nature, it is still incomplete. Problems if incompleteness, indeterminism, inconsistency and incomputability abound in science; they appear in all fields including mathematics, physics, chemistry, biology, neuroscience, linguistics and computing. It is not difficult to see that *if* material objects are symbols of meaning then they would be incompletely described by physical theories. This is because if we know the meaning then we can completely predict the physical properties but if we only know the physical properties then we cannot completely predict the meanings. Meanings are underdetermined by physical properties although physical properties are completely determined by meanings. The incompleteness of science can be viewed as an outcome of this underdetermination of meanings by physical properties (science is trying to describe a world of meanings in terms of physical properties and thereby failing to predict the meanings). Thus, *if* material objects are symbols of meaning, then the incompleteness in current science can be fixed by shifting from a physical to an informational view.

The informational viewpoint will also resolve issues concerning the nature of the mind and concepts, the hard problem of perceptual qualities, intentions and the problems concerning choice and morality. The idea that there are two kinds of matter—gross and subtle—therefore presents an alternative path of scientific evolution, with *prima facie* the promise of not just fixing the problems in current science but also widening its scope to bring the observer within rational inquiry.

This book undertakes an analysis of the philosophical and conceptual differences between Sāṅkhya and science and what these differences could mean for the evolution of science. When Descartes framed the mind-body divide, he aimed to keep the mind out of science, apparently to avoid the conflict with the Church. The subsequent evolution of science has been very successful in describing matter, but that success has come at a great cost—the incompleteness of scientific theories and the exclusion of mind from science. While there is resistance to change the materialistic ideology in science today, it is noteworthy that the inclusion of the mind into science can also be done via a naturalistic theory. This theory will be broader and more complete, but it will involve radically different concepts and natural laws than current science allows.

2

A Different Kind of Science

The important thing in science is not so much to obtain new facts as to discover new ways of thinking about them.
—*William Lawrence Bragg*

Empiricism, Objectivity and Reductionism

Modern science is founded on three key ideas: (a) sense experience is the only way by which we can test our theories about nature, (b) behind these sense experiences are material objects that cause the sense experiences, and (c) all material objects are built out of elementary particles that can be described mathematically, and everything is produced from these particles. Science has been successful in applying these three principles to describe a variety of phenomena using mathematical theories. But are these ideas correct? Let's first examine them in greater detail.

Science believes that the best way to test the truth of a claim is through sense experience, namely sound, taste, touch, sight and smell. This idea is called Empiricism and it arose because of the need to separate things that we find meaningful from the things that are true. Different ideas appeal to different people, but science can only work with things that are true. Sense experience helps us verify if what we regard as meaningful is also true, and that is a way of stepping outside our human biases to find the nature of reality. Sense experiences put us in a shared rather than a private world of experience. Of course, sense experience gives us the sensations of colors, tastes, smells, sounds and touch, which are still a human way of knowing the world. Is science just a human criterion for truth, or something that transcends our humanity?

Scientists do not believe that sensations are anything other than our human way of knowing the world, although scientists also claim that we are constrained to know the world through these human methods of observation. And yet science aims to transcend these human methods of observation. Therefore, while sense experiences give us the ability to validate truths, science aims to find what lies 'behind' these experiences, and transcends our human ways of knowing, to get to some reality that exists prior to our knowing it. But what is this reality?

This leads us to the second key idea in science which is that reality is ultimately objects, which are individuated and real independent of our methods of observation. Philosophers have debated the meaning of the word 'object' and Descartes defined it as something that has a definite position in space. Objects can have other properties besides position, and the world is built out of things which have different physical properties that *appear* to us as sound, taste, touch, smell and color. But science claims that rather than studying sensations themselves we must study the properties behind these sensations, which is how nature exists prior to being sensed by us. The key idea here is that the way nature exists is different from how we experience it, so science must attempt to describe how nature really exists rather than how it appears to us.

But how do we go about describing how nature exists prior to our sensing it? How can we get behind the sensations if the only thing that we can perceive is sensations? The short answer is creativity, but not just any type of creativity. Creativity in science is the search for the simplest, most elementary ideas. Science assumes that all objects are ultimately built out of very simple parts that combine in various ways to form complex things. Belief in the simplicity of nature is a premise that has been useful in formulating theories and it is a good working hypothesis about nature. Thus, sensations are not reality because they only represent our human way of knowing reality. The objects behind these sensations are also not real because these objects are complex combinations of more elementary things. Reality is the most elementary things. This idea is also called Reductionism and represents a method by which we attempt to reduce the complexity to elementary constructs until they appear very simple to us. And this endeavor requires lots of creativity.

Note how the practice of science depends on our ability to observe the world through senses, on our ability to imagine what might lie behind these sensations, and upon our creativity in finding the logically simplest ideas that can be used to explain the sensations. But science keeps the processes of observing, imagining and creating outside of its theories. Even though science depends on many human processes—which don't have a scientific explanation—this dependence is not explicitly acknowledged in science. In a sense, the scientist as a human is outside the world that he or she aims to describe. The scientist observes the world dispassionately, thinks scrupulously and creates theories with honest intentions, but we cannot talk about passion, honesty and integrity as something science needs to define or explain. At the very least, these notions cannot be easily reduced to states of physical objects.

We are living in an age of a mind-body divide where science depends on the mind to form theories of nature, but that mind has no explicit role in the world or within scientific theories of nature. Immense successes in describing material objects independent of the mind have created a paradox in science: How will we describe the mind—that creates science—using science itself? The main premise today is that *given* science has been successful in explaining and predicting the nature of reality so far, it will also be successful in explaining the mind using the same assumptions that have worked thus far. Is this premise correct?

The Problem of the Observer

Observers too have a material body that can be measured and known like other material phenomena in science. But humans also have a private world of meanings, sensations, thoughts, feelings, judgments, personality, and choice, which cannot be *sensed* although they can often be *known*. For instance, we might see a person and say that he is angry or happy; that he understands an idea or is confused about it. These claims are based not upon the actual experience of anger or happiness which that person is undergoing. They are rather *inferences* we draw from sensations of a person's face or body language. These inferences attribute to the observer states of being happy or sad, which cannot be reduced to physical states, although we can infer the mental state based on the physical state. We find that such a correlation between mental and physical states is quite useful in explaining the person's behavior, and the successes in explaining these behaviors makes the idea of mental state real. Note how everyday explanatory approaches are no different than science in this regard, even though everyday descriptions are not very rigorous. There are thus at least two ways in which we can describe the physical state of a person: (a) as sensations about this bodily state, and (b) as a mental 'behind-the-scenes' explanation of that state. We might distinguish them as observation and theory about a person.

Behind the public representations of the internal world of experience, lies the internal world, with which we are all familiar privately, although scientists have struggled to define it for two reasons. First, if the mental state is unlike the physical state, then how could we explain mental states using theories about physical states? Second, are we even sure that there is always a mental to physical state mapping? For example, does anger always manifest in quivering of the lips? Or does confusion always lead to a quizzical expression on the face? We know that body language and facial expressions are not always a reliable source of knowledge about a person's mental state. And this deficit in inferring the mental state from physical state raises an important question: How will science *methodologically* address the struggle to define the internal existence of an observer in terms of observations of physical states? Is there a reliable scheme by which scientists can infer mental states from the measurements of physical states such as mass, length or speed?

Neuroscientists believe that the study of the brain holds such a promise. By studying electrical activity in the brain we can know whether the person is happy or sad, and that is a significantly better indicator of the person's mental state than their facial expressions or body language. Of course, neuroscience is still far from forming a complete catalogue of physical to mental state mappings. But, granting that such an exercise could indeed be completed in the future, we still would not have solved the *linguistic* problem of describing mental vs. physical states. For instance, does the ability to map mental to physical states imply that these two are identical? Some neuroscientists claim that given that we can infer mental states from physical ones, mental states are in fact physical states; that there is no difference between a person's brain exhibiting certain electrical activity and the person's thinking or feeling or willing. But other neuroscientists disagree on equating the mental with the physical states. They argue that *being* in a certain physical state is different from *being* in pain. By looking at someone's brain state, we can get knowledge of a physical state from which we can infer the mental state. Such an inference, however, only amounts to *knowing* the physical state in the brain, not experiencing the pain itself. The real understanding of pain comes to us because we have ourselves been in pain. We understand that some physical states mean some mental states because we extend our mental experiences into the experiences that others have. These inferences are based on correlations between a subject's reports of mental states and observations of their physical states.

There are then clearly two kinds of observer problems that science is faced with. First, how will science address the problem of describing the internal *experience* of a person in a way that makes sense to that person? Second, how can science address the problem of *knowing* the mental state of a person by observing physical states? As we can see, these two problems require different methods. The method by which we verify private experiences—i.e. introspection—is different from the method by which we verify public inferences of those private experiences—i.e. measurement. In fact, given this methodological difference, can we call the attempt to explain private experiences 'science'? And if we were to call it science, how does this new science relate to the old one where we described everything in terms of public experiences?

We find ourselves at a point in the evolution of science where we need to draw a distinction between *knowing* and *experiencing* within science itself. Through observations of the brain's states we can *know* if a person is in pain although we don't *experience* that pain. A scientist experiences the physical state of the brain. But the person whose brain is being observed experiences the pain itself, although he may know nothing about the brain. Knowing the brain and experiencing the brain are therefore different things. In current science, knowing and experiencing are identical: we experience a chair and we know a chair. The study of the observer however creates a divide between knowing and experiencing: a neuroscientist knows that a person is in pain although he does not experience that pain. Of course, he does experience the results of his experiment, but that is not the same as the experience of pain itself. Before we can solve the problem of scientifically studying the observer, we need to develop a view of reality that allows us to distinguish between knowing and experiencing within science.

A Symbolic View of Reality

Think of what happens when we read a book, such as a travelogue. On reading a travelogue, we *know* about an author's experiences of travel, although we don't experience the travel itself. The symbols in the book represent *information* about the traveler's experiences, although reading the book isn't the same as traveling itself. Of course, we could imagine those experiences, but our mental reconstruction of an author's descriptions of travel may differ from the experiences of the author, and certain things in the author's experience may never be reconstructed.

A neuroscientist studies the brain quite like we read the travelogue. She can infer from the brain knowledge of what the brain's owner is experiencing although she won't have those experiences herself. Observing the brain is not much different than observing a person's behavior; both provide information about the person's mental state, although we still don't know how to read brain states, and we have a significantly better ability to read body language. A deeper understanding of the brain will give us insights into the person's mental state, just as body language and behavior now tell us about mental states. In that respect, both approaches are behaviorist. However, just as the mind cannot be reduced to the body language, although it can be used as an *explanation* of the body language, similarly, the mind cannot be reduced to the brain, although the mind can be used to explain brain chemistry.

We might say that the brain is the travelogue of the travel the mind is undertaking; that the travelogue is *manifested* due to the travel, which allows others to know about that travel. By manifesting the travelogue, the brain allows others a peek into its private experiences, because the brain's state can be seen as a *description* of the corresponding mental states. Reading the description is however not identical to having the experiences and even if we knew about the brain state, we may still not have the same experiences as the brain's owner. The observation of the brain or body language, however, does not prevent others from having the same experiences; in fact, an empathetic observer may feel the pain of others, rejoice in the joy of others, or obtain a profound understanding of other's experiences to the point that they have similar if not identical experiences. A powerful speaker can convey his mental states to a rapt audience, even though what their senses receive are only sounds and sights. These familiar examples tell us that speech and body language can themselves represent the mental state, although the people who are inattentive or who do not empathize with the speaker may not derive the same level of experience from these sounds and sights.

The derivation of meaning from physical states is easily seen in the appreciation of abstract art or classical music where artistically savvy people understand intended meanings while others do not. And yet, there are at least two ways in which we can view the perception of meaning. We might, for instance, say that the meaning of art and music only resides in the observer's mind, but not in the musical and artistic works themselves, which are nothing but physical properties. Or, we might say that the meaning really exists in art and music, although its perception depends on the observer's ability to decode it.

Which of these positions is true? By committing to the former idea, we lose the ability to assert that some object is a book, music or work of art, because the meaning is only in the observer. In this view, there is no such thing as a work of art or of music; it is only our perception that makes it so. In other words, objects have no meaning because meanings are created by the mind. But if meanings are only creations of our minds, then nothing that we experience can be applied to reality. Now, if reality does not have meanings, then how does the reality comprising the brain create meanings? If artistic or musical objects do not encode aesthetics, then how can the brain encode those experiences, since the brain is also an object? This problem is fundamentally unsolvable except to say that all experience is an illusion; that there is no such thing as experience or meaning. The notion, therefore, that music or art only reside in the mind leads to the conclusion that there is no mind and hence no art and music. This is the situation with the current physicalist view of nature. The latter position, however, creates no such problem. We allow the fact that art and music are real properties of matter, although some people may not perceive the artistic pieces as works as art because they do not yet comprehend the language of the author. If they were to develop artistic sensibilities, then the *same* object would be a source of meaning.

If we adopt the second position, then we can say that reality is an objective *description* of mental states, and our interaction with that reality creates either knowledge or experience depending on the extent to which we can read it. When reading a travelogue, a reader is not limited to only obtaining knowledge of the author's experiences; the reader may also reconstruct the author's experiences in his mind, if those descriptions are sufficiently vivid. Our minds have a way of interacting with descriptions to generate experiences, although, there is a difference in vividness between the direct experience of travel, and the indirect experience of reading about that travel. Experiences arise when observers interact with matter, but matter is objective information about the experiences that matter may potentially effect in the observer. Knowledge can be objective but experiences are subjective, and experiences can be created from knowledge. To allow for this view of nature, we need to understand how matter can encode information about experience.

Our ability to derive experiences from a travelogue depends on our understanding of the *language* that encodes meanings in the description. If we did not know the language, we would see squiggles or shapes but not meanings. It is our familiarity with the language which allows us to interpret those squiggles as meanings. There are then two ways in which we perceive the travelogue: (a) as physical properties, if we do not know the language of encoding and, (b) as representations of meaning, if we know the language. This is easily seen in the case of a neuroscientist as well. About fifty years ago, neuroscientists could observe the electrical activity in the brain, but they did not have a good understanding of the brain's architecture: i.e. which parts of the brain perform which kinds of functions. While they could observe the electrical activity, they could not *infer* subject's mental state from it. With greater developments in neuroscience, that inference has been made easier.

In a sense, the neuroscientist has learnt to 'read' the brain whereby she can translate experiences of the brain's electrical impulses into a description of mental states. We still wonder about how physical states lead to mental states, but this problem can be greatly simplified by assuming that there is a language in which matter encodes meanings in physical states. The observer of these physical states can decode meanings from these observations, provided she has learnt to read the language of encoding. For a neuroscientist reading the brains of others, the translation of brain states to mental meanings still requires some effort, but that is because she doesn't yet fully know the meaning of the encoding language. However, we can surmise that this hurdle will eventually be overcome and neuroscientists may easily translate knowledge of physical states into a description of the subject's mental states.

The idea that physical states themselves can encode meanings can help us solve the problem of mind-body interaction. This interaction is now through *language*. The physical state encodes meaning into words, while the mental state encodes meanings in the mind. The physical encoding and mental meaning are distinct but related. That is, a certain kind of meaning has a certain type of physical representation. We may now suppose that physical and mental states are related, and there is something in the physical state that qualifies as a representation of mental meanings. Physical and mental states are semantically identical but exist as two different ways of presenting the same meaning. The physical world exists as a 'word' that objectifies meaning as a symbolic token. That token corresponds to the experience of meaning in the mind. If the mental meaning is the experience of yellowness, then the physical state is a physical encoding of the meaning yellow. If the mental meaning is the experience of a judgment, pleasure, concept or choice, then the brain physically encodes these in matter as tokens as well.

The important philosophical point to recognize here is that everything we can experience, we can also express in language objectively. All our experiences can be objectified as descriptions, and therefore there must be something in matter that allows us to encode meanings. The conversion of these concepts into the experience of meaning requires an additional step of translating linguistic symbols to meanings, but we have created the possibility that, by studying the physical states, we can *know* all mental states, although we might not *experience* them. To view physical states as knowledge of mental states, we must use the language of representation. Thus, a physical state can first be seen as knowledge of someone's pain, and if that knowledge is vivid, and we identify with it, it can also lead to the experience of pain. Likewise, we can convert a token of yellow into the sensation of yellow, a token of motion into the experience of activity, a token of truth into the experience of belief, and a token of identity into the experience of personality. Language can encode all aspects of our experience, and meanings in language can be objectified. Therefore, it is possible to suppose that all aspects of our mental existence can be objectified in matter, although that objectification only pertains to the *knowledge* of the mental state, not its *experience*.

Mind-Body Inversion

The symbolic view inverts the relation between mind and matter that modern science has held since the time of Descartes. In modern science, matter is reality and the mind holds descriptions of that reality. Science therefore believes that matter is logically prior to the mind and the mind came about through the development of matter. This idea underlies the modern theory of biological evolution in which living beings evolved at a later stage in the development of the material universe. In Sāṅkhya, the mind is reality while matter is a description of that reality. The mind came prior to matter and matter was manifested as the act of describing the mental state. Reality can exist without its description, although the description cannot arise without some reality. In that respect, mental states are logically prior to the physical states and minds can exist disembodied. However, matter cannot exist without the mind. In fact, matter is a consequence of the mind. This means that all physical objects have been prior created by some mind, as a description of their mental state. Descriptions are needed to communicate subjective experiences since they objectify them. Matter therefore helps in the communication between different minds because it acts as a *medium* of communication between the observers. When the mental state has been objectified in matter, matter has to be described in terms of the language used for mental states. Again, this inverts the relationship between mind and matter within science. In current science, minds are described as properties of objects. However, semantically, matter can also be described in terms of mind.

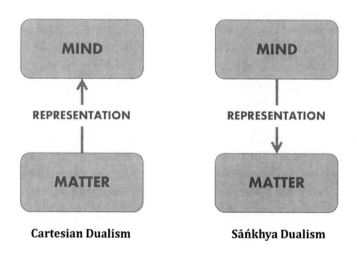

Figure-1 Mind-Body Inversion

In the travelogue analogy, the mind is the experience of the travel, while the travelogue is an objectified description of that travel. The travelogue thus follows the travel. Of course, we can argue that the experience of travel itself was created by the presence of some real-world objects. But we must also acknowledge that these objects are travelogues of people who came prior to the traveler and created those objects. In other words, objects are conceived in the mind before they are created in reality. This is opposite of what neuroscientists today believe: they think that experiences are created by matter, which has no prior mental origin. The symbolic view of nature inverts the relation between meaning and matter, and matter thus follows the creation of meaning. It should not surprise us therefore that the Vedic view does not accept the evolutionary theory about the advent of life. However, we must also recognize that the evolutionary view is a natural consequence of assuming that mind is a description of matter. This belief was created by Descartes who separated mind from matter and treated mind as something that holds ideas about matter. By inverting the relation between mind and matter the evolutionary thesis is also denied, because the development of the body depends on the existence of the mind, not vice versa.

Since matter is a description of mind, everything that is in the mind, can also exist in matter, although as an objectified description of that mental state. Our mental states include sensations, concepts, judgments, intentions and morals, and all these mental entities can also exist in matter as a symbolic representation of that mental experience.

By objectification, every aspect of the observer's experience can be communicated to others as knowledge of their experience. We know about others' experiences simply by observing their behaviors, bodily language or brain states. And we explain these behaviors using theories about senses, mind, intelligence, ego and consciousness. Explanations of matter based on features of the observer's sensory apparatus will invoke ideas such as that the observer senses sensations, cognizes concepts, constructs propositions, forms intents, and seeks morality. The theories of nature based on such ideas will be quite different from theories in current science. Unlike current science, where matter creates sensations, concepts, propositions, intents and morals, the new science will claim that sensations, concepts, propositions, intents and morals create different physical properties in matter. The scope of science under the new approach is also much wider as science now includes every aspect of the observer's experiences as a property that exists in matter.

When Descartes created the mind-body divide, the mind was private and we could not know a person's mental state by looking at their bodily state. This contradicts both everyday intuitions and observed facts. Of late, neuroscientists and biologists have found numerous correlations between mental and physical states, which have blurred the mind-body distinction, sometimes leading to the view that the mind and the body are identical. This equating of mind and body creates a new problem: If mind and body are identical then how do we explain sensations, concepts, propositions, intentions and morals based on theories in physics and chemistry? This is called the 'hard' problem of consciousness, where the hardness pertains to difficulties in explaining the experience of pain or the sensation of yellowness in terms of physical properties. The language of experience and the language of science have gone so far apart that we now have extreme difficulties in mapping these two languages, even in the case of ordinary sensations. And the gap between these two languages only increases as we go beyond sensations into the study of concepts, propositions, intents and morality.

These problems, however, do not arise in the symbolic view. The body is a description of the mind, and mental states are correlated with physical states, as reality and its description. But the body or the mind do not reduce to one another. The mental state is *experience*, and the physical state is a *description* of that experience. We can *know* the mental state by studying matter but we may not *experience* that mental state. The symbolic view therefore is consistent with everyday intuitions about our ability to know the mental state from the physical state, and these intuitions have been confirmed by neuroscience and biology in recent times. The symbolic view avoids the problems of the Cartesian mind-body split, because we can now envision the interaction between mind and body based on the fact that matter has mindlike properties. The symbolic view greatly extends the scope of science from studying nature based on sensations to studying it based on mind, intelligence, ego and consciousness. In fact, the symbolic view tells us that to study wider phenomena we need a deeper understanding of the observer.

A New Kind of Empiricism

Of course, if this extended science is to be empirical, then it must produce new kinds of experiences. These new experiences can be classified into two broad groups. First, if the mind sees concepts, intelligence sees propositions, ego sees intentions and consciousness sees morals, then, in order to devise a science of concepts, propositions, intents and morals, we must employ the empiricism of mind, intelligence, ego and consciousness. This requires the development of perceptive abilities in the scientist where he or she can see new types of realities. Such an approach is very hard on the scientist. Second, it is possible that concepts, propositions, intents and values have *effects* even on the world of sensations, and these effects can be measured within the scope of current experimental observations. This approach requires new types of concepts and theories but no new sensations; science can be done using touch, taste, smell, sight and sound. Of these two kinds of sciences, the former is clearly more interesting but the latter is obviously more practical.

Traditionally, to do science, a scientist has to be trained in theory and experiment, but not required to develop specialized faculties of observation; everything in science should be observed using sensations. The approach in Vedic philosophy is contrasting because here, to see something new, the observer has to develop new sensory faculties. The classic Vedic approach requires the practitioners of science to be convinced that mind, intelligence, ego and consciousness are additional types of sensory faculties, and they must then develop their sensory abilities to see the world through mind, intelligence, ego and consciousness. This approach will be a non-starter in the case of modern science, where everything must be seen, tasted, touched, smelt or heard. This book therefore attempts to adapt Vedic philosophy for the contemporary context in a way that has never been done in the Vedic texts themselves. The adaptation is that we would like to see the effects of the existence of mind, intelligence, ego and consciousness using our conventional sensations of sound, touch, sight, taste and smell. Clearly, we cannot see or taste the mind. But the mind produces *effects* which can be seen, tasted or smelt. The novelty will be that the *explanations* of such sensations cannot be based on conventional ideas about material objects. The explanations must instead be based on properties drawn from intuitions about mind, intelligence, ego and consciousness. This requires us to dig into our intuitive base about the observer, to obtain new ideas. But the scientist is not required to develop new perceptive faculties. Traditionally, science conceived and sensed objects. Theories in science were about objects, and we thought that reality is objects. Now, science must conceive meanings and its theories will be about meanings, but these meanings will be available as sensations. Traditionally we looked at the measurement of a particle and said that if the measurement is true, then the particle is real. Now we will look at some sensations and say that if these sensations are true, then concepts, propositions, intents and values are real. If a theory provides a predictively accurate description of nature, then the concepts in that description are real. Sensual validity of a theory about the mind thus reinstates the truth of mental concepts, even though we never see the mind itself.

The Methodological Shift

Realizing this view of science requires a shift from a non-semantic to a semantic style of descriptions. The basic difference between the two is that a semantic description is always in relation to an observer's *senses* while a non-semantic description is always in relation to other material objects. Measurements against objects are *quantified* as numbers, whereas perception through senses discovers *types* in nature. The shift to semantic descriptions requires seeing the world in terms of types rather than in terms of quantities. This means that since observers can perceive color through their senses, then color is real. Since they can classify the color into whiteness or redness, these concepts are real. Since there can be a meaning of peace associated with whiteness, that meaning is real. Since the concepts such as whiteness can be combined into conceptual objects—such as a white flag—those object-concepts are real. Since someone can desire peace, the desire is real. And since that desire can be based on someone's morality, morality is also real.

There are thus many forms of realism in Vedic philosophy beyond the realism of current science. Each type of realism corresponds to a different type of sense. Sensations are reality for the senses, properties are reality for the mind, objects are reality for the intelligence, intents are reality for the ego and morality is reality for consciousness. These are encoded in matter, but in different ways. That encoding makes all realities objective, but their meaning and theory is based on the observer. We can of course study the symbolic properties in matter in relation to other material objects. For instance, because the mind gives meanings to objects through a contextual relation, we might say that objects have contextual properties. Similarly, since intent refers to a mental state about the world, objects must have intentional relations. By attributing such newer properties to objects we might conclude that there are just physical properties but no mind. While this approach is not technically wrong, it foregoes the fact that arriving at new theories itself requires an analysis of mental experiences, and not of physical states. Physical states help reaffirm the existence of such properties in matter. But such an analysis is not adequate to develop the theories.

While scientific theories of matter should formulate new properties in matter—e.g. contextual properties and references—the intuitive base for these properties lies in how we perceive the world as meaning rather than how things exist objectively by themselves. Current science maps properties in measured objects to properties in measuring instruments, and then maps properties in instruments to meanings in senses. Thus, we create the illusion that science studies objects as they exist independent of observation. This approach can also be extended to deeper aspects of the observer—i.e. mind, intelligence, ego and consciousness—because all aspects of the observer are represented in matter and can be observed. However, the formulation of such theories will have to invoke our understanding of the mental experiences rather than just that of physical states. For instance, the fact that a travelogue refers to a travel cannot be seen if we just analyze the physical states of the paper on which the travelogue is imprinted. To see that a symbol refers to a fact we must invoke the idea that the mind is able to hold meanings about other things. *If* there were no mind, these properties would also not exist in matter. The existence of the mind makes meanings real in matter, and, without understanding the mind, we can't create physical theories that, essentially, take features in the mind and encode it in matter.

Historically, the inclusion of the mind has been perceived as a methodological problem because the mind represented our personal opinions about reality, not reality itself. Opinions could be marred by biases, illusions, hallucinations and mistakes. Empiricists thus chose to use primary properties because they did not seem to suffer from these methodological problems. But physical measurements don't solve the problem because there can be mistakes in the experimental setup, errors in the measuring instruments, or in the human interpretations of observations. To circumvent this problem, induction was added to empiricism as a conceptual supplement, and experiments have to be performed repeatedly—and expected to produce the same results each time—for these experiments to be regarded as facts. Experiments must also be conducted in different times, places and using different apparatus to eliminate spurious results. The fundamental problem of illusion or mistakes is therefore not solved by choosing to describe reality in relation to other objects. The problem is rather solved by induction[3], by varying the time, place and apparatus, and through a broad consensus amongst a group of scientists after they have repeated the results.

This is essentially no different than how we agree if something is red. The notion, therefore, that primary properties are somehow superior to secondary properties is false. It represents a metaphysical assumption in science that reality is logically independent of the observer and the observer is an accident of reality, not a cause of it. The converse—that reality reflects properties of the observer—is also a metaphysical premise, but has more interesting implications: it allows us to apply all of ordinary language to describe reality, rather than the limited language of current science. Accordingly, there would be more experiences that correspond to reality and science would thus be much broader. Specifically, there are phenomena that require theories which cannot be derived by generalizing sensations. Such phenomena require theories that generalize the mind, intelligence, ego and consciousness to produce new properties, and explain phenomena in terms of these newer properties.

The semantic style of descriptions should begin with sensations because higher constructs in the observer are based on sensations. Concepts depend on sensations. Propositions of facts depend on concepts. Intentions and purposes depend on propositions. And morals depend upon a person's intents. Language begins in the comprehension of basic sensual modes, like color, taste, smell, touch and sound. Current science describes sensations physically, by a two-step process in which properties in the measured objects are mapped to the properties in the measuring system, which are then mapped to sensation meanings. Under the view that nature is basically meaningless, and meanings are a creation of our minds, science creates non-semantic theories of sensations. This makes it harder to bring higher aspects of language within science. For example, we can talk about why someone 'likes' the color yellow or 'loves' to eat sweet things, but we can't say why someone would like a frequency, love an electron or desire a mass. Note how modern science reduces color to frequency and taste to electrons. This reduction works in the context of a physical explanation of measurements. But it is severely limiting when science tries to build higher theories of experience, because the notions of concept, proposition, intent or value can't be related to physical states. By creating non-semantic theories of sensations, science creates problems in describing higher aspects of experience.

Non-semantic theories are a conceptual dead-end for science, when the most interesting aspects of science—understanding the working of the mind—is yet to come. To address these unsolved problems, science needs a method that permits greater parts of ordinary experience into science. Higher aspects of ordinary experience depend on a semantic treatment of lower aspects. Unless we can treat sensations and actions semantically, we cannot describe the experiences of mind, intelligence, ego and consciousness in science. This means that properties in matter that correspond to experiences of the mind, intelligence, ego and consciousness cannot be understood, unless sensations and actions are described semantically. To describe reality semantically, we need to relate it to the observer's senses, not to material objects. Current science describes matter in relation to material objects. The ensuing description now contends with the problem of how these relations create experiences in relation to observers—e.g., how the mass of an object creates the touch sensation of heaviness. Science has been partially successful in explaining some of these sensations—e.g., the explanation of heaviness in terms of mass. But there are equally many ordinary experiences like smell and taste that have no explanation in terms of physical properties, despite much advancement in the study of elementary matter.

For example, why do sulphur compounds have a pungent smell? Why does chlorine create bitter taste? What molecular properties in sugar make it sweet? Why does sodium chloride taste salty? We seem to know everything about these chemicals from an atomic and molecular structure standpoint. In fact, each of these molecules is known to be very simple, and their structure and physical properties are well-documented. Why then can we not explain the diverse tastes and smells of these molecules? Modern science relegates these problems to the study of the brain and observational apparatus. Science claims that nature is already perfectly described in terms of current physical properties. The *perception* of this nature in terms of tastes or smells is an altogether different question and requires a separate theory. The problem is not one of knowing what chemicals *are* in terms of tastes and smells, because tastes and smells are 'human' features. But when humans are described as chemicals, the explanation of perception of taste and smell that was deferred from physics into biology now faces a dead-end. If chemicals outside the body don't have smell and taste, then how can these same chemicals *create* the sensation of smell and taste in the body?

Current science divides the problem of describing matter in terms of smells and tastes into two separate problems: (a) the problem of describing matter in relation to other material objects, and (b) the problem of understanding how matter is perceived by observers. In Vedic philosophy, these are not separate problems. That is, we would not describe matter in terms of properties of other objects, which science calls 'standards' of measurement. This is because the choice of a standard and the quality it embodies (sometimes called the *dimension*) are both arbitrary. Science first chooses a conceptual framework and then formulates laws in that framework. To validate these laws, measurement standards are selected. If the laws are successful, then the conceptual framework, the laws and the measuring standard are collectively validated. Modern scientists recognize that the choice of a measuring standard is arbitrary; we can measure mass using a kilogram instead of a pound. What most scientists are unprepared to acknowledge is that the choice of mass as a property of nature in terms of which we describe nature is also arbitrary. We can choose some logical combination of current concepts and then formulate a different set of laws using those new concepts, and then choose a different set of measuring instruments that embody those conceptual properties. Science, as a method, would work perfectly even with that new choice of concepts, laws and standards.

It is an accident of history that science uses the concepts of mass, charge, momentum, energy, etc. because these concepts were created in the context of describing the phenomena that scientists chose to study at some point in history. If Newton had been trying to explain black-body radiation instead of falling apples, then lack of prior validated concepts in terms of which thinking was carried out could have led to a different set of concepts, laws and standards. If science had begun by the study of heat rather than motion, then motion today would be described in terms of heat, rather than heat in terms of motion. The irony of current science is that it is subject to historical conditions in which phenomena studied later are described in terms of concepts that were formulated earlier. The concepts formulated earlier arose in the context of trying to describe a different phenomenon. What would happen if we reverse the order of phenomena? Won't we describe all phenomena in new, different ways? If we change the history of science, we will most likely also change science itself because the reference of scientific laws, concepts and standards is the phenomena science *chooses* to describe. Such a science is more arbitrary than we currently like to acknowledge. It is a contextual, historical and cultural description of nature, governed by our ways of thinking and the kind of problems we choose to solve.

A less arbitrary science would pick a more universal reference and define properties of matter in relation to that. In Sāṅkhya, that standard of reference is the observer. This does not mean that every observer's experience is real. It only means that it can *potentially* be real, and therefore the world should be described in terms of the observer's possibilities. An observer can know the world in terms of sensations, properties, objects, intentions and morals. Each of these categories is further sub-divided into other categories, which are embedded in ordinary language. We can combine these categories into new categories, thereby creating new vocabularies. Fields of science that involve incompatible concepts are basically different vocabularies to describe reality. The ability to create diverse vocabularies allows a massive diversification of knowledge. But, all vocabularies describe the same reality, and must ultimately be unified. Such unification within the individual fields of science still remains a dream, and the unification of diverse sciences is not even on the table yet. A deeper understanding of observers however can bring these dreams to fruition, because all fields of science ultimately arise in relation to some or other of the observer's faculties.

This however requires a radically different approach to science itself. The reference of concepts, laws and standards should not be the objects and phenomena that we seek to describe. The reference should be the observer and its sensual faculties, which are not subject to our choices. Of course, a particular observer may have an enhanced sense of smell or may be deaf or blind. This limits a specific individual's experiences but it does not limit the formulation of theories in relation to a generic observer whose capabilities we suppose are partly manifest in each one of us. Similar to how current science progresses by abstracting specific objects into mathematical objects (e.g., particles and waves) a new science can proceed by abstracting specific observers into a generic set of observational capabilities. Many of these capabilities are already known to us. Other capabilities may require development of the observational faculties themselves. The methodological shift in science is, therefore, the shift from trying to understand what matter is, to trying to understand what the observer is. *If* our theory of the observer is correct, then it will imply certain properties in matter, and validation of these properties will reinforce our theory of the observer. As current science progresses through theories about matter, a new science can also proceed with theories about the observer. The challenges in trying to understand nature in terms of a universal law and particle today in science now transforms into the challenge of trying to understand diverse observers in terms of the properties of a universal observer. I don't presume that a new approach to science will make it any easier, as far as knowing the whole truth is concerned. But we can be sure that this new science will be a far better approach than the current one for two reasons: (a) we are already familiar with many parts of our experience that science doesn't explain today, and (b) we know the language in which we communicate and correspond about these experiences to others. Thus, both the experiential and linguistic basis of these experiences is known to a great extent. Making this language rigorous and generic will help us formulate theories, and objectivizing these theories into physical symbol-states gives us a definition of material reality.

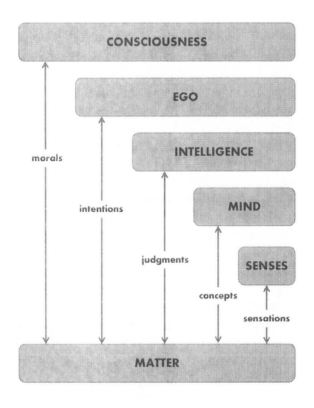

Figure-2 Enlarging Scientific Empiricism

To formulate such theories, science requires a *semantic* view of senses, mind, intelligence, ego and consciousness. The current description of sensations in terms of non-semantic physical properties is eventually detrimental to the progress of science. A science that studies matter in relation to different aspects of the observer would not be limited to observing the world based on sensations, let alone a non-semantic view of sensations. We will rather explain material states based on the state of the observer. For instance, we can perceive whether a person is angry or happy; whether they like or dislike us; whether they understand or are confused. We describe these phenomena by appealing to the mental state of the person: we say that the person *looks* happy and therefore there is a mental state behind that look which actually makes him happy. In other words, we use a theory of the mind to explain bodily expressions. Modern science is attempting the reverse: it is trying to explain the mind based on the physical state, and this physical state is construed based on the study of objects devoid of any mental state.

In the symbolic view, each symbol has a semantic state which current science describes as a physical state devoid of meaning. To understand the semantic state, theories need to describe the meaning in the symbol using types drawn from senses, mind, intelligence, ego and consciousness. In such descriptions, the types will be quite different, although the sensory measurements will not change. Through such an observation a new science will 'infer' what current science cannot, from the same sensations. This inference is not identical to direct sensory encounter with properties, objects, intents and morals, but it is a theoretical construct *in lieu of* the ability to have those types of experiences directly. Accordingly, theories based on new types of intuitions drawn from the observer's faculties will explain the world differently than the theory based on non-semantic states. We can see that this science (as a theory) will be radically different from current science, even at the level of sensations. The new science will allow us to see new properties in matter that arise through interactions with observers. We will have to acknowledge that there are many aspects to matter that embody sensations, properties, objects, intentions and morals.

From Matter to Information

The idea that matter is symbolic requires a shift in the practices of science from thinking of things to thinking of information. Reality is not things whose information we store in the mind. Reality itself is information. The observer acquires this information and perceives it as sensation, concepts, propositions, intentions and morals. If information is fundamental, then its description as objects must create problems not just in physics but in all other areas of science. Indeed, these problems have become pervasive in modern science. They have been encountered in mathematics as incompleteness and logical paradoxes, because mathematics cannot distinguish between objects and meanings[4]. They have been seen in physics as indeterminism and uncertainty, because physics describes things but not meanings in those things[5]. They are seen as problems of semantics in computing and artificial intelligence. They are seen in biology as the ability in the molecules to hold information about the organism. These problems point to a fundamental role of information in science, because without including information as a basic category, mathematical and causal pictures in science are incomplete.

But why aren't physical theories already describing information? What is missing from current theories of matter and mathematics? The key missing piece in modern theories of matter and mathematics is that information has two aspects—quantitative and qualitative— but the objectification of this information has discarded the quality of information. For instance, when we perceive the yellow color, we have a quality and a quantity. When this perception is objectified into frequency, the quality is lost. Modern theories of matter and mathematics were derived by objectifying sensations. Classical physics postulates that behind all sensations is a *particle* with various properties. Mathematics similarly objectifies our notions about extension and quantity into numbers. All other sciences use this model of objectification. These objectifications leave out the semantics in objects. Science equates frequency with color, but frequency and color do not have the same type of qualities. This leads to the idea that the object being seen is not red; it just *appears* to us as being red. When this idea is extended, the meanings associated with red are false. Objects created by combining sensations are imaginary. Intentions formed based on such objects are unreal. And morals that evaluate intentions are fantasy.

To reinstate semantics, it should be possible to assert that the thing that appears red is red; that the experience of redness is not an illusion of the mind. Of course, the physical object is not the experience of redness, but it can be the *knowledge* representation of the mental state that made the object red. If someone calls that thing red, his claim is true *objectively* not just as a manner of speaking between human beings. The ability to describe the world in terms of sensations, in a new semantic way, requires a science where matter encodes knowledge, similar to the linguistic encoding of experience. This linguistic encoding is not identical to experience, but it is also not totally different from experience. The world exists as a travelogue and by sensing it we know and experience travel. The world must thus be described as a *linguistic* objectification of experience and not as a *substance* objectification behind that experience. Both experience and matter are described using a *type* language.

Vedic science and modern science differ in how they objectify experience. Experiences are objectified as particles, things or substances, in modern science. The same world is objectified as language, in Vedic science. The problem of how matter gets meaning through perception by the senses and mind arises in modern science. No such problem arises in Vedic science, because matter never lost meaning to begin with.

Two important things are needed for an informational view of nature. First, there must be a language in nature by which physical states can be seen as semantic states. Second, a view of reality in which experience gained in a scientific experiment can be applied back to reality as objective information. Current science describes objects in relation to other objects, which are seen non-semantically. Thus, we say that an object has mass, but it does not have heaviness; or that it emits light with a frequency but it does not have redness. Eventually, mass and frequency have to be converted into some sensation for science to be empirical, but this conversion remains outside scientific *theories*. Theoretically, we say matter is mass and frequency. Experimentally we observe that as heaviness and color. Why not describe matter in terms of heaviness and color, applying these properties back to reality? We don't need an additional 'layer' of interpretation that converts physical properties into sensations; we can also treat the physical state of an object as a symbol of information about its perceptions, if there is a language.

An entirely new array of physical possibilities opens up *if* nature natively has a language to encode information. This is because, nature that has so far been described in terms of physical properties, can now be described using semantic properties. The possibility that there is a native language in which nature encodes information makes a completely new science possible. In this science, we will not say that an atom has such-and-such mass; we will rather say that it has the color 'red'. Accordingly, we will not say that my body moves towards the red object because of force, but say that I tried to grab an object because I wanted to eat an apple. The phenomenon of movement is the same, but there are two different descriptions—and consequently explanations—of that phenomenon. The new type of explanation comes handy if the physical explanation is inadequate. Therefore, semantic explanations ride on the problems of incompleteness, uncertainty, indeterminism and logical paradoxes in science. Meaning in the latter case is not a post-hoc addition to the physical state. It is rather the *cause* behind the phenomena.

To read the world as signs, we must have learnt the language by which the world can be seen as signs. Depending on the type of language we use to interpret the world, our interpretations will yield different kinds of information within the same physical reality. For example, computer bit sequences can be interpreted as decimal, hexadecimal, or octal numbers. To interpret bits, we choose a language— an encoding scheme—that converts the bits into voice, video, pictures or data. The world appears as objective states to the scientist, but the same world can appear as meanings to one who knows how to 'read' those states in terms of a language of meanings. Modern science assumes that nature is itself meaningless and that we give meanings to material objects by calling them chairs and tables. This is a flaw in theory construction, and in how we objectify sensations into physical properties. The very same experience can be also objectified in a different way, informationally. The science and order discovered through such observation would be different. The basic question therefore is: Does nature have a language? This question cannot be answered definitively without assessing the causal and empirical implications of semantic theories. What we can, however, predict is that if nature was semantic, then a physical theory would not adequately explain phenomena. For instance, the order of the letters in this book can be explained only if we see the book semantically; if we see the book as physical properties, it would be impossible to explain the order of the squiggles inside it. Similarly, changes in our facial expressions on hearing good versus bad news would be inexplicable unless we accounted for meanings. Almost every behavior of living beings requires meaning before it can be understood. Thus, a semantic view of nature can be applied in areas where current theories of science are incomplete and fail to account for the phenomena at hand in terms of physical properties. There is no dearth of such problems in modern science: they abound in physics, in mathematics, in computing theory and in biology. A science construed in terms of semantics is also empirical, but more powerful than the science of non-semantic properties.

The semantic view of nature has several distinct aspects. First, it includes ideas like 'white,' 'red,' 'sweet,' 'pungent,' etc. which have objective existence even before being perceived. Second, it includes properties like 'color,' 'taste,' 'smell,' 'sound' and 'sight' which make ideas such as 'sweet' sensations, such as sweet smell, sweet taste, sweet sound, etc. . Third, it includes object-concepts that are created by combining sensations and concepts. For instance, ordinary words like 'table' and 'chair' denote macroscopic objects. The above three include almost all verbs, adjectives and common nouns in language. They also include the ability for concept denotation; for instance, white denotes the idea of peace and red denotes the idea of passion. Fourth, language comprises of pronouns—'I', 'we,' 'us,' 'them,' 'this,' 'his,' etc. which represent an observer's personal relations to the world, and the idea that we have purposes that drive us towards our goals. Fifth, language consists of words that denote morality, goodness, happiness or suffering in life. In Sāṅkhya, these categories correspond to senses, mind, intelligence, ego and consciousness, as deeper kinds of meanings derived from the same material object. Thus, we can say that reality has sensations, properties, objects, intents and morals. Each of these can also denote or describe other things or ideas through reference; both the object and its description are, however, semantic (types) and not physical (quantities). Language embeds the structure of the observer in matter to describe all aspects of the observer's subjective states within ordinary language. Modern science describes nature in terms of the dynamics of atoms and molecules. Sāṅkhya describes the same nature in terms of the effect that nature causes in us—namely sensations, cognitions, perceptions, purposes and morals. Vedic science externalizes properties in experience into properties of matter. Thus, the Vedic elements called Earth, Water, Fire, Air and Ether are externalization of sensations. The idea that sensations can denote taste, touch, sound, sight or smell is an externalization of type cognition in the mind. The notion that sensations and properties are combined as objects is an externalization of intelligence. Beliefs about ownership of things or that something is Beethoven's symphony or Picasso's painting is an externalization of ego. The notion that objects and actions are righteous and virtuous is an externalization of the moral sense (called *mahattattva* and sometimes *chitta* or 'contaminated consciousness). It is now possible to study sensations, properties, objects, intents and morals within matter, while invoking an understanding of the observer's faculties.

3

Foundations of Vedic Science

*The entire universe is perfused with signs, if it is not
composed exclusively of signs.*

—*Charles Sanders Peirce*

The Problem of Realism

Modern science believes that it is discovering the nature of reality
through observations although whether reality can be derived from
observations has never been answered in Western philosophy. We
commonly believe that reality is something that lies 'behind' our perceptions, and science formulates theories about this reality. If the theories are empirically successful, science claims that our theory must be
right and hence a description of reality. But there is always a possibility that a different theory of reality could explain observations equally
well. This is called the underdetermination of theory by experiment,
and refers to the possibility that there are many theoretical explanations for the same observations. Indeed, one basic aim of this book
is to show that nature can be described in a radically different way
from the style of theoretical description adopted in current science.
If theories are underdetermined by experience, then we can never be
sure about the truth of our theories, even if they are very successful.
This is then the problem of realism: How do we know that our theory
of reality is true, given that other equally successful theories can, in
principle, be formulated?

The history of science is replete with theories that were thought to
be true at one time, but later gave way to a different theory that unified

more than one phenomenon. Thus Newton's mechanics is better than Ptolemy's cycles because Newton described both terrestrial and celestial gravitation using a single theory. Maxwell's electromagnetism is better than the separate theories of electricity and magnetism because of the unification. Einstein's relativity is better than mechanics and electrodynamics because it unified ideas of motion in mechanics and electromagnetism into a single theory. Quantum theory is similarly better because it unified theories of matter and radiation. In this progression of science, there have been several descriptions of the same phenomena, and it is therefore possible that we still don't have the final theory of reality because there are still phenomena unexplained by science. Just as adding new phenomena to science have changed the theories in the past, similar types of changes are foreseeable in the future. This very likely scenario also implies that until we have explained all phenomena, our theory about any particular phenomena may be an inaccurate description of nature. The only way we can get to a correct theory of anything is if we have a correct theory of everything. This fact, however, raises serious practical concerns in science. How can we describe all phenomena in nature when we have limited access to only a small fraction of possible phenomena? How can we be certain about a part of the universe, without being certain about everything in the universe? This problem is fundamentally unsolvable in current science because we have no direct access to reality. We *infer* reality from observations, and there are many ways to infer, as the history of science amply shows.

The problem of realism in Western philosophy goes back to Socrates who articulated the Western view of experience through the allegory of the cavemen who see the world through the shadows cast on the cave's walls. These shadows, Socrates said, are created by things and people behind the cavemen, which cast a shadow on the wall because of the fire burning behind the cavemen. The reality is, for these cavemen, 'behind' them and they have no access to the real world, except through the imagery being cast on the walls. If those images were in fact an exercise in shadowgraphy created by an expert artist's hands instead of real people and things, the cavemen would not be able to know. The cavemen would postulate the existence of people and things, when in reality it was just a clever artist. Socrates thus concluded that we can never know the true nature of reality, unless we can engage with it directly.

In the early days of empiricism, Bishop Berkeley articulated a similar view where we only have access to perceptions and reality is simply a construction from this perception. We cannot know the true nature of reality, because reality is 'behind' those perceptions. No matter how successful our theory of reality may be, it still remains potentially false.

Contrast this with the Vedic viewpoint where reality is in 'front' of our perception, not 'behind' it. Think of a man looking into a mirror. He sees his image, similar to the images seen by cavemen. But, unlike the images seen by the cavemen, the image in the mirror is created by the observer himself. The person looks in the mirror to know himself and by seeing himself he forms theories about himself. Unlike the cavemen who have no access to reality, however, the man in the mirror has direct access to himself, even without the mirror. In both Socrates's and Berkeley's view, we try to understand reality through its images but we have no way of knowing reality because it is constructed from observations. Our theories are our best guesses based on the imagery of perception and we have no way of verifying our theories, other than to refer to experiences from which they were derived through a logical, but potentially mistaken, process. However, in the Vedic case, the knower is the thing known and experience is created by reflecting the observer in the mirror of material nature. The experience of the world is one way for an observer to know himself when he is reflected in nature's mirror. The observer, however, also has direct access to his consciousness through introspection. The observer can thus know reality perfectly because he is the reality being known. Theories of the observer created by analyzing perceptions can be validated through those perceptions. But the underdetermination of reality by experiment can only be solved if we have direct access to that reality. This direct access is methodologically forbidden in science but it is imminently possible in Sāṅkhya. In Sāṅkhya, a theory of reality is not final unless it describes the observer completely.

While all theories of experience formed by studying the experience are potentially false even in the Vedic approach, they can in principle be verified through direct introspection by the observer since the reality is the observer itself. The observer has no direct access to reality in Western philosophy but the observer has direct access to reality in Sāṅkhya because the observer is the reality that he is trying to discover. This basic insight about the Vedic way of thinking is so important to understanding Vedic science that its significance cannot be overstated. In Vedic philosophy, matter is essentially undifferentiated like a mirror prior to reflection. Matter is differentiated into experience when the observer's consciousness is reflected in matter. All experiences therefore have a prior origin in the observer itself. This, of course, does not mean that if I'm seeing a table, then the table is created by my consciousness. It only means that the table was created prior by some consciousness in a creative act, by objectifying meanings that originally existed in that person[6].

All experience, in Vedic philosophy, is created by objectifying meanings in consciousness into matter. While individual experiences may correspond to things that another consciousness may have objectified in matter prior to my experience of it, the *theory* constructed by analyzing this experience is the theory of the observer and it pertains to the capabilities of observation, not a theory about a specific individual consciousness. Conscious experience in Sāṅkhya originates through choices and these choices are present in matter as the *language* in terms of which we describe experiences. The atoms in reality are the alphabets of this language. The language of choices can be expressed in several *models* that include matter, senses, mind, intelligence, ego and morality. Everything that exists in consciousness can thus be expressed in experience through one of the sensory faculties by which we experience and the theory of reality consists of the alphabets and its models.

Three Notions of Reality

The modern notion of reality packs at least three distinct ideas which are not always satisfied in every type of philosophical realism. First, we believe that experience is a source of knowledge about reality and thus *corresponds* to reality. Of course, if experience was always correlated with reality, there could not be errors and hallucinations. On the other hand, if experience was always false, there could not be knowledge from experience. The correspondence theory of experience therefore is neither trivially true nor trivially false. Given this fact, the second notion of reality says that experience is *caused* by reality. I see the Sun as yellow, not because the Sun is yellow (correspondence) but because light rays from the Sun travel into my eye and make it seem yellow (causation). Again, this view is neither trivially true nor false. The problem in considering it trivially true is the linguistic gap between cause and effect: how light becomes the sensation of color has not been explained. Obviously, there is something real that causes a change to my senses, so it could not be trivially false either. Causation too is therefore not obviously true or false. Third, by reality we often mean the thing that remains unchanged through the changing phenomena; phenomena are temporary appearances, while reality is unchanging. The problem now is that reality cannot be directly perceived by the senses, since senses will only obtain phenomena. How can we know about reality if we cannot sense it? We can see that all notions of reality are problematic in some way.

Figure-3 Three Notions of Reality

Scientific realism rejects the correspondence view of reality. Experience and reality, science claims, are not similar, and should therefore be described by different words—experience in terms of taste, touch, smell, sound and sight, and reality in terms of mass, charge, electrons, quarks, etc. Of course, science cannot totally reject correspondence as it will undercut empiricism: If senses are not sources of truth, then how can we ever know reality through experiences? Scientists therefore postulate that reality is material objects that cause experiences in the observer. However, mapping objects to experience does not explain how physical properties become sensations. In modern times, the conversion of physical properties into sensations is often seen as a special type of physical process in the brain, although no theoretical explanation of that process currently exists. Science also postulates that material objects persist through state changes, even though the notion of an object apart from its states has been problematic in science. For example, when a particle moves in space, the identity of the particle is unchanged (it is the same particle) while the state (position) is changed. This notion of realism is now known to be false in atomic theory because particles change state probabilistically and discretely which contradicts the idea that there is a material entity 'behind' the phenomena that persists and causes the changes. Physicists have to now accept the idea that atomic theory only deals with order amongst phenomena, and not reality.

Each of the three scientific notions of reality is problematic in a different way but science has not been able to replace them with other notions. The correspondence notion is rejected because if the world were the way it seemed to us, there would be no need for science (we could just as well observe nature and believe perceptions to be real). The causal view is problematic because how physical objects cause mental experiences is yet to be explained. The idea that there is something that persists behind phenomena also can't be sustained because the idea that objects in two distinct states are the same object is now suspect. Given these problems, there is a grave crisis of realism within science, but most scientists are either unaware of these problems or don't give enough serious consideration to them. The belief is that if science works (i.e. it makes successful predictions) then we should not have to worry about reality. Pragmatically, however, scientists claim to discover reality because science works. There is hence a double standard about realism in science. When faced with problems of realism, scientists claim that the question is irrelevant because science works. But, in other contexts, science claims to describe reality simply because science is successful.

In Vedic philosophy, matter is a phenomenon, not reality. The conscious observer is reality, and phenomena are created as experiences in the observer. There is hence a reality underlying phenomena, which persists as unchanged individual existence through those phenomena, but that reality is not material. The consciousness that underlies experiences is non-material although it creates material phenomena by embedding meanings in matter. This view states that all material objects are created and destroyed but their cause must be eternal, because otherwise the cycle of creation and destruction of objects cannot be sustained. For instance, if objects are destroyed then there must be another agency that creates them. But, if this other agency creates objects when they did not exist, then it can also create them when other objects exist.

Phenomena themselves are of three kinds—(a) conscious experience, (b) unconscious causes, and (c) material objects. The first thing to emerge from consciousness is an unconscious 'personality' of the soul, which 'covers' the soul with tendencies and desires. From this unconscious cause conscious experiences emerge. Note that, in the Vedic view, there can be experiences even when there are no material objects; these experiences are created by the unconscious. Obvious examples are dreams and hallucinations which are caused by deep-seated, unconscious fears and desires. From the conscious experience, matter emerges. For instance, we first have ideas and then objects are created according to those ideas. Once the objects have been created, they can be perceived and they become a source of ideas for other observers. But the object originates as an idea. Since personalities, experiences and objects are successive creations, they are considered 'phenomena' and not 'reality'. Consciousness is the only reality which in turn creates phenomena. This view doesn't deny the existence of objects, but it doesn't treat them as 'real' in the specific sense that they are not eternal. Matter is therefore not reality but a phenomenon. The material world is experienced as sensations, properties, objects, intentions and morals, and these too are phenomena, although different from the external objectification of these phenomena. Finally, the cause of experience is a subtle unconscious realm that constitutes a living being's personality, tendencies and preferences, which is also a phenomenon, as it changes. Only the soul is real, because it persists through phenomena, and exists when phenomena do not.

The three types of phenomena together with reality constitute four types of *sound*[7] in Vedic philosophy. Conscious experience is *madhyamā* sound (this includes waking and dreaming experiences). This experience generally corresponds to an 'external' reality called *vaikhari* which is not 'behind' but in 'front' of our experience. Experiences are caused by a subtler *paśyanti* or causal sound that remains dormant in the observer as its unconscious, and is therefore 'behind' the experience as its subtle seed. Through all the phenomena, there is something that remains unchanged, which is *para* represented by the free will of consciousness. Thus, there is reality in front of experience, behind experience and above experience which help construct the experience.

The Vedic notion of *vaikhari* is the correspondence notion of reality, namely that reality is that which corresponds to experience. *Vaikhari* basically means speech-like sound that objectifies meaning into symbols. Gross material objects are called *vaikhari* and they are objectifications of meanings in the observer. The senses therefore experience color as redness and matter encodes this meaning as the sound (vibration) of 'redness'. The experience of redness and the word redness are not identical but they can be described using the same word—i.e. redness. Unlike modern science where reality and phenomena are described by different words, in Vedic philosophy, they are described using the same *words* although the words represent different things. It is now possible to say that when I see a red apple there is indeed a red apple. The apple in an observer's sensation and that in the external world are different, but they are related by the same word. The linguistic divide between experience and reality (which appears as the mind-body divide) does not arise because the mind and the body interact through language.

The Vedic sound of *paśyanti* corresponds to the everyday causal notion of reality although causes too are phenomena and not reality in Vedic philosophy. A cause is created as a consequence of some prior action. It is destroyed when the result of the action has been reaped, although by that time, another cause may be created. The creation of these causes and effects can be controlled by consciousness, but most often they continue unhindered. Consciousness begins to play a role in the causal flow only when it wishes to get out of the cycle of cause and effect. Consciousness, now, chooses to destroy the cycle of cause and effect, by performing only those actions which do not generate a reaction. Inherent in this view of causality is the idea that every action has two consequences—(a) a result, which we ordinarily call its 'effect'; for instance the effect of pushing a cart is that it starts moving, and (b) a reaction, which is the moral consequence of the action. The reaction stays dormant and is later activated by Time. Nature is governed by choices and their reactions which constrain or enhance the freedom of choice. Choices include patterns of thinking, desiring, judging, planning, and acting. The freedom is the boundaries of the system in which the individual participates and is able to choose. These boundaries include everyday notions of systems such as teams, organizations, societies, nations and cultures. The results of individual action determine which kinds of contexts a soul can participate in; these contexts cannot be chosen. The Vedas state that nature creates contexts under the influence of Time. This implies that collective phenomena such as economies, societies, ideologies, religions and nation-states are creations of Time, not of the individual choices. Individuals can participate in these systems as a result of their past actions, but they cannot create these systems.

The *para* sound is that which exists even when phenomena do not, and it is the choices of consciousness. Even in Western philosophy, reality is supposed to be that which exists even when there is no observation. But in Western philosophy reality is that material object that exists prior to being known while in the Vedic view reality is the observer when there is no observation. Every phenomenon in Western philosophy requires some material object, while every phenomenon in the Vedic view requires some observer. Since phenomena include even material objects, matter is not considered reality in Vedic philosophy. Every material object, rather, has a conscious observer as its cause. Thus, even a stone has *para*, *paśyanti*, *madhyamā* and *vaikhari*. The matter that makes up what we sense as a stone is in fact information manifested from a subtle body of senses and mind that can experience, which is manifested from an unconscious realm of causes, which cover the consciousness of a living being. The difference between a human and a stone is not that one has a mind and consciousness and the other doesn't. The difference is that the mind and senses in the stone are not developed to the point of demonstrating the abilities of consciousness. The soul's choices are constrained by limitations of his causal, subtle and gross bodies. While we cannot perceive the soul, the soul is that which remains unchanged and ties changing states as states of some *object*. Without such an object, there would be changes, but no causes.

The Vedic view reconciles correspondence, causality and eternity notions about reality in Western philosophy although the correspondence and causal views are not seen as reality. Experience (*madhyamā*) and matter (*vaikhari*) correspond because of language. Causality (*paśyanti*) and experience (*madhyamā*) are connected through a moral law. Finally, the conscious soul acquires a causal, subtle and gross body due to its desires to experience matter and objectify itself in that matter. The soul (*para*) is the ultimate cause of change, but *paśyanti*, *madhyamā* and *vaikhari* are also intermediate causes of the same experience.

Object Equals State

Modern science individuates matter into distinct objects even before we know their properties although we cannot identify these objects without knowing their properties. The notion that there is a particle even when we don't know any of its properties is a metaphysical assumption in science made to justify scientific realism—namely, the idea that matter exists objectively even when we don't know about it, and when we know it, our knowledge pertains to that object. Under this view of science, we assume that matter is individuated into distinct *objects* which, additionally, have a *state*. For instance, physics postulates that particles have position and momentum. While position and momentum are used to identify the particle, there is a difference between these dynamical properties and the particle itself: the *same* particle can have many positions and momenta. Therefore, at least logically, there is a difference between the particle and its state. While we cannot know the existence of the particle without knowing its state, the notion that there are individual particles is needed in science to claim that there is a reality which changes state while, in some respect, reality itself remains unchanged. If there are only changes but nothing persisting through these changes, then what is that reality which science describes in its theories?

In Vedic philosophy, matter is fundamentally undifferentiated. That is, matter does not exist as objects. Rather, objects are created when information is added to matter. In other words, information gives state to matter, by individuating it into separate objects. Information is the *state* of matter, and this state is the individuality of the object, or how it is different from other objects. In Vedic philosophy, therefore, there is a difference between matter and its state, but no difference between objects and their state. The state of matter is that it is individuated into objects by information. The state can be *described* in language, and pictures and books can hold information about an object's state. The state of an object can therefore also exist in other objects, and this gives rise to the possibility that we can create descriptions of state, and hence descriptions of objects. The object that describes other objects has two kinds of information: (a) that pertains to its own physical properties and (b) that pertains to other objects. In current science, the second type of information doesn't exist because science only describes an object's physical properties. Since the identity of an object is its state, an object has both physical and semantic identities. These identities are known through experience and what we get in experience is objective information, not matter. Indeed, we can never know matter as it exists without information because if there is no information then there are no objects. Adding information to matter makes matter *knowable*. In short, the study of reality is the study of the information that exists in matter, not of matter itself. Matter without information does not have an identity and without information, matter is not distinguished into objects. The identity and individuality of objects is the information that distinguishes one object from another. This information can be abstracted out of an object, and kept in other objects, senses, minds or intelligences.

Matter and information are separate categories in Vedic philosophy; they are both eternal, but their sources are different. Matter is eternal as an inactive and dormant substance (actually, we will see later that this substance is just space-time). It is existence without activity, consciousness and pleasure. Information, however, originates as alphabets of language from consciousness and these alphabets objectify meanings that consciousness can experience. These meanings include the way in which consciousness senses, acts, knows, judges, intends and enjoys. Consciousness too can exist in a state when it is inactive, does not have experiences and does not enjoy. In such a state, consciousness is very similar to matter, except that it has the *potential* to be active, conscious and enjoying. Matter does not have these potentials. In that sense, the inactive state in matter is permanent and is matter's fundamental property, while the inactive state in consciousness is a *choice*. When consciousness chooses to be active, conscious and enjoying, it objectifies forms of knowing, acting and enjoying into a primordial language of symbols. These symbols are objectifications of choices in consciousness and they represent exactly the manner in which consciousness *can* know, act and enjoy. Different living beings can mutate these elementary symbols into complex symbols. That is, every consciousness is different in its individual choices, but all choices are mutations of an elementary language of fundamental choices. This language is originally created by God, whose capacities to know, act and enjoy are qualitatively similar[8] to the manner in which living beings know, act and enjoy.

The language in nature represents the *atoms* of information. When information combines with matter, the choices of consciousness are embedded in matter and become the individuality or separateness of objects. Consciousness therefore does not create matter, although it creates individual objects out of undifferentiated matter. The existence of fundamental objects in nature cannot be justified based solely on the properties of matter, because these properties are themselves produced by choices. They can however be justified based on the properties of consciousness, or the linguistic choices in terms of which consciousness creates objects. Matter and consciousness in Vedic philosophy interact through language. The alphabets of this language are elementary choices of consciousness. Forms that objects can take are forms that consciousness can know, use and enjoy. If forms in matter were not based on the choices of consciousness, then we would not be able to know, use and enjoy matter. Consciousness interacts with matter when forms in matter are extracted into consciousness and when choices in consciousness are represented in matter. Everything that we can know, do and enjoy can be represented in matter, through this language of choices.

Information that originates as choices is embedded in matter as *forms* of knowing, which include how we sense matter (taste, touch, smell, sight and sound), how we think of matter as properties, how we combine these properties into complex objects, how we create intentions and ownership of objects and how intentions are based on various morals. Without choice or language, matter is formless. But matter is given a form by distinguishing and dividing matter into objects using language. Every form of distinction or individuality that exists in matter also exists as a fundamental distinction in language and the conscious observer. This isomorphism between the world of objects, the world of symbols and the world of observers is central to Vedic philosophy, and forms the basis for both its mystical and material descriptions. Empiricists recognize that matter can only be known in terms of our abilities to sense and know. But empiricists do not believe that matter *exists* in the same forms as we know it. This creates a paradox about how experiences are created from matter. This problem cannot be solved unless reality and experience have the same form.

Matter Produced from Dualism

The isomorphism between objects, symbols and experience also influences the Vedic mystical viewpoint because it implies that the reality seen in the universe has its roots in the choices of consciousness. The variety in the universe does not originate in matter itself. Rather, it originates as information in consciousness. This means that consciousness is superior to matter and gives *form* to matter. Matter is a medium of communication between observers, although matter is not the source of information. Information is rather created by consciousness and it can be destroyed by consciousness. The Vedas state that there are at least two kinds of information. Material information, the Vedas state, is based on duality and distinctions: if something is red, then it must not be blue, hot things are not cold. Duality leads to clash, conflict, contradictions and struggle between opposites. We struggle to reconcile differences and there cannot be perfect harmony in the material universe. To find perfect happiness, the Vedas state that one must capitulate to another non-dualistic mode of information in which forms are not created through distinction and duality. In this mode of language, there are assertions, but no negations. Now, the redness of an object doesn't imply that the object is not blue; something is hot, but it doesn't mean it is not cold. This mode of communication is devoid of clash, conflict and contradictions. But it is also devoid of knowing matter through distinctions.

Dualism and non-dualism are two forms of logic. Dualism enters language through the principles of non-contradiction and mutual-exclusion in dualistic logic. According to these principles, something must be either hot or cold (non-contradiction), and it cannot be anything other than hot and cold (mutual-exclusion). Non-dualistic logic preempts these principles. Now, the same thing may be described as warm, instead of hot and cold. Different individuals may perceive the same thing as hot, cold, and warm. Once non-contradiction and mutual-exclusion are dropped, reality need not be either hot or cold. Without duality, reality is hot, cold and warm all at once. The debate about whether reality is hot or cold is over, but the dialogue is not. Two individuals who have different beliefs about reality as hot and cold can converse about their experiences, and they will also treat it as *real* from the other person's perspective about reality. There is, hence, no contradiction between two individuals calling the same thing hot and cold. To understand why this is so, we need to recognize that our experiences are a product of our choices. Two individuals can see reality differently because they have different choices, or ways in which they perceive the same reality. Prior to these choices of perception, reality is all of its possible interpretations simultaneously, which choices can pick and elect.

Dual and non-dual uses of logic have their basis in two different ways in which we use choices. First, we may wish to know ourselves as individuals who are different from others, and this difference constitutes the basis of ordering (counting) things. Second, we may also wish to know ourselves as different individuals although that difference does not imply ordering (counting). In the dualist mode of logic, difference implies that one thing is superior (has more length, more mass, or more of some other property) than the other. In the non-dualistic mode, there are differences but there is no ordering because ordering depends on picking a standard scale relative to which comparisons take place. If all living beings are equally real and individual, and no one is smaller or bigger, then a standard cannot be picked and there is no counting. This non-dual mode of logic applies to what Vedas call the spiritual world. This spiritual world becomes the material world when a standard is picked because then distinctions, duality, conflict and counting begin[9].

In Vedic philosophy, matter and spirit are two different modes of language that employ different forms of logic. Mysticism based on non-dualistic logic and materialism based on dualistic logic are similar in the sense that the two languages employ the same words, sensations, concepts, propositions, intents and morals. But they are different because the underlying logical principles differ. Consciousness is spiritual and it should follow the non-dualistic mode of language. However, consciousness also has the ability to use dualistic language. The choice of language determines what consciousness experiences. Matter and spirit are therefore choices; they can be studied rationally and described linguistically, although they involve two different approaches to language and logic. By shifting choices, the material experiences are unmanifest and spiritual experiences are manifest, because all experiences are ultimately the products of choices. This view has direct consequences for the study of matter, because matter must now be described in terms of choices of consciousness and how choices are embedded in matter.

A Linguistic Reality

Matter in the Vedic view is a medium of communication between observers. In everyday communications, a sender objectifies meanings as symbols into matter, assuming a linguistic convention. The receiver must use the same linguistic convention to decode that meaning. The choice of convention represents the *protocol* of communication and to correctly communicate, the sender and receiver must use the same protocol. By using different protocols, communicators will receive identical *data* but derive different meanings—i.e. experiences from them. Inherent in every communication is therefore a choice of language. In Vedic philosophy, nature itself has a language in which meanings are encoded by physical states. This language transcends the linguistic conventions commonly used in everyday life. Nature's language, however, is not material. The Vedas state that the universe begins with language, which represents abilities in consciousness to consume and create meaning. All living beings have the same native abilities to process meaning, and they can potentially understand the same meanings. The meaning processing ability is, however, modified by a living being's senses, mind, intelligence, ego and consciousness. If something cannot be encoded into language then it also cannot be experienced. Conversely, if something can be experienced, then it can also be encoded in language[10].

Current science chooses a subset of nature's language obtained by objectifying sensations into physical properties and discards the rest. The choice of subset is itself not incorrect; what is flawed is the idea that this subset will explain everything in experience. In the scientific view, an experimenter encodes the energy, momentum, mass or charge of a particle, and the observer interprets the world according to these properties. This language is *incomplete* because it does not contain all the elementary semantic memes such as the ability to perceive color or taste or concepts like yellowness or sweetness. The scientific language is constructed by objectifying sensations, and every measurement of a physical property must in turn be mapped to an ordinary sensation.

However, in the process of objectifying, the words that describe sensations have become different from the words that describe physical states. For instance, the sensation of color is objectified as a frequency. This objectification has led to two problems. First, it makes the explanation of sensations impossible because how frequency becomes color has to be explained by a series of steps, in which each step only represents a new physical property although not a sensation. Once we separate the languages of experience and reality, there is no way to bridge them. Second, the objectification has made it impossible to study representations of meaning into matter. For instance, a position cannot represent color, and color cannot denote a state of the mind. Semantics in science requires that: (a) primary properties should be mapped to secondary properties—e.g., position can denote color, (b) matter should be described in terms of secondary properties—e.g. that a sunset can be yellow or apples can be red and, (c) secondary properties should be mapped to other secondary properties—e.g., redness can denote passion and yellow can denote knowledge. Semantic languages include all basic memes of experience. They also allow for the ability to map one meme in sensation to another meme in concept, context-sensitively.

From a non-semantic view, current science understands almost the entire universe except for the small but complex parts we call brains. From a semantic view, we understand the universe very little because we cannot assert almost anything in ordinary experience. If reality has to be described in terms of experience, then current science is mistaken in reducing sensations, properties, objects, intents and morality to primary properties. There is a counterpart of every experience in matter, but matter and mind are correlated as a sign and its meaning. The words that suitably describe experience can thus also be adequately used to describe material objects. The language of science can therefore be developed from an analysis of the basic elements of experience.

Nature as Word-Meaning

Sanskrit is the nature's language in Vedic philosophy and the laws of nature are the rules of grammar and phoneme-morphism that govern symbol combining. One important difference between Sanskrit and other languages is that alphabets in Sanskrit are directly meaningful while alphabets in other languages like English are generally not expected to be meaningful. Studies in phonosemantics[11] are, of course, discarding this view of language even in case of ordinary languages such as English, as it has become increasingly evident now that words and meanings have a tight correlation even in a language like English. The correlation is more rigorous and direct in Sanskrit. The alphabets of Sanskrit are elementary choices. Linguistic choices are manifest at the level of words, sensations, properties, objects, intents and morals, describing different parts of experience. Sanskrit is therefore a *natural* language in which consciousness can understand meanings, because its alphabets represent the manner in which consciousness chooses. In Sanskrit, the word-meaning association is given by the fact that letters themselves represent basic memes. Dictionaries are used for Sanskrit only because we do not comprehend the meanings of the alphabets themselves. But the sounds of Sanskrit words can be used to manipulate matter, indicating that word-meaning relationship is *natural* and not merely *human*.

This objective relation between sound and meaning creates the possibility that meanings can be objectively encoded in matter. Note how the objective encoding of meanings in matter is today precluded by our assumption that meanings are only in the mind. We also suppose that since minds evolved out of matter—which is without meaning—meanings and languages emerged late in the evolution of the universe, and these meanings are basically epiphenomena of human minds. There is still nothing in science that explains the existence of meaning, although scientists are certain that there could not be anything fundamental in nature that natively allows us to encode meanings. If, however, consciousness creates meanings through its choices, which give rise to objects, then matter must support the possibility of encoding meanings in objects. Indeed, now, objects are symbols created from meanings.

The Vedas describe creation as the process of manifesting words and meanings. Words are called *śabda-brahmān* and meanings are called *artha-brahmān*. *Śabda* or sound is the Vedic term for information. *Artha* denotes material elements through which these meanings are expressed, and which we regard as instances of the concepts. The concept is *śabda* while the material entity that encodes that *śabda* is called *artha*. *Śabda* is represented at various levels of experience including sensation, property, object, intent and morals. This means that an ordinary word like 'car' can denote sensation (e.g., redness), property (that cars have shapes), objects (that a car can be used to transport), intention (that I own a car) and value (that owning a car is a good thing). The same *śabda* is manifest at various levels, creating various types of experiences. *Śabda* denotes primordial alphabets while a*rtha* denotes all material elements in which these alphabets are embodied. The material elements include Earth, Water, Fire, Air and Ether, which embody sounds as sensations of smell, taste, sight, touch and sound, respectively. They also include subtle senses, mind, intelligence, ego and consciousness[12] which experience material objects as concepts, propositions, intentions and morals.

The Vedic notion of *śabda* and *artha* is different from the Western notions of word-meaning. Following Descartes, for instance, we would presume that meanings are in the mind and the meanings are about matter. In the Vedic view, even the mind is material, although a more subtle type of matter than the five gross elements. Similarly, senses, intelligence, ego and consciousness (sometimes called *chitta*) are also material. These elements combine with information to create mental or physical objects. Therefore, objects in the mind are meaning, just as objects in the world are meaning. The word behind these meanings is different from both mind and matter. Both mind and matter are produced from information to create atoms and complex objects and atomicity extends to all aspects of the gross and subtle bodies, not just to the atomicity of the gross elements. Thus, we can talk about 'mental objects' just like we can speak of physical objects[13]. All material elements can hold *śabda* or sound-meaning. This sound-meaning is originally meanings that consciousness can experience, and sound-meanings are created as expressions of the ability in consciousness to experience meaning. The material elements are carriers of meanings and they are produced from meanings. The sound-meanings combine with the elements to form objects. The sound-meanings are used by living beings to create different kinds of meaningful things in the world.

To understand the distinction between *śabda* and *artha* let us take the example of a travelogue again. The travelogue may be written on a piece of paper, a magnetic tape, computer disk, etc. We can decode the information on paper by seeing the writing, and we can decode the information on the magnetic tape by listening to the tape. The information obtained through seeing or hearing is identical, although the same information is physically expressed in different ways through sound and sight. The fact that information can be impressed into matter using properties that facilitate our hearing or seeing is incidental to the meaning of that information. Current science emphasizes the physical properties that help us see and hear, rather than the information that is conveyed through these properties. In Vedic philosophy, however, these physical properties are the medium and not the message. Matter is the medium for conveying the message and different types of material elements enable the same information to be encoded in different ways allowing us to gather information by hearing, touching, seeing, tasting and smelling, as well as thinking, judging, intending and valuing the objects.

Each medium is capable of representing the same information by using different physical properties: paper through the shapes of squiggles, magnetic tape or disk through the orientation of very small magnets, etc. The information itself is logical but the medium is material. In the same way, *śabda* is the logical content and *artha* is that content embodied in a medium. The same *śabda* can be encoded in different material elements. The knowledge is the same in each case, but the experiences derived from these combination objects are different. But there is also a sense in which *śabda* and *artha* are closely related and the meanings we experience are the meanings we can know. For instance, we can know and experience the color yellow. Color and yellow are therefore both *śabda* and *artha*. Nevertheless, *śabda* is the primordial cause while *artha* is its effect. Primordial matter has no distinctions until sound combines with it to create various objects and properties. Therefore, if matter has taste, it is because there is a primordial concept for taste in the language. The diversity and variety of material elements in nature is reconciled in the fact that all this variety originates as the choices of consciousness.

Sound is a divine creation and embodies all linguistic distinctions possible in the universe. Everything that can be known in nature is subject to distinctions that already exist in language. These distinctions are embedded in matter to create different objects. But since everything in nature is a product of applying language distinctions to primordial matter, all these products can be described by language. This idea is very important because it implies that everything in nature can be communicated through language, and hence there can be a language that describes every aspect of nature completely. Current science uses mathematical theories to model nature. However, mathematical symbols are only tokens; they do not carry meaning. In fact, a person unfamiliar with mathematical symbolism will not be able to understand the squiggles or signs on a paper describing mathematics. We therefore commonly assume that the signs are meaningless and the human mind gives these squiggles meanings. The Vedas however assert that beyond this human interpretation of meaning out of squiggles, there is an objective language that can encode meaning in matter. Using this language meanings can be encoded in nature in an observer independent manner, and this allows us to study meanings objectively. A book that holds meanings holds it in two ways—medium and content. The medium is paper with physical properties while the content is the printed words. However, the paper too can be described using words (e.g., color, texture, thickness, etc.) in the same way that the content is understood. Information therefore takes on two forms in the everyday world—a part of information becomes matter sensed by the senses while the other part remains meanings grasped by the mind, intelligence, ego and consciousness. Both these types of information are ultimately products of language.

In the Vedic view, there are four types of sound called *para, paśyanti, madhyamā* and *vaikhari* and these correspond to four stages of consciousness called *transcendent, deep-sleep, dreaming*, and *waking*, respectively. In the *para* stage, sound individuates different souls through differences in their native choices. In the *paśyanti* stage, sound is a subtle material covering of the soul formed on the basis of past experiences. This covering is unconscious during dreaming or waking stages, but tempers the native choices of consciousness through its prior impressions. In the *madhyamā* stage, sound denotes experiences in senses, mind, intelligence, ego and consciousness. In the *vaikhari* stage sound is encoded as objects. The four stages of sound-meaning map to the four stages of experiences and the living being experiences different kinds of meanings in each of these stages. In the *vaikhari* stage, meanings are viewed as objects, or objective knowledge. In the *paśyanti* stage meaning is perceived as the unconscious mind that rules over the conscious choices. In the *madhyamā* stage, the same meaning is viewed as conscious experience and choices. Ultimately, in the *para* stage meaning is seen as the individuality of the soul that transcends the unconscious.

The symbolic view runs deep through Vedic philosophy and brings the following important difference vis-à-vis modern science. In modern science, the ultimate reality is matter. In Sāṅkhya philosophy, matter includes not just gross elements behind sensations but also the subtle senses, mind, intelligence, ego, consciousness, and an even more subtle causal covering of the soul, which impels it to know and act. But all of these put together are still inadequate to explain the variety in the universe. Each of these elements merely constitutes a type of object differentiated from primordial matter by the application of linguistic choices. The informational variety is created by God who creates alphabets using which a living being may encode information into matter. Information originally comes from God, and the universe cannot be explained without reference to the information that God puts into the universe as alphabets that consciousness can know. God and individual consciousness are qualitatively similar in that they can both understand and speak the same language. Thus, the creation of meaning by God is also accessible to the individual living being. Matter, however, is separate from God; it is eternal, although not always differentiated into objects. God injects information into material carriers, creating varieties of objects.

Three Types of Bodies

Generally, all living beings in the material creation possess three kinds of bodies. The first is the gross material body comprising of the elements Earth, Water, Fire, Air and Ether. These elements are not the Earth or Water of ordinary experience. They are symbols that represent information about sensations of smell, taste, form, touch and sound, respectively. The second body is called the subtle body that comprises senses, mind, intelligence, ego and consciousness. This body creates all of our waking and dreaming experiences. Beyond the gross and subtle bodies, there is another deeper level of reality that controls the working of the subtle and gross bodies. This third body is called the causal body and constitutes all the unconscious propensities in a living being that preceded entry into the material creation. A universe in the Vedic philosophy is covered by layers of

Earth, Water, Fire, Air, Ether, mind, intelligence, ego and consciousness, and this constitutes the living being's waking and dreaming
experience. However, there is matter that lies outside the universe
of waking and dreaming experiences and controls them. The causal
body is unconscious because the living being becomes conscious
only after entering the universe and consciousness (as sensual experience) is itself produced from this subtle, unconscious matter. The
universes are submerged into a *kāraṇa* or causal ocean and the living being's body is also therefore called the *kāraṇa* or causal body.
This body comprises hidden and latent desires and the personality
of the living being, which determine how the living being wants to
know and act in the universe. Psychologists like Freud and Jung have
extensively studied the unconscious and its control over conscious
experience.

In Vedic philosophy, there is a distinction between the soul which
is eternal and the consciousness of the waking and dreaming experience which is created within the universe as the experience of the
senses. This consciousness is also sometimes called *mahattattva*,
which is a material element and can be created and destroyed. *Mahattattva* is the greatest element in the material creation, and it embodies the moral principles that govern an individual living being. From
this morality, intentions are created; from the intentions, objects are
created; from the objects properties are created; from properties sensations are created; and from sensations, material objects are created.
Mahattattva is however not the eternal consciousness of the soul,
although it is a representation of that soul in matter as the experience
of morality. We might also call it material choices or judgements about
the *value* of the material world. It is only when we value the world that
we know it; when the same world is devoid of value, the consciousness is withdrawn and the experiences cease.

Higher than the waking and dreaming consciousness is awareness of the unconscious realm. A living being becomes aware of the
unconscious only when he transcends the material universe, and
goes beyond the layers of senses, mind, intelligence, ego and sensual
experience. The unconscious represents a soul's impressions from
past lives, including from past universes. These impressions are outside dreaming and waking experiences although they create the moral

individual called *mahattattva*. Even when a living being exits the universe, he is not fully 'purified' of his unconscious desires and there is every chance that he can fall back into the material creation. But consciousness of the deep-sleep state brings a living being face-to-face with his impressions and he can see how these were created in past lives. Beyond this consciousness of the subtle personality and latent desires based on past impressions, lies a pure consciousness and personality. This pure consciousness is not free of desires and choices. Its choices instead give the soul a *form* which can be described in the language of elementary choice alphabets.

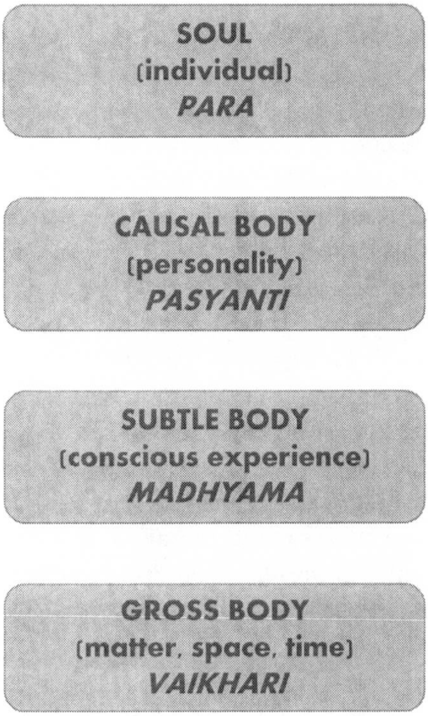

SOUL
(individual)
PARA

CAUSAL BODY
(personality)
PASYANTI

SUBTLE BODY
(conscious experience)
MADHYAMA

GROSS BODY
(matter, space, time)
VAIKHARI

Figure-4 The Three Bodies of the Soul

The Vedas prescribe that to discover this consciousness and its true nature we must purify ourselves of the consciousness of the waking and dreaming states, then exit the universe and free ourselves of the causal and latent desires. When the living being has freed itself of the other types of consciousness, which are described as 'coverings' of the living being, the latent consciousness becomes manifest again. At the end of the creation, the waking and dreaming experiences are destroyed but the unconscious desires and memories remain and the living being is merged into God's body, entering the 'deep-sleep' state of awareness, waiting for the universe to spring again. This state is exactly like the experience of deep-sleep and a living being is said to be in a deep-sleep outside the universe. When the universe is created again, the living beings are woken up, assigned a subtle and gross body and the waking and dreaming experiences begin again. Thus, the Vedas state, the cycle of birth and death, and creation and dissolution continues eternally unless a living being frees itself of the lower three types of consciousness.

The three bodies—gross, subtle and causal—are three stages of the development of experience, called waking, dreaming and deep sleep. There is a transcendent state of experience beyond these three stages, which is a spiritually perfected state of existence where the living beings have discarded their material coverings and are free of the three kinds of bodies. The native consciousness of the soul interacts with the causal body. The causal body interacts with the subtle body and the subtle body interacts with the gross body. Thus, the three bodies arise due to desires in the soul. These desires are tempered by past experiences, and develop into types of morals, intents, objects, properties and sensations, and then into material objects that objectify these experiences.

All three types of bodies can be studied scientifically but in different ways. The gross body must be studied as an objective representation of our sensations through senses, mind, intelligence, ego and consciousness. The experience of this subtle body is itself a symbol of a deeper causal realm of past impressions, desires and results of activities. The causal realm is in turn a symbol of the native personality of the soul. The native personality of the soul is reflected first in the causal body, then in the subtle body and finally in the gross body. The gross body is a symbol of the soul's propensities, how these propensities are conditioned by its past experiences, as well as how the past influences the present conscious states. There are thus many ways in which the gross body can be studied and its properties can be attributed to current mental states, past unconscious experiences and to the soul itself.

The Limits of Empiricism

Philosophers of science shudder to think about this observer-depen-dent nature of science. If science is in fact observer-dependent then how could we construct a 'universal' science? How could we claim that there is an objective reality whose properties are independent of our methods of knowing? If the properties in nature depend upon our methods of knowing then science would vary from one observer to another. This is where a philosophical revision to the nature of reality is needed. In Vedic philosophy, different observers can and often will see nature in different ways. Different species of life for instance have radically different ways of viewing the same reality. All these ways of viewing and describing reality are 'real' in a specific sense: they all *work* for those species of observers, because they are all empirical. The criterion for truth in science too is that science works empirically. If a scientific theory makes correct predictions, we can conclude that the theory describes reality. But we must also acknowledge that there are many ways to describe nature that work equally well, and the empirical successes of these descriptions themselves do not single out a particular theory of nature. Different species of life can for instance model nature in different ways and it works for them, according to their own viewpoints, quite well.

This fact is sometimes called *underdetermination* of reality by expe-rience. That is, reality can be described by many theories and expe-rienced in many different ways. This is important because we need to grant that all these varied theories—which may be constructed by different kinds of observers, including those in different species of life—are all 'real' as far as empirical successes go. We cannot choose between these theories if the only criterion for theory selection is empirical utility. Most scientists don't take underdetermination very seriously. They believe that eventually there will be one theory that describes everything, according to our viewpoint, and then we will not need to talk about the possibility for many theories, at least from a human perspective. What they ignore is that if the description of nature depends on observers then there should be *experiments* in which the empirical outcomes depend on the experimental setup. These experiments are not done by different species of life; they can be done by different members of the human species. In such experiments, there are many ways to describe nature and descriptions will depend on the *choice* of experimental setup. These setups are an objective, material counterpart of our senses and the mind, which are instruments we use to create observations. The important thing here is that when the experiment is changed, the observations are also changed empirically, so the view is *objective* and not *subjective*. That is, we are not talking about having a personal opinion about the nature of reality, but about objective facts in nature.

Experiment-dependent observations have been found in atomic theory. These experiments show that the 'same' reality can be described in many ways, like we might taste or smell the same food and use different words to describe it. Even if we use the same words (such as sweetness, which can denote smell or taste) their meanings will be quite different, as they correspond to different experiences. Even within current science, therefore, we are past the stage where matter has to be described in a unique way, although these implications are still not understood. The implication of underdetermination is that the question of reality cannot be settled simply by the empirical successes of our theories, because there are many ways in which we can describe nature, all empirically successful. The question of reality must be settled by arriving at a conception of reality that helps us reconcile an infinite amount of observer-dependent *interpretations* of reality with that reality. That is, we need a theory that explains how a single reality can produce many different interpretations, all *consistent* with that reality[14]. Reality must be consistent with many possible interpretations of that reality, and this realization injects a role for choice even at the level of theory formation.

Scientists currently believe that there is only one reality that is to be described in one way, by one theory. So, there is a one-to-one mapping between reality and its description. If in fact it turns out that the mapping between reality and its description is one-to-many, then that fact would require some basic shifts in our view of science. The most important shift is that we need to talk about how changes to our description of nature depend on the *interpretational stance* we take vis-à-vis nature. Our interpretational stance represents our choices, and by applying these choices we can change how we see this world and describe it in our theories. Since gross matter is only a symbol of our experience, by changing our experiences, we are not merely talking about a private idea, but about objective reality. Mind and matter are not two disparate things, and matter cannot be described without the mind. Rather, the description of matter depends on the interpretational stance we take towards matter, which is represented by the mind and senses.

With a revised theory of interaction between matter and the observer's senses, we will solve the empirical problem of explaining how different types of theories explain different experiences, but we still would not have solved the need in science to know the universal truth. If in fact there are many descriptions of nature, each of which appears to work for different observers, which of these descriptions is *real*? Which of these descriptions should be regarded as the preferred mode of describing nature? Obviously if these descriptions are all equally real from an empirical standpoint, then we cannot base our preference for theories on the empirical successes of theories. All descriptions are equally true and empirical truth in science has reached a limit because neither verificationism nor falsificationism will work.

This dead-end, as far as empiricism is concerned, requires a fundamental shift. We cannot now say that there is a universally true description of nature because that description works in some experiment or another. We must now talk about which description is *right* and *wrong*. Different descriptions are the products of different choices, and although all of these choices seem to work, there must be a preferred or correct choice. We cannot decide between choices at the level of matter, although we can ask ourselves: Which choice is the right choice for *me*? This constitutes the domain of morality and that of meanings about why we find some knowledge *significant* to us. The Vedas describe that the question of right and wrong is relative to a species and to the social role and status of an individual within a given species. Each such role and status specifies its own right and wrong. While many choices may work empirically, they are not always right. Rather, choices have to be associated with responsibility and accountability based on one's role in life.

When we make a choice to know and use the world in a specific way, the choice acts back on the individual. Choices therefore are not free because they react back on us. These reactions alter subtle and gross bodies and change the course of life. The Vedas call this the *law of karma*. *Karma* acts on different living beings in different ways. The consequences of different actions are different for different species, social statuses, genders and responsibilities of a given role in life. We intuitively understand this idea: for example, killing in a war is acceptable for a soldier but not acceptable for a civilian. Our subtle bodies exist in a subtle system that we call a *role*. Like gross material particles are collected into an ensemble, the subtle material particles are also collected into a role. In different roles, senses, mind, intelligence, ego and consciousness are expected to act and know differently. They have the ability and power to act even in ways incompatible with their role, and this is where the accountability in using our choices becomes very important.

The laws in current science apply equally to everything, including all living beings. However, in a moral science, the laws of nature are different for different species, roles and statuses in life. The moral science is also objective, because it can be articulated in a language. The moral science also deals with symbols, although these are symbols of the causal body, and their properties can be known in waking and dreaming experiences. Thus, while everyone can learn about the laws that apply to action in different roles, the laws don't apply to everyone and everything in the same manner. The laws are different for different living beings. Since there are many possible empirical descriptions and uses of nature, empirically true science is still incomplete, because it doesn't single out a particular theory that a person in a given role, social status or phase of life must use. To overcome this shortcoming, there is a need for theories and laws that apply to a specific species and social status, because the reactions of choices will act upon us differently than they will act on other living beings. Our choices in the material world have empirical consequences, but they also have moral consequences. The science of moral consequences solves the under-determination of scientific theories which affects the science of empirical consequences.

Questions of right and wrong will now ask: Is it *right* to hold such-and-such view of reality given that I am in a so-and-so species of life, charged with this-and-that duties, and accountable towards such-and-such members of this-and-that species? The actions of a person are judged not just by its empirical successes but also based on whether the person should do them. Eventually this science leads us to a theory of morality or what is also called the law of *karma* that decides the consequences of actions. The most common consequence is that if a living being adopts a certain viewpoint about nature, he would be transferred into a species of life where that viewpoint is acceptable behavior.

The moral science of values and signification is however still not complete. This is because a person might say: going to a different species of life is quite consistent with the ideas and ideals I hold dear. So, how is being a human being any better than being a tree or an animal or a bird? This question leads us to the next important facet of Vedic philosophy where we are required to inquire about the nature of happiness enjoyed in a particular species of life. Our philosophy of nature now takes another radical turn: we are not discussing what is *right* or *wrong* anymore but what is *good* or *bad*. Happiness is good and distress is bad. But what someone regards to be happiness is relative to that individual. The things that a dog or a goat considers happiness may be considered distress by humans. So, how could we judge the dog's experience from our viewpoint? This may seem like idle argumentation but it is related to a deep point in Vedic philosophy, namely that happiness and distress are not the products of mind, senses, intelligence or ego, but created by the consciousness. A morally correct action itself produces pleasure in consciousness whereby we feel peaceful and satisfied, even though the action my produce difficulties for the other senses. This means that happiness and distress are different from emotions or sensual, mental, intellectual or intentional pleasures. In many mystical and spiritual philosophies therefore a distinction is drawn between the pleasure of the senses and the idea of happiness. People might say that the possession of goods does not lead to real happiness, because happiness is characterized by peace and contentment. Questions about *good* and *bad* are thus concerned with a deeper level of happiness and not with pleasures.

A discussion of happiness is the vista to the nature of the soul and its entanglement in the material creation. Note how the laws of *karma* are compatible with the existence of the soul but don't require its existence. Buddhism in fact speaks about the mind and the transmigration from body to body without talking about the soul. Buddhism attributes happiness and suffering to a living being's illusion but does not explain why that illusion conditions the soul. The Vedic philosophy is that the unconscious body of the living being consists of *māya* which conditions the soul to think that it exists in a specific time and place and possesses certain knowledge, preferences and abilities. When experiences accord with this limited sense of the self—that *māya* has created for the soul—the soul creates happiness out of itself. When the experiences don't accord with the individuality, the soul creates unhappiness. There is hence no objective or inter-subjective criterion for happiness. The criterion is subjective. Of course, both suffering and happiness in Vedic philosophy are illusory, because they depend on our limited vision of ourselves as beings in time and place, with limited knowledge, abilities and preferences. These limitations of *māya* are not the true personality of the living being. Rather, *māya* creates an illusion of a limited personality and constrains the living being to think itself as constrained. This realization is enough to put a living being on a path in search of its real personality.

The above discussion hopefully shows how questions of soul, transmigration and salvation are relevant to science. Current science describes nature irrespective of its relation to the observer's senses and minds. This science has its limitations, and will fail to account for observed differences when the experimental setups are changed. Changes to this science require the additional idea that our observations are relative to the observer's senses and mind. Different observers can choose to describe nature in different ways, and there are many ways to know and use the world, which work equally well as far as empirical successes are concerned. However, these empirical successes do not necessarily imply that we are choosing the right theory and technology. Modern technology for instance gives us tremendous powers through weapons and instruments that help us exploit nature to our benefit. But this exploitation of nature is not without its adverse consequences. Without a firm basis for analyzing right and wrong, and how our choices act back on our subtle body, it is hard to change the current course of science.

The next step therefore requires the formulation of laws that connect choices in the subtle body with their consequences—i.e. a different subtle body. The study of this action and reaction forms a new science of actions that specifies the consequences of choices for different individuals in different roles in society. The human society is classified in the Vedas according to the *varna-aśrama* system of classes and stages of life and many people think that this is a caste system unjust to certain classes of people. They need to realize that *varna-aśrama* is based on a subtle science of choices and the consequences of one's choices are different based upon which *varna* or *aśrama* you belong to. The *karma* produced by an action is different for individuals in different classes and states. The classification is therefore objective and scientific, although we are unaware of the science by which choices create consequences[15].

Finally, we need to understand how happiness and suffering depend on the causal body and not on gross or subtle bodies. What gives me happiness may be saddening for another person, so this difference cannot be accounted for in terms of the state of the external world. It can be partially accounted for in terms of the type of mind that experiences it. But, ultimately, happiness is a function of who we believe we are, and that personality is outside the waking and dreaming experience. The personality manifests in our waking and dreaming experience but the subtle repository of our desires and past experiences is hidden from the waking and dreaming experiences. Thus many people are born artists or musicians and we cannot trace their tendencies to their waking or dreaming experiences. We might argue that tendencies in the living being are due to the experiences in the past life, and therefore they are part of the subtle body. But Vedic philosophy tells us that these tendencies survive even the dissolution of the universe, when both the subtle and gross bodies are dissolved and even the material ingredients making up these bodies do not exist. Therefore, if our tendencies existed in the subtle body, then they would be finished with the subtle body during the annihilation of the universe. However, these tendencies survive the annihilation and they are therefore outside the material creation. Our experiences leave behind impressions that are stored in a subtle unconscious realm which is outside the waking and dreaming stages of experience within the universe. The tendencies we are exhibiting in the present life therefore are not just products of past lives in the present creation, but also due to an uncountable number of lives in prior creations as well. The present universe and our present body are created based upon these subtle impressions that exist as our unconscious which is the realm of our latent desires for different kinds of life forms.

Each of the three kinds of bodies involves a science subtler than the previous. To understand these sciences, we require three shifts in thinking. First, current science studies the question of true and false, based on sensations, and this study is (believed to be) universal and applicable to all matter. But, as we've seen, this way of doing science is also underdetermined because each individual can choose a different way of describing reality. The study of nature based on empirical criteria therefore will reach a limit when we realize that there are many true descriptions of nature that are equally good empirically. Different species of life, for instance, view the same nature differently. Since questions of ultimate truth cannot be settled merely by the empirical successes of our theories, a new criterion about right and wrong must be invoked. We must ask—given that there are many possible truths, which truth represents the *right* way of knowing and using reality? This gives us a new science of choice and responsibility in which our choices have to be used according to our role and status in the universe. This science is not universal, but it applies to a class of species, roles and statues in life. But, ultimately, the laws of choice also cannot decide the best type of knowledge or action for me as an individual because there are many right things, all consistent with a species, role or relation in society. We might say that some choices are good for a role and status in society, but which amongst these possible choices must *I* as an individual make? One question about choices must eventually be asked: What is the action or knowledge that results in *my* happiness? The answer depends on the type of conditioned or pure personality and what one consider happiness or distress based upon prior impressions in past lives.

In Vedic philosophy, therefore, science progresses from a purely objective study to an inter-subjective criteria based on morals to a purely subjective criteria based on individuality and personality. While universal principles can be articulated in each such science, these principles leave room for choices of right and wrong and judgments of good and bad. We are therefore free to choose a type of sensation and theory to describe the gross material world, because we find the theory *right*. We are further free to pick from amongst many right viewpoints a specific viewpoint because we individually find it more pleasurable. Physical, moral and personal outcomes depend on the nature of choices.

The Problem of Contextual Knowledge

Perhaps the hardest notion to understand from the perspective of modern science is the idea of a whole within which the parts get a semantic identity. This is hard because modern science thinks in terms of objects and not in terms of systems. A system is a collection of objects, but since there is nothing material about a collection, science supposes that there could not be causal effects of collecting something, and the collection is causally irrelevant to science. Since we don't sense wholes like we taste, touch, see, smell or hear objects, it is hard to ascertain their properties and effects. The solution to this problem is that while the boundaries of collections cannot be sensed, they produce effects which can be sensed.

This means that the effect of a context is perceivable in an object, because it alters the state of that object, although we cannot perceive the context. Classical physics began with the idea that both causes and their effects must be perceivable. This is not true in general since concepts like electrons and protons cannot be sensed, although their effects can be perceived. Furthermore, this idea is also not true when science postulates 'action at a distance' because the so-called 'force' which acts at a distance cannot be perceived. Theory trumped experience in science because the force could not be observed other than

through its effects. It was acceptable to postulate such fictitious entities as long as they helped explain experiences. In a similar vein, context cannot be measured by senses, but it can be used as a theoretical
construct.

The success of a theory in explaining phenomena implies the reality
of the theoretical constructs postulated in the theory, even though the
theoretical constructs themselves cannot be observed. Similarly, even
though we cannot directly observe a collection, it can be postulated as
a theoretical construct whose effects can be perceived. This notion of
'scientific realism' is inadequate in the sense that if theoretical entities can never be observed, how can a scientist intuit such realities?
Vedic philosophy offers a solution: all theoretical entities are perceivable by the mind, intelligence, ego or consciousness, and theories
emerge from something that the observer can think, judge, intend or
value, even though we cannot directly see, taste, touch, smell or hear
them. In a sense, therefore, the scientist evolves science not based
on sensations but based on ideas whose effects change sensations.
In classical physics, most of the scientific ideas—e.g. mass, charge,
momentum, space and time—were generalized from sensations, just
as the concept yellow is the generalization of a certain type of color
sensation. Semantic science however requires ideas that will never
be generalized from individual objects. However, they can be generalized from object collections and relations between objects. While
senses perceive individual sensations, the mind, intelligence, ego and
consciousness are involved in aggregating and relating the world of
things together. In that sense, when using ideas about collections
and relations, we have already stepped beyond the ordinary world
of sensations, although not beyond experience itself.

Collections and relations cannot be sensed but their effects can, and
they are therefore theoretical constructs that can be used to explain
sensations. These theoretical constructs originate in the abilities of the
mind, intelligence, ego and consciousness to think, judge, intend and
value, not in the perception of sensations. To understand semantics,
science has to intuit ideas from a part of experience that goes beyond
sensations. These theories will be understood, not by pointing to something that can be sensed, but by appealing to ordinary notions about collections and relations which can be thought, judged, intended or valued.

The Problem of Universals

Universals are thought to be opposed to the idea of contexts, since it is commonly believed that ideas combine and relate only in the real world, but not in the ideal world. In the Platonic ideal world, all ideas exist as pure individuals, not as collections or relations. This sort of idealism suffers from the glut of ideas since if there was a complex idea formed out of collecting or relating other elementary ideas, the combination or relation too must exist as a pure individual in the ideal world. Platonic idealism is therefore flawed because it is not parsimonious. In science, the complexity of the universe is derived by mutating elementary things called atoms. Science aims to be parsimonious by using as few concepts as necessary. By allowing perfect instances of everything to exist eternally as individuals in the ideal world, Platonism doesn't help explain the *origin* of complex ideas from simpler ones. The Vedic outlook is also idealistic, but in a different sense than Platonic idealism. In Vedic philosophy, there is a core set of elementary ideas represented by the alphabets in language. These ideas are, however, not the only possible ideas. Like alphabets can combine to create words, sentences and paragraphs through rules of combining elementary memes, there is a fundamental role for relations and combinations in generating new ideas.

Ordinary language uses many ideas that are directly related to sensations. For example, the abilities to see, taste, touch, smell and hear are elementary ideas. These ideas are divided into many modes of perception, such as the abilities to see color, form and intensity as modes in seeing. Similarly, the abilities to hear tone, pitch and rhythm are modes in hearing. Colors and tones themselves are divided into many types, creating more ideas such as yellow and red for color or different notes for tones. Beyond the ideas gained and generalized from the senses, there are other ideas created by combining and relating these elementary ideas. For instance the idea of a pot combines several sensations. Similarly, ideas about intentionality and morality are deeper ideas. Combining, relating, judging and valuing are elementary ideas, but different from the ones that we sense. In Vedic philosophy, therefore, the elementary ideas include not just the basic memes from senses (e.g., taste and smell) but also memes represented by the mind (thinking), intelligence (judging), ego (intending) and consciousness (moralizing).

All elementary memes are produced from the choices of consciousness. However, given that these choices can represent sensual, mental, intellectual, intentional and moral memes, the full expression of these choices requires the development of various types of cognitive and conative faculties. Senses, mind, intelligence, ego and morality are thus developed to express the full range of choices in consciousness. The ultimate Platonic world of ideas in Vedic philosophy is consciousness, from which all possible ideas originate. But this Platonic world is not an ideal world of ideas; it can also be embedded into matter just as Aristotle thought that forms are embedded into matter. Consciousness as the source of all ideas is embedded in matter to create specific types of individual things. These things may be aggregations and relations of more elementary types, because the relation or collection is also an elementary idea. Consciousness is the Platonic world from which all ideas are created. Each consciousness mutates and combines elementary ideas in different ways, thereby creating various types of sensation, thinking, judging, intended and moralizing. These choices limit the possibilities of consciousness in deference of being a specific type of individual.

This fact brings out the tension between universal and particular in Plato's philosophy, since, as Plato himself said, no individual is as perfect as the universal. The world of particular things is an imperfect reflection of ideals in the world of universals in Plato's philosophy. In Vedic philosophy, however, the universal becomes a particular through a choice. As a universal, consciousness is merely the possibility of being a particular. Choices convert the universal into a particular. This is unlike Plato's ideals where these universals are reflected in matter. This might seem to suggest that choice is an accidental covering of consciousness and impersonal interpretations of Vedic philosophy regard this covering as an illusion. Becoming free from choices is therefore seen as a return from particular to universal, and that unified, undifferentiated universal is called *Brahman*. However, personalist interpretations of Vedic philosophy regard choices as an innate aspect of consciousness, although different from its existential feature. The existential feature subsists as the possibility of choices, while the individual realizes these possibilities.

In Vedic philosophy, universality is only one feature of consciousness. The universal possibility is complemented by individual choices. With choices, the universal becomes individuals, but these are not material individuals. The singular, possible universal becomes many particulars through choice. Both the universal and the particular are ultimately not ideas or things but living beings. God too is an individual and His consciousness is qualitatively the same as other living beings. The difference between God and other living beings is that He can enact all possibilities simultaneously. In that respect, all other individuals only partially experience the possibility, but God enacts all the possibilities at once. He is therefore the completeness of experience. The power of choice is called *śakti* in Vedic philosophy and God's *śakti* allows Him to be all possibilities (even contradictory ones) simultaneously. Thus, he is simultaneously the perfect hot and cold, big and small, light and dark, because of His *śakti*. Other living beings are similar to God in the sense that they have the same possibilities. But, they don't have the same type of *śakti* or power of choice to become contradictory things at once.

The Three Features of Knowledge

Vedic philosophy describes consciousness as existing in three states. First, consciousness is the possibility of choices, which creates a language from which other types of things can be created. This language is incomplete without choices that combine memes into complex ideas. Therefore, choices are the second feature of consciousness. With choices, an individual is produced, and this is the third feature of consciousness. The Vedas state that consciousness is natively individual given that choices are an inextricable aspect of consciousness. Nevertheless, it is possible to decouple the individual into a possibility and a choice. This triad of language, choice and individuality applies not just to consciousness but also to the ordinary world. Let's explore its application through the idea of a *pot*. We can understand the idea of a pot in three ways.

First, we might look at various pots and see their different shapes, sizes and functions as alternative possibilities of the idea of pot. Second, we can assert that these differences are created by choices. Third, we might say that there is a perfect pot that embodies differences of pot variety. In other words, the idea of pot can be derived from generalizing the concept of many imperfect pots, or it can be derived by abstracting the perfection from a perfected pot. Plato only took the first route to ideas, but in Vedic philosophy, the second path is considered the real origin of ideas. That is, the ideals come from the ideal individual who externalizes His ideals into ideas. These ideals are then modified into imperfect instances of an idea that was derived from the perfect ideal.

AN INDIVIDUAL POT　　　THE POTNESS CLASS　　　THE IDEAL POT

Figure-5 Three Notions of Pot

These three states of knowing are respectively called *Brahmān, Paramātma* and *Bhagavān. Brahmān* is the pure possibility of a something, e.g., the idea of a pot. *Paramātma* represents the choices that convert possibility into an individual. *Bhagavān* is the perfect individual. Of course, in Vedic philosophy, these three states of knowing are applied not to pots but to knowledge of the absolute truth as possibility, choice and perfect instance. But the same idea can also be grasped through other objects.

The reality is consciousness, underlying all phenomena. All living beings including God have the same *type* in the sense that they can potentially make the same choices. This possibility embodies itself as the *language* of symbols which they can understand and use. When the spiritualist sees everything as one type, he basically sees abilities of consciousness which are *possible* in every type of individual being. This understanding is not incorrect, but it is not the whole truth, because a consciousness has free will by which it chooses to be something specific, given that it can potentially choose everything possible. The complete understanding is that all souls have the same type, but due to free will they choose to be something specific. All souls constitute *Brahmān*. They have capacity for choice by which they become individuals and this individuality is *Paramātma*. But, there is still an original perfect instance called *Bhagavān*. His personality first becomes the Supreme Type, and then expands to create many (incomplete) instances of that same type. These instances all have free will (they are of the same type as God) but they use that will in different ways, becoming different persons.

This spiritual philosophy in the Vedas reduces the problem of knowing the nature of an object to knowing oneself as an individual person. All persons in the universe have the same type because they have the same possibilities of experience in consciousness. These possibilities are reflected in matter as sensations, properties, objects, intents and morals. By knowing these abilities we can understand the nature of consciousness, as the Universal Type. After that, we can choose what we want to be. The study of matter is a window into the nature of the self as consciousness and its abilities. Material science can tell us that there are several different categories of meanings, and they are experienced by consciousness because consciousness is capable of them.

4

The Vedic Theory of Matter

What we observe as material bodies and forces are nothing but shapes and variations in the structure of space.

—*Erwin Schrödinger*

The Realism of Sensations

Early in the history of Empiricism it was recognized that what science calls primary properties (length, frequency, momentum, energy, etc.) are not directly accessible to us. These properties are known through sensations (smell, taste, color, sound and touch), which are called secondary properties. Empiricists argued that we have no way of knowing whether the world actually has primary properties; all we can know is that we have some sensations. But philosophical terminology played an important role in the subsequent evolution of science: the physical world was considered 'primary' and the world of sensations 'secondary' although the empiricist argument was that primary properties are derived from secondary properties, by objectifying secondary properties.

The terminology betrayed an important bias in our worldview, where we think that our experiences are created by the external world, comprised of objects, which is different than how we experience these objects. Given this bias, science progressed by *objectifying* our sensations into physical properties. This bias is not entirely wrong because to know if our theories are true, experiences must correspond to reality. For the experiences to correspond to some reality there must in fact be some reality. Fundamentally, therefore, there is no flaw in

93

assuming that there is an external reality to which our experiences must correspond. However, the manner in which this objectification was carried out also created a schism between the language of experience and the language of science, because objectification assumed that objects are fundamentally different from how we observe them. Science, for example, objectified the sensation of color into the frequency of light which is emitted when an atom transitions from a high-energy to a low-energy state. This description made it impossible to assert that objects are in fact red or green; we say that reality is atoms which *appears* to us as red or green. All everyday descriptions of nature based on sensations now ring hollow because sensations are just appearances and not reality.

The reduction of sensations to classical properties leads to the view that nature indeed has properties like mass, charge, energy, momentum, etc., while properties like color, taste, smell, touch and sound are only mental byproducts of the physical properties. The senses are thus not sources of true knowledge about reality, because reality is *never* how it appears to us. But if reality is never like its perception, then how is reality perceived in the brain? The idea that reality and perception are different is a type of mind-body dualism in which we employ two different languages to describe reality and experience. The mind is however represented in the brain. If matter has physical properties but no perceptual qualities, then how is the brain getting those perceptual qualities? The problem of the brain alters the landscape of discussion on whether sensations are real, because if sensations are not real, then science must explain how physical properties create sensations in the brain.

The Vedic view is that reality holds *information* about sensation although reality itself is not sensation. The external world is symbolic and represents a description of experience. When we perceive a red color, the sensation of redness in the observer is the creation of the observer's senses. Corresponding to this sensation are two kinds of representations—one in the brain and another in the external world. They both encode information about redness, not about primary properties like frequency. The external world (and the brain) is *knowledge* of red and the observer has the *experience* of red. External reality is the symbolic representation of the experience of redness, similar to the word 'red' which has a specific sound and physical form that denotes the meaning redness. The senses convert the information about red into experience of redness. This allows us to assert that when I see a red object, the world is in fact really red, without claiming that the world is sensations. There are thus two kinds of redness— knowledge and experience. What we call sensations is the experience of redness, but there is another kind of redness that exists symbolically as a representation of experience. This is a fundamental shift in thinking because it collapses the divide between the languages used to describe reality and their experiences. In current science, reality is primary properties while sensations are secondary properties. If, however, reality itself encodes redness, then both reality and its experience can be described by the same word—i.e. red—without reducing reality to experience or vice versa.

You might argue that things we claim to be red are not always perceived as red. For instance, in darkness, a red object may be seen as black, and in blue light it might appear purple. How then can we apply the idea that there is in fact a red object when we don't always see it as red? Science solves this problem by contextualizing the outcome of measurement on experimental setup. If the experimental setup is changed, the outcome of measurement will also change. A similar contextualization needs to be done in the symbolic view as well. We must say that the external world is a symbol of redness but in order to comprehend that symbol we need to 'read' it according to the norms of language in which it was encoded. This may include, for example, viewing objects under white light. This criterion is not new for us. It exists in science and in everyday methods of interpreting facts into meanings. A computer disk can store pictures in decimal, octal or hexadecimal representation schemes. If the picture was stored in the decimal scheme but is read in the octal scheme, the picture would be garbled, although even that garbled picture would be intrinsically related to the picture as it was intended to be interpreted. When meanings are encoded using symbols, a *language* is used to convert meanings into symbols. The linguistic conventions that were used in encoding must be used for decoding as well. Seeing an object under blue light when it was intended to be seen under white light changes the linguistic interpretation. The resulting experience produces a new meaning, related to the original meaning, just as we could read a binary encoded number decimally.

This view dramatically changes the reality in science from things to meanings. That is, reality itself encodes properties of red, sweet, hard, pungent or cold although not as sensations. Reality is objective information that defines how it was encoded to be perceived. The same language can be used to describe reality and its sensations and the senses become sources for the nature of reality. That is, when we see red, the reality is potentially red. This is a far cry from modern science where reality is always primary properties and can therefore never be red.

A Theory of Elements

The Vedas state that for every type of sensation, there is a type of material atom that represents—and hence objectifies—that sensation. Thus, Ether is the element that corresponds to the sensation of sound, Air to the sensation of touch, Fire to the sensation of sight, Water to the sensation of taste and Earth to the sensation of smell. There are at least two naïve interpretations of this idea. The first interprets these ideas in terms of ordinary concepts of fire, water or earth. The second sees elements as 'substances' similar to Greeks. These interpretations are naïve because ordinary concepts about water and earth are not directly associated with taste and smell, while the Vedic notions are, although water and earth do have taste and smell. Furthermore, the Vedic elements are not substances, because the notion of substance is something that is eternal and in Vedic philosophy matter is a phenomena and not reality. But, most importantly, naïve views are dissimilar to the Vedic notion because the elements are created from the senses, similar to how the mind creates ideas. To understand the Vedic view of matter, we must therefore first understand its view of senses. In the current philosophy of perception, a 'sense' is that which observes reality but doesn't create reality. In Vedic philosophy, all senses are capable of creating and consuming information. Like the mind can create and understand concepts, senses can also create and consume sensations. The creative potential in the senses is seen during dreams, hallucinations and visions. The Vedas state that during the creation of the universe, matter is manifested from the senses, quite like ideas are created by the mind. The creation of matter from senses is mediated by *tanmātra* which are basic sensation-meanings. The senses produce sensation-meanings (like the mind creates concepts) which are externalized into objects as symbols of sensations. Conversely, the senses extract the *tanmātra* from material objects, just as the mind grasps concepts from the objects.

There are three important consequences of this stance towards material properties. First, material properties are not logically prior to senses and sensation. Rather, sensation is produced by senses, which is then objectified as physical properties. If senses are needed to produce the objectification of sensation, then senses are logically prior to the material objects. Second, since objects are created from *tanmātra* (information about sensations), objects must be described in terms of the sensations they create in observers. The notion that nature is primary properties that cause secondary properties in the observer is inverted in the Vedic view. Matter is the objectification of secondary properties. When these objects are compared to other objects, nature is seen as primary properties. When these objects are perceived as *types*, they can be seen as symbols of secondary properties. Thus, primary properties (e.g., frequency) are created from secondary properties (e.g., color). Indeed, in the correct description of reality, nature is a *symbol* of color but it can be described as frequency. Third, the senses do not just *perceive* sensations, they can also *create* sensations. Dreaming, hallucinations and misperceptions are examples in which sensations are created by the senses. The translation of dreams and visions into reality involves ideation and action, which the Vedas state is done by the mind and senses.

The current view of sensation in science is founded on the Lockean thesis that the mind is *tabula rasa* or a blank slate which absorbs data from the external world, although it does not create the data. While Locke acknowledged that the mind does create ideas by combining the ideas obtained from the world, he claimed that the mind of a child at birth is blank and must acquire ideas from the world before it can create any new ideas. In Vedic philosophy, the mind at birth is not a blank slate and it carries impressions from past lives which are embodied in the unconscious. The mind is therefore shaped by past impressions which enable the mind to create new ideas, besides acquiring them from the world. But even more profound than this is the idea that, originally, all matter is produced from sensations which were created by the senses. In other words, material objects are not prior to their observations. Rather, observers are prior to sensations which are prior to objects.

The idea that senses produce sensations which are then objectified in matter changes the way we look at matter. Material elements are actually symbols of the sensations; they objectify sensations within matter in the sense of describing them. Ether is therefore the symbol of perceived sound; Air is the symbol of touch; Fire is a symbol of color and form; Water is the symbol of taste and Earth is the symbol of smell. An observer's senses interact with these symbols to create sensations, quite like we might read a travelogue and derive first the knowledge and then the experience of traveling. There can be different types of tastes, smells, sounds, touches and colors and the states of atoms are objectifications of these sensations. In other words, if we see a color, then there exists an objectified symbol of that color in the observer's brain. And if that experience is not an illusion, then there is also a direct physical correlate of that sensation in the external world. Since my brain state can be about someone else's brain state, the brain state and states in the external world are both representations of information content.

The Vedic solution to the problem of perception rejects the idea that there are objective physical properties like mass and charge. There is, however, in Vedic philosophy, information in matter that describes how this matter can be perceived. The information is objective in the sense that if different observers used the same procedures to 'read' this information—i.e. if they have the same types of senses that observe—they will obtain the same type of sensations. The ability to encode information in matter changes the ideology about matter. The external world does not have mass or charge although there is information whose effect we *model* as the presence of mass and charge. Mass and charge are thus not reality, but they arise as physical properties when we measure objects against other objects rather than against an observer's senses. The same reality can also be modeled as information, rather than as physical properties like mass and charge. Of course, information has a physical existence, because otherwise we could not assert the existence of some reality behind the sensation of reality. For information to exist physically there must be some real physical properties that encode information. So, if mass and charge are not real, then what are the real physical properties which encode information within matter?

In Vedic philosophy, the physical world is space-time and all other properties in matter are created as modifications of space-time; we can say that all physical properties are essentially properties of space-time. Thus, Ether is the first material element and all other material elements emerge from it. Reality represents information about experience, which is encoded in space-time. Without information, space-time is symmetric (and the symmetry properties of space-time have been used in physics to define conserved quantities like momentum, angular momentum and energy). Adding information breaks symmetry. This asymmetry now appears as space-time *forms*. Relativity Theory shows how mass emerges from space-time curvature. Subsequently, many theories were formulated to convert other dynamical properties to space-time forms. The remarkable insight from these theories is that matter is not needed to account for experiences. Rather, a vacuum is sufficient to account for everything. The vacuum, of course, is, in one sense, empty but its vibration, bending, twisting and swirling represents physical properties. Current space-time theory does not see forms in space-time as symbols of information. Rather, current physics interprets these forms as mass and charge which is incorrect. A semantic interpretation will see space-time forms as asymmetry which can denote semantic information.

To encode information, symbols must be extended; a point particle cannot symbolize any idea. In written languages, extended forms are used to encode meanings. That shapes and forms can represent meanings is well-known. Through such encoding, meaning does not reduce to extended forms, although the spatial form becomes a sign or token of the meaning. A variety of distinct forms can be used to encode different types of meanings, and to know this relationship between meaning and form, the natural language of forms must be uncovered. Many meanings are denoted not by static forms but by patterns of activities. Material objects are already known to have various types of motions—translation, rotation, revolution, expansion, contraction, bending, etc. These patterns of change can also be applied to spatial forms to encode meaning. Every meaning in experience can be encoded in a language and every word in the language can be reduced to some space-time form. Space and time therefore suffice to encode all types of symbols.

A naïve interpretation of elements leads to the idea that these elements denote either substances or things like water, fire, soil, air and space. The elements are, however, neither substances nor everyday objects. Ether, Air, Fire, Water and Earth are different types of information that represent sound, touch, sight, taste and smell. Ether encodes tone, pitch, and audible forms. Air encodes heat, weight and roughness, sensed during touch. Fire encodes color, shape and brightness, which are seen. Water encodes flavor, softness, and intensity, which are tasted. Earth encodes flavor, intensity and sharpness of smell. These elements are therefore symbols of information. All these symbols are created from space-time which acts as the medium for encoding information. Like data can be written to a magnetic disk, Ether is the element that allows the encoding of all information as sound vibration, or words that represent meanings. When the sound is condensed, or when more information is packed in the same space, touch is produced and this condensed form of sound is called Air. There are two ways to look at Air. First, we can see it as a larger amount of information than that which existed in Ether. Second, we can view this larger amount of information as being created by elaborating the information that existed in Ether; for instance, if the sound in Ether was the concept of 'hot' then the element of Air elaborates the idea of heat to a level where the sense of touch can feel the heat. Thus, one can know about heat by hearing the sound, and also by touch. Things that can be touched can also be heard, but not vice versa. The touch therefore develops from the elaboration of sound.

Subsequent elements like Fire, Water and Earth are similarly developed by further elaboration of the information that forms Air. For instance, if the sound in Ether represented 'sweet smell', then this idea will require something that can be touched, seen and tasted, before it develops into something that can be smelt. The development of sound into other elements is similar to how we can create a rough sketch of a building before the building is constructed. As the building is defined to greater levels of detail, more refinements are added to that sketch until the sketch itself becomes the building. Thus, underlying everything that we can touch, see, taste or smell are ideas. Things are elaborations of those ideas and a space-time form gradually becomes a thing as information is added to elaborate the idea. Everything originates as an idea. As ideas are developed by adding details, physical things are produced.

The Origin of the Elements

The Vedic theory of elements has similarities to modern theories about information communication. In modern wireless communication, information is carried upon a wave 'carrier'. This superposition of the carrier and information is called modulation. Electromagnetic waves are *modulated* to carry voice, video or data. In one sense, voice, video and data are nothing but vibrations of the wave. But, in another sense, when those vibrations are interpreted by a linguistic convention, the wave's physical properties have meaning. Thus, the physical vibrations of an electromagnetic wave can also be described as a picture, video or book. In a similar way, in Vedic philosophy, the successive elements of Air, Fire, Water and Earth are created by adding information 'within' the previous element. To add information, the previous element is divided into smaller parts and the structure of that division represents additional information. This is similar to modulation where information is added on some 'carrier' to create a finer structure. Thus, Air is a modulation of Ether, Fire is a modulation of Air, Water is a modulation of Fire and Earth is a modulation of Water. During modulation, information is added to a carrier, and the carrier thus acquires a finer structure.

The Ether encodes sensual information about sound, but conceptual information about touch, sight, taste and smell. When further information is added to Ether, conceptual information about touch, sight, taste and smell is converted into sensual information about touch, sight, taste and smell. The sensual information is therefore only a refinement of the conceptual information. As some idea becomes more and more detailed it creates sensations *corresponding* to that idea. If, however, the idea is abstract, then it appears to us as sound. The Vedas describe that material objects emerge from the Ether. All material objects are information which is first encoded by the mind in the Ether. At this point, the object in question is only a sound vibration. This vibration can be heard but cannot be touched, seen, tasted or smelt. Subsequently, as this sound is refined by adding more and more details, the information object becomes increasingly more 'dense' and it can be sensed through touch, sight, taste and smell. The object of smell and the sound of smell have the same concept but the object of smell elaborates the concept.

Compare this idea with how a painter develops a painting through multiple stages. First, the painter may sketch a broad outline of the painting on a blank canvas, giving it an approximate form. In case of a landscape, this may be the shapes of a mountain, tree, river and house. Next, he may add some details into the form, such as defining the branches of a tree, the doors and windows within a house etc. Next, the painter may add colors to this outline, giving it more texture and details. Finally, the painter may frame the painting making it a work of art to be hung on someone's private wall. Just as a painting develops from concept to abstract forms, to more detailed forms, to things we can touch and see, in a similar way, the Vedas state that matter develops from concept to thing by adding refinements to sound. As information gets more dense and detailed, the senses can grasp it as well. When the information is scarce, only the mind is able to grasp it. Thus, as Ether, a thing can only be heard. As Air, it can be heard and touched. As Fire, it can be heard, touched and seen. As Water, it can be heard, touched, seen and tasted. As Earth, it can be heard, touched, seen, tasted and smelt.

In physical communication, the receiver compares the received signal against a standard reference signal to decode the information. While physical theories distinguish between the measured object and the measuring device, both are fundamentally made of the same matter. This isn't the case for observation, because objects exist as knowledge while sensation exists as experience. At the point of sensation, the information that existed as Ether, Air, Fire, Water or Earth is added to the senses to create sound, touch, sight, taste and smell. But, so far as we can draw a parallel between a sense and a measuring instrument, we can see that a sense is similar to the unmodulated carrier in a communications device. If Air is the modulation of Ether, then to sense touch, the sense must be like Ether which was modulated to create the element of Air. Thus, Sāṅkhya philosophy states that the element of Air is created from the sensation (*tanmātra*) of touch, which is created from the sense of touch, which is created from the element of Ether. Similarly, the element Air leads to the sense of sight, which creates the sensation of color and form, which then objectifies into the element Fire. An intricate intermingling of subjective and objective elements is a unique aspect of Sāṅkhya and it defies realist or idealist characterizations.

Perhaps the most difficult aspect of Sāṅkhya (from a modern scientific standpoint) is the idea that the mind becomes the sense of hearing, which gives rise to sound sensation which creates the element Ether. This is hard because science is in the search of the origin of space-time and in Sāṅkhya space-time comes from the mind although modern science believes that minds are properties of objects created within space-time. In Sāṅkhya, matter is created from space-time which is created from mind, through the sense of hearing and the sensation of hearing. So, how do concepts in the mind become the sense of hearing?

The Vedas state that the mind has several functions, which include thinking, feeling, willing, knowing and acting. Concepts are thinking but the mind also desires these concepts, wills the concepts, plans to acquire them and then acts on the process of acquisition. The senses in Vedic philosophy are a development of the mind's activity. Thus, a concept in the mind becomes the sense of hearing when we have desired a concept, decided to acquire it, developed a plan to acquire it and are now in need to act towards the acquisition. This need to act develops into the sense for activity. For example, the mind can think the concept of 'passion'. It can then desire passion, will to be passionate, develop a plan for passion and needs to start acting passionately. The activity for passion is produced by an element called *prāna* which converts the plan into the perception of activity in the senses. For instance, the plan for passion may now become the sight of redness, the touch of softness, the sound of sensual music, the aromas of excitement and tastes of intoxication. Essentially, the senses now acquire the plan, which is now a 'thought' for the senses. Like the mind, the senses too desire this plan, will the plan, refine the plan to greater levels of detail and then execute the plan. The execution of the plan produces sensations called *tanmātra*. These sensations combine with the Ether to produce sound-objects through a similar process. The sound-objects then develop into objects that can be touched, seen, tasted and smelt.

When we desire an idea, the desires first manifest in the sense of hearing which is the ability by which we can hear more about the idea. The sense of hearing gives rise to the sensation of hearing, which objectifies as the element of Ether. Sound is therefore often the basis of further development of desire. When the senses and the mind hear this sound, the desire may be strengthened. When this strengthened desire further acts on Ether, a new type of desire for touch is created which becomes the sense of touch. From that sense emerges the sensation of touch, and then the element of Air. The sense and mind now experience the touch and the desire further strengthens. This new desire now acts on the element of Air and produces the desire for sight, which then produces the sensation of sight and then the element of Fire. In this way, all elements are produced from thought when consciousness applies its desires to matter. When the desires cease, all the elements withdraw into their causes, which occurs at the time of universal dissolution.

The senses are material, similar to objects, but they are different as desire and the object of that desire. The object of desire is produced from the desire. Consciousness is the original element and also the original desire. As desire develops, the senses for morality, intentions, objects, properties and sensations are created, which in turn create their respective objects. The senses now combine with their objects to fulfill the desires. There are hence two kinds of information—one that exists as desires within the senses and another as objects of the desire.

The ability to convert thoughts in the mind to things in matter forms the basis of Vedic material technology where a powerful mind transforms its thoughts into material objects simply by desiring. This science has been lost due to two reasons: (a) the mental development needed to convert ideas into objects is lacking today, and, (b) the Vedic technology that described how even a relatively underdeveloped mind could fulfill its desires by performance of rituals and chanting of Vedic *mantras* has also been lost. Both factors have contributed to the decline in understanding the role played by the mind even in material objects.

Besides the desire in the senses and the objects of that desire, there is the *power* of action needed to combine the two. If the senses have the power, they can acquire the objects on their own. But, if they don't, then they can still acquire the objects by satisfying other beings who have the relevant power. These empowered living beings are called *demigods.* The sense, the object and the power are respectively called *ātmika, bhautika* and *daivika.* The senses may desire arbitrarily but they cannot fulfill those desires if they don't have the relevant powers to actually combine with the desired objects. The Vedas therefore describe rituals and technology by which the senses can be satisfied by satisfying demigods. Beyond this mundane satisfaction of the senses, the Vedas also state that the soul is freed from matter when it stops desiring. When the desires cease, the senses withdraw into the mind, which withdraws into the intelligence, which withdraws into the ego which withdraws into *mahattattva* which withdraws into primordial matter, called *pradhāna.* Recall that primordial matter is differentiated into mind and objects by the choices of consciousness. When choices cease, different concepts in the mind and different objects also cease to exist.

The mental activity of desiring produces the sense of hearing which develops into the sound which exists as vibrations of space-time. In Vedic philosophy, therefore, the space-time within the universe is always vibrating and there is no such thing as empty space-time. This is related to the recent discovery in cosmology that the universe is filled with a background radiation and that over 60% of the universe is dark energy. This dark energy is not due to material objects but exists in space itself. Unlike science, however, where the vibration is seen as energy, in Vedic philosophy, this vibration represents information and space-time locations which, by holding that information, become distinguishable. That is, space-time is not uniform. Rather, the vibration of space-time when understood semantically constitutes the basis of distinguishing space-time locations. In a sense, each location is a different meaning, similar to how kitchen and bedroom are semantically distinct locations in a house. The meaning of a location is tied to mental activities that produced that location which implies that different types of minds inhabit different locations in space. Space-time is therefore not empty and not the most fundamental ingredient of the universe. Beneath that space-time are the senses which create sensations based upon properties in the mind. The senses are therefore the cause of the space-time. Underlying the senses is the mind, and beyond the mind are intelligence, ego, *mahattattva, pradhāna* and, ultimately, consciousness.

Absolute Space-Time

Physical theories describe vibrations using mathematical equations. The technology developed using such a physical theory, however, also describes the same vibration as meanings of voice, video and data. This technology employs man-made linguistic conventions in which electronic receivers and senders decode and encode information using a specific type of protocol convention. The main difference between Vedic and modern science is that the former recognizes a natural language in which information can be encoded in matter in a way that our *senses* can perceive these things as color, taste, smell or touch unmediated by technology. Our senses too are senders and receivers of information and in that sense they are also like electronic transceivers. The language employed in the senses and in electronic transceivers is however different. If the language used in encoding and decoding information as physical states were known, then matter could be described as taste, touch, smell and sight, just as electromagnetic waves are described as voice, video and data. In one sense, there is nothing other than a vibrating vacuum. In another sense, there is a world of things which can be perceived.

The use of language to interpret physical states into semantic states currently requires a mind. But, if there is indeed a natural language by which physical states naturally encode meanings, then why isn't current physics capable of capturing that information? The reason for this is that current physical theories describe matter in terms of differential equations which always underdetermine reality in some way depending on the order of the equation. First order differential equations underdetermine up to a zeroth order differential which represents a constant. Second order differential equations underdetermine to a first order differential which represents a derivative between two variables. The basic variables in a space-time description are x, t, and θ that respectively denote a position, time and angle. First order differential equations underdetermine the exact position, time and angle. Second order equations underdetermine $\partial x/\partial t$, $\partial \theta/\partial t$ and $\partial \theta/\partial x$ which represent constant rates of linear and angular motion and the wavelength or frequency of vibration. Third order equations underdetermine second order differential variables which represent the acceleration of these quantities. Physics recognizes the indeterminism as the Equivalence Principle in Relativity which says that all frames of reference are equivalent as far as physical laws are concerned. In other words, *if* there was a property associated with absolute location or constant motion or constant acceleration, it would never be detected by any physical measurement.

Problems however arise when physical states are used to encode meanings. For instance, when data is encoded in a magnetic disk, an absolute reference frame is assumed. If all directions were equivalent, then the +z direction that encodes the bit 1 will be flipped into the –z direction that encodes the bit 0 if the coordinate system is inverted along the z-axis. The equivalence of reference frames will now invert the meanings associated with physical states. For instance, if +z denoted the description of an object that is hot while –z denotes the description of an object that is cold, then by inverting the z-axis the descriptions of nature will be inverted although the temperature of the objects will not be changed. If the +z statement was earlier true, the axis inversion will now make the statement false. It follows that when objects denote meanings we cannot arbitrarily change coordinate axes because locations, directions, durations and extensions themselves are representations of physical properties. Coordinate system changes will preserve meanings only if the linguistic convention that maps a point in space-time to a meaning is also changed.

For instance, if +z denotes hot and –z denotes cold, then a coordinate system inversion will preserve meanings only if in the new coordinate system –z denotes hot and +z denotes cold. It thus follows that if material objects have to denote meanings—and these meanings are universally communicable—then there has to be a universal mapping between coordinate systems and meanings.

If we change the coordinate system, then we must also change the *language* that maps physical states (words) to mental states (meanings). For instance, if we invert the coordinate system around the z-axis, then the mapping between temperature and direction needs to be inverted as well. If +z denoted hot, then after the change –z will denote hot. Note how the mapping between meanings and directions remains intact in this scheme. The *convention* by which we call that direction however changes. This convention is irrelevant to any physical theory; it is only relevant to the convention in which some experimenters discuss with each other. For instance, there can be two observers whose coordinate systems are inverted. One looks at an object and thinks that the object is at +z and therefore it means hot while the second looks at the same object and thinks that it is at –z and therefore it means hot. Their eventual conclusions—namely, that the object means hot—are invariant in both cases, although they arrive at these conclusions in two different ways.

Now, the key point is the following. If the information denoted by a physical state is invariant across coordinate system changes, then from the standpoint of the *senses* these coordinate system changes cannot be detected. If two observers with mutually inverted coordinate frames detect the same meaning—e.g., that the object being measured means hot—then this outcome exhausts the empirical content of the theory. It does not matter if the object in question is in front of us or behind us. Being in front or behind is a relative position and that is irrelevant for the question about the real meaning in the symbol, because the meaning in the symbol itself remains unchanged by a coordinate frame change.

We are now led to a simple but startling conclusion. *If* matter can encode meanings (which are communicable), then there is an absolute space-time. The absoluteness of this space-time pertains to the meanings denoted by material objects and not to the coordinate systems of current physics, which can be arbitrarily chosen. However, when a coordinate system is transformed, the meanings associated with that coordinate system must also drag along. For instance, if +z becomes –z, then the meaning of hot associated with +z will now drag into –z. Nothing truly changes in the real world; we simply have decided to call hot things cold and cold things hot. As long as we drag our entire vocabulary with the coordinate system change we can consistently communicate. The direction—whether we call it +z or –z—continues to denote the idea of hot. This fact opens up a new way of looking at space-time. Why should we call space-time locations, directions, durations and extension using coordinate numbers since they are arbitrary anyway? We can also call these properties by the *meanings* they represent. For instance, we can call some direction as a representation of the idea of hot, which remains invariant across various coordinate transformations. The equivalence of various frames now leads us to the idea that if matter denotes meanings, then this equivalence is identical to an absolute frame.

However, the absolute reference frame is a frame of ideas or types rather than a frame of quantities. The quantities +z and –z can change but the type denoted by these quantities cannot change, because if the type did change then a hot object will become cold simply by a coordinate transformation. This gives us a radically new way to conceive space-time wherein space-time locations, directions, durations and extensions denote types rather than quantities. The quantity space-time is relative and arbitrary but the type space-time is absolute and invariant. We can also call this space-time of types a *semantic* space-time. In such a space-time, an object at a different location has a different type. To move objects in this space, we must change their meanings or types.

In Vedic philosophy, Ether is an absolute space-time. Its absoluteness however is not based on quantities but based on types. For instance, there are absolute up and down directions, not because we cannot flip the coordinate axes but because the up and down directions denote meanings which cannot be changed even if we flip the axes. If matter encodes meanings, and if +z represents hot and –z represents cold, then flipping the axes will not change the temperature of the objects. In some sense, these objects have a definite location, direction, duration and extension which do not change even if we flip the coordinate axes. In current physics, objects do not denote meanings, and we only measure the *values* of properties inside a coordinate system but we do not *interpret* these values to derive the meaning. If objects were to denote meanings, then we would interpret the meanings from the physical states and we will see that these interpretations are invariant across coordinate system transformations. These invariants represent the empirically real observations; the values from which they are derived are not empirically real. That is, we can know whether the world is hot or cold but whether the object points in +z or –z direction is not real.

Science is the study of invariants and if matter denotes meanings then these meanings remain invariant across coordinate transforms. Since these meanings are encoded by space-time properties, the space-time of measurable invariants also remains unchanged and therefore there is an absolute space-time in nature that encodes these meanings.

The question of whether a universal space-time exists is equivalent to the question of whether there is a natural language of meanings. In this language, there is an absolute meaning associated with locations, times and directions. If this idea is correct, then by moving an object from one location to another, by pointing it in a different direction, or by doing an experiment at a different time, we will cause a change to its meaning. Such changes will be detected by the senses and the mind, and they will therefore be empirical. To reinstate meaning into the study of matter, science needs to treat space-time as a semantic domain rather than as a physical domain. A physical domain is described by relative coordinate frames while a semantic domain will be described by an absolute frame. The absolute frame encodes meanings while the relative frame denotes the words. We can use different words to denote the meanings but the variation in the words still preserves the meaning.

Vocabulary and Choice

In current science, we can count objects from a particular reference frame, but we cannot describe the reference frame itself.

Relativistic equivalence is based on the idea that the observer cannot know whether he is in a moving or stationary reference frame, or that the forces he experiences are due to its own acceleration or due to other matter in the universe. Relativistic equivalence can be restated more broadly as the claim that we can know the world but we cannot know ourselves. Equivalence claims an inability to represent knowledge of the observer (i.e. the reference frame) within the observer's reference frame.

In Vedic philosophy, an observer can know himself by becoming aware of his choices. Choices constitute a reference frame and by becoming aware of one's choices, an observer can represent himself to himself, creating self-knowledge. Obviously, to represent one's choices as a description, a language of choices is needed. Language is therefore essential not just to describe the world, but also to know oneself. In Vedic philosophy, the self-knowledge function of language is more important than the world-knowledge function. Indeed, since the world springs from choices, the language of choices describes the world in the same way that it describes the self. For this knowledge to be communicable, different observers must use the same language. In other words, they must all be capable of natively understanding and using the same types of choices, and describing themselves in those choices. The Vedas state that all living beings have the same native potential choices and by that they are natively capable of knowing themselves and others.

The language of choices allows us to know the world in just the way we want to know ourselves. In other words, to see the world in terms of how we want to perceive, conceive, judge, intend and choose ourselves. Different aspects of the observer express a different subset of the language of choice, and each such subset is inadequate without another part of the language. Thus, for instance, objects are inadequate without the senses. The objects have sweetness and the senses make this the sweetness of flavor, tone, color, etc. The senses are inadequate without the mind which divides the perception of sight into properties such as color, distance, direction, form, and size. The mind is inadequate without the intelligence which combines the properties such as color, size and form into the cognition of an object. The intelligence is inadequate without the ego which generates different intentional purposes for an object. The ego is inadequate without the moral sense which judges whether the intentions about the object are right or wrong. The moral sense is inadequate without the soul which determines if this right or wrong makes us happy or sad. For counting to complete, there must be an entity that can count itself. That entity is consciousness. It is fully capable of knowing itself and describing (representing) itself to itself.

Indeed, the material body, senses, mind, intelligence, ego, moral sense and consciousness are all descriptions of the observer to itself. Current science interprets these experiences as descriptions of the world while Vedic philosophy treats these experiences as descriptions of the self. These descriptions are constructed from choices which use a language that everyone can understand, although they may choose to *be* different propositions in the language. Representations in terms of the language of choice are fully communicable if everyone has the same native potential abilities of choice. Thus, if the method by which we know ourselves is also the method by which we can know the world and other living beings, then the language of science and that of self-knowledge are not different. By elevating the discourse to self-knowledge, Vedic philosophy does not preclude knowledge of the world. Rather, it sets standards for the *language* in terms of which any knowledge must be expressed.

If self-knowledge and world-knowledge are described using two different languages—like in the mind-body divide in current science—then the way we know ourselves will always be radically different from the way we know objects in the world or other living beings. The languages of the body and mind will never meet and we could never make the world a source of self-knowledge or describe the self by the objects in the world. We would also not be able to communicate our self-view to others because the material medium in which we represent involves a different language than the content that is being represented.

Current scientific language describes the world but not the observer. This idea is precisely stated in the theory of relativity as the inability to express the knowledge of the observer in the observer's reference frame. If all coordinate frames are equivalent then we can describe objects but we cannot represent the knowledge of the reference frame in that reference frame. Thus, we can surmise that the world is moving but we can't know if we are moving. In Vedic philosophy, all reference frames are products of our choices and we can know our choices. To the extent that we can know our choices, we can know that we are moving. This knowledge would be manifested in the fact that if we choose an arbitrary reference frame and then derive the meanings of reality from the measurement of objects, there will be only one reference frame in which the *semantic* laws of nature will hold true. For instance, if objects denote meanings by their directions, and our arbitrarily chosen reference frame says than an object is pointing in +z direction which in our arbitrarily chosen language denotes the meaning 'cold' then such a theory will predict that energy will flow from other objects that we will consider hot. If this frame is actually flipped with respect to the absolute reference frame, then we will observe that the energy does not flow in the way we predicted. We will see that the energy will flow from the cold object to the hot object, violating the laws of nature. There is hence only one reference frame in which the laws of nature will hold true. Then we will have to align our reference frame to fit the natural laws.

If laws deal in physical properties then the same laws are true in many reference frames, and the truth of the laws cannot be used to determine the state of motion. If, however, the laws deal in semantic properties then there is only one reference frame in which the laws will be true. If we stick to the idea that all reference frames are equivalent, this will imply that each reference frame has different laws. In one frame of reference, the energy will flow from hot to cold and in another reference frame the energy will flow from cold to hot. If an observer insists that his reference frame is the absolute reference frame, then he will find laws of nature that differ from the laws of the other observers. If, however, the observer accepts some universal laws of nature, then he would have to acknowledge that his reference frame is different from the reference frame in which the laws of nature are defined. Such an observer can use the discrepancy between empirical observation and predictions of the natural laws to know his state of motion because there is only one frame in which observations will be compatible with the predictions of a semantic theory. This knowledge will correspond to an observer's self-knowledge of his state of motion.

In a similar way, other forms of meaning can be used to determine deeper kinds of choices beyond motion.

The choice of reference frame now translates into different laws. This does not mean that there are many laws of nature, one for each observer. It only means that *if* an observer thinks that his reference frame is the absolute reference frame, then he may discover laws that are different from the real laws. The observer can, however, also know that each frame involves different laws. If Vedic philosophy is correct, then there will also be a reference frame in which the laws cease to exist. That is, the observer can make choices but these choices don't have consequences. This reference frame represents a *type* of choice which frees the observer from the reactions and consequences of his actions. If someone wishes to get out of the cycle of cause and effect, he may adapt his choices to enter a reference frame that is not constrained by laws.

Ultimately, all laws of science are laws of choice, but we perceive these laws in different ways. Current laws tell us about consequences of choices at the level of sensations. Deeper laws will tell us consequences of choices in terms of concepts, objects, intent and, eventually, morality.

In Vedic philosophy, the goal of the study of lawfulness in nature is to get out of the control of the laws. Within a specific observer's frame, the laws discovered by the observer depend on his choices. The observer can interpret this choice as the need to adapt his choices to obtain the 'desired' kinds of laws. He can also interpret the choice as a single law that is transformed according to the reference frame. The second kind of interpretation can help the observer come out of the lawfulness of nature because he can see that there is a reference frame in which the laws cease. Thus, the study of lawfulness in nature can illuminate the observer about the choices that will free him from the laws of nature.

From Phenomena to Reality

Since Earth, Water, Fire, Air and Ether objectify the sensations of smell taste, sight, touch and sound, matter is described in Vedic philosophy in terms of its perceptual properties. A macroscopic object is comprised of many sensations—e.g. an apple consists of the sensations of red, round and sweet. In that respect, a macroscopic object is built up of many atoms. At the grossest level, atoms are symbols of sensations; i.e. they are objects that encode information corresponding to the sensation of those objects. When an object changes state it produces different sensations. Ideally, we like to think that behind this change is some immutable, unchanging reality, that causes changes to sensations and by understanding this reality we can predict changes to sensations. According to Vedic philosophy, however, there are not one but several realities underlying sensations. Of these, the ultimate reality is the individual conscious entity. But there are also intermediate layers of temporary phenomena similar to sensations. These include properties, objects, intents and morals. As successively deeper kinds of phenomena, they can be seen as causes of the previous level of phenomena. For instance, properties can be seen as causes of sensations, objects as causes of properties, intentions as causes of objects and morals as causes of intentions. Sensations, properties, objects, intentions and morals are all phenomena, but the fact that they are successively deeper makes it possible to say that the deeper phenomena cause the grosser phenomena.

Consciousness is the ultimate cause of all phenomena in Vedic philosophy. This ultimate conclusion is generally considered adequate for someone who wishes to transcend all phenomena. But this conclusion is insufficient for a scientific understanding of the phenomena themselves. Although consciousness is the ultimate reality, it interacts with matter not directly but through several layers of semantic phenomena.

Behind the phenomenon of changing sensations, properties, objects, intents and morals there is an eternal soul that causes these changes. But, if this conclusion appears like a big leap, then it is also possible to say that behind the phenomenon of changing physical states, there are changing senses that cause physical changes. Behind the changing senses is a changing mind, behind the changing mind is a changing intelligence, behind the changing intelligence is a changing ego and behind the changing ego is a changing morality. Which of these two alternatives is more interesting? The answer depends on whether you are a mystic or a scientist. To the mystic, the ultimate conclusion is more interesting because it helps his search of a reality beyond changing phenomena. To the scientist, the study of the phenomena is more interesting, because he can sense, know, judge, desire and moralize with his senses. Current science is opposed to mysticism because reality in science is material. Vedic science is consistent with mysticism because reality here is spiritual. But the Vedic science is also scientifically richer because there is a greater variety in types of possible phenomena.

Current science is a study of order amongst sensations. When theories of sensations are inadequate, the incompleteness can be bridged by bringing properties into the study of phenomena. But properties cannot fully solve the causal problem because these too are phenomena caused by another deeper reality. Methodologically, however, this approach to solving the incompleteness of phenomenal sciences sets an important precedent, namely, that if a theory is incomplete then the reality in that science should be reformulated as a type of phenomena, to be explained by a deeper reality. The transition from sensations to concepts is, therefore, not a final move for sensation-based sciences, but the first in a series of moves. The quest for reality stops only when the theory of some appropriate level of phenomenal experience is consistent and complete and the reality depicted in that theory would now be the ultimate reality. Of course, this is similar to the approach already adopted in current science except that we can now also predict the stages through which scientific development must pass to reach that ultimate state. This prediction of deeper levels of reality described here can help accelerate the otherwise conservative process of scientific development.

Scientific development through layers of meaning should be interesting even to the transcendentalist because this development indicates all that consciousness is capable of, because it is the abilities of consciousness that are reflected in matter. In monistic approaches to transcendentalism these abilities are irrelevant. The monist is only interested in transcending all phenomena. The pluralist is however also interested in understanding how variety is created, because this variety is not limited to matter. When properties of consciousness are reflected in matter, matter is described in terms of the capabilities of consciousness, and this implies that the variety exists in consciousness. For instance, if sensations are real, then matter can be described in terms of properties of color and taste. There are other similar descriptions in which matter is described in terms of conceiving, judging, intending and moralizing capabilities. The monist is right in saying that in matter there are only phenomena and not reality. But the pluralist is right in saying that the study of phenomena indicates the properties of reality. The monist is wrong if he concludes that since the variety in matter is a phenomenal illusion, then, ultimately, reality must be an undifferentiated oneness. If anything, the plurality is caused by consciousness and not by matter. It is matter which is differentiated from an undifferentiated state by the effect of consciousness. By taking away consciousness matter is collapsed into an undifferentiated state, not into individual observers.

Many philosophers believe that the idea of a reality different from observations is superfluous. They insist that reality is observation, and we must discard the idea that there is something 'behind' the observation, because we can never reach this reality. But this argument raises the question: If science is not studying reality, which exists independent and prior to its observation, then why describe sensations in a way different from how an observer experiences them? If reality and sensation are identical, then scientific theories must describe sensation in terms of sounds, colors, tastes and smells, and not speak about mass, charge, electrons, protons, etc. There is also a more basic problem about change, namely that change is defined as the motion of objects. If a succession of sensations exhausts what science can say, then this succession cannot represent the idea of motion, because motion involves something that changes position without changing its identity. If there is no reality, there can also not be motion, because different sensations cannot be connected as successive states of the same physically real object.

In classical physics, the succession of objects states is linked by the hypothesis of a particle, and physics believes that the same particle moves through different states. In the Vedic view, the succession of states is connected by the individual consciousness, and the Vedas state that a living being continuously acquires new bodies. This raises important questions about what we really mean by an 'object' that connects phenomenal states. Is the object material or a spiritual entity?

This used to be a fruitless metaphysical discussion until the dawn of atomic theory, which forbids continuous state transitions. In fact, different states are different particles, not states of the same particle. In that respect, we cannot say that the same particle goes to a new state, because the new state is a new particle. Now, a particle that jumps from one state to another is actually a particle whose *identity* is transformed from one particle to another. This jumping or transformation cannot be causally predicted. The notion that consciousness shifts from one phenomenon to another discretely involves no such causal problems because the shifting of states is based upon a choice, which can be discrete. In the Vedic view, my body is continuously changing as phenomena, but the soul that experiences these phenomena remains unchanged. The soul is therefore the real object underlying the phenomenal states.

The idea that phenomenal states can change discretely under the influence of choice is consistent with the idea that consciousness is the 'object' that connects phenomenal states. The existence of choice is however inconsistent with the idea of material particles as objects. The problem of missing causality in atomic theory can be solved by adding a role for choice. But the addition of choice to the scientific repertoire requires a new view of matter, because choices cannot interact with classical particles. The interaction of matter and consciousness is an unsolved problem in current science. This problem can be solved if choices are modeled as linguistic information that can exist both in consciousness and in matter. But, now, matter is a semantic entity, which needs to be described differently that its description in current science. The transition from a non-semantic to a semantic science has the following rationale. Non-semantic science is incomplete, and the indeterminism shows that there is a room for choice. For choices to actually exploit the indeterminism, consciousness must interact with matter.

The problem of consciousness-matter interaction is solved in Vedic philosophy through the idea that meanings can exist in both consciousness and in matter, and consciousness and matter interact by exchanging meanings. We might say that consciousness and matter are two different *models* of language, such that the same meanings can be experienced by consciousness and objectified into matter. During creation, the variety in the consciousness is objectified in matter. The material variety constitutes phenomena that are always changing. To do science, these phenomena must be connected as changes *of* something that doesn't itself change. Science must also find the *cause* of changes. Consciousness is the cause and the unchanging object underlying phenomena.

Contexts in Perception

One of the key problems of perception pertains to illusions and meanings. One might ask: Why put them together? The answer is that both involve a context-sensitive interpretation of some objective facts. Take the example of visual illusions. Two lines that have the same length can appear as longer and shorter. Two objects that have the same color can appear to be darker and lighter. Two things at the same distance can be appear to be closer and farther. In perceiving such illusions, the illusion is not limited to any given individual, time or place. Everyone sees these illusions every time. Even if we are told that two things are equally long, equally far or have the same color, we will not see them correctly. Illusions can however be removed by adding, deleting or changing something in the perceptual field. In a sense, we are all hardwired to misperceive objects in some way, but that misperception is context-sensitive.

Successively deeper forms of meanings also involve similar context-sensitive patterns, although the freedom and choices in interpretation grow as we move from gross to subtle. For instance, most people will perceive a skull-and-bones sign as denoting danger, even when they don't necessarily read the language in which the text under the sign says 'danger'. But other signs such as road signs may not have a universal interpretation. Unlike sensations, where the senses generally perceive an illusion universally, the mind interprets much of the meanings based on its prior knowledge. Objects too are context-sensitive, but involve an even greater familiarity with the context. For example, someone who jumps a stop sign will be described as a 'law breaker.' To arrive at this conclusion, one must have prior knowledge of traffic laws in a given geographical location. Successively deeper kinds of meanings become more and more contextual. For instance, morality and values are almost entirely a personal property. Intents are less personal, as a number of other individuals with similar backgrounds may share similar intents. Objects are even less personal as people with different intents, but with the same knowledge (e.g., knowledge of laws) can arrive at the same conclusion. The mapping between properties and sensation is more universal and perceptual illusions are almost universal in a species. Physical properties are observer independent. This illustrates the fact that reality can be measured, perceived, conceived, judged, intended and enjoyed in different ways, such that it successively gets more and more personal to the observer involved in it. Thus, successively deeper forms of experience are more amenable to choice control, as they depend more on the context.

In Vedic philosophy, the universe is manifest through stages that objectify meanings originating in consciousness into symbols of meaning in matter. Each stage involves a choice, since one level of manifestation does not determine the other. Thus, a moral value is satisfied by the fulfillment of many goals, and a goal can be motivated by many types of morals. Similarly, a goal can be justified by many objects and an object can create many goals. An object can involve many properties, and a property can partake in many objects. A property abstracts many sensations, and a sensation can be described by many properties. A sensation can pertain to many objects, and an object can give many sensations. There are unique stages of meaning because these stages underdetermine each other. The relationship between different stages of meaning is fixed by a choice, made possible by a context.

Choices help interpret a physical object in terms of many sensations (e.g., when we choose to touch rather than taste an object), a sensation in terms of many properties (e.g., when sight is divided into form, distance, color, size, and direction), a property in terms of many objects (e.g., when the property of color is used to construct a table versus a chair), an object in terms of many goals (such as when a table is used to study or eat), and a goal in terms of various moral values (e.g., when eating is supposed to support survival versus when survival is supposed to support eating). The reverse process can also occur, thereby creating intentions from morals, objects from intentions, properties from objects, sensations from properties, and physical states from sensations. Our experience comprises of top-down processes of defining and bottoms-up processes of abstraction. Higher aspects of experience are underdetermined without the lower aspects and lower aspects are incomplete without the higher aspects. Only the combination of consciousness, ego, intelligence, mind, senses and physical states specifies all features of experience. Accordingly, a science that only deals in physical states is an incomplete explanation of our everyday experience.

Each interpretation of lower-meaning into higher-meaning or definition of higher-meaning into lower-meaning involves a context. Without a context, there is a many-to-many relationship between semantic entities. An object can produce many sensations and a sensation can be obtained from many objects. A sensation can lead to many properties, and a property can be obtained from many sensations. A property can produce many objects and an object involves many properties. An object can create many intentions and an intention is fulfilled by many objects. An intention can satisfy many morals and a moral can lead to many intentions. To convert many-to-many mappings into a one-to-one mapping, a context is required. In synesthesia, the subject is presented sounds but he perceives color; the physical property is described as sound but the sensation is described as color. In scientific measurements, similarly, color may be measured by the sound of a detector. Thus, sound can be sensed as color and color can be sensed as sound. Countless other schemes of converting physical properties to sensations are possible. The sensation-property mapping requires a context in which sensations and properties may be described by different words. Using such a mapping, color can be denoted by different space locations. In every spoken and written language, a wide variety of meanings are conveyed through a few linguistic or verbal signs. Similar contextual mappings are needed for objects, intentions and morals as well.

The context is called *prāna* in Vedic philosophy. *Prāna* maps different *models* of language. Things, sensations, properties, objects, intents and morals are different models of language. Within objects, Earth, Water, Fire, Air and Ether are different models of language, present in sensations. All these models are correlated when language is used to denote things, sensations, properties, objects, intents and morals by the same symbol. For example, a red rose can represent a thing, a sensation, a property, an object, an intention and a morality, which are all the same red rose. But there are also connotative uses when the rose can for instance denote the concept of one person's love for another; the rose may be intended as an apology for their past misdemeanors, etc. There are many ways to express love, apologize or please someone, and to use a rose for that requires mapping meanings into things. *Prāna* represents the context-sensitive mapping amongst different models.

The Vedas state that the subtle body of the living being—consisting of senses, mind, intelligence, ego and consciousness—is 'carried' by *prāna*. *Prāna* attaches the subtle body of senses, mind, intelligence, ego and consciousness to the gross body of the five elements. During observation, the relation between space-time forms and sensations is established by *prāna* and during action sensations are mapped into space-time forms. If *prāna* is missing, then forms will exist but they cannot be perceived by the senses. Or meanings will exist in the subtle body but they will not cause changes to matter. At the time of death, *prāna* detaches the gross body from the subtle body and carries the subtle body to a new gross body and reattaches there. The attachment and detachment of *prāna* from the gross body means that the subtle body exercises control over only that part of the material world which we call our body. By the development of the *prāna* this capacity can be extended to other living beings and other parts of the universe besides our individual bodies.

The notion of *prāna* can be understood analogically through the idea of coordinate systems in mathematics. A coordinate system maps algebraic forms to geometric forms. An algebraic form can represent many geometric forms, and vice versa. The relation between a geometric and algebraic form is established through a coordinate system. This is similar to the mapping between space-time forms and sensations, or between sensations and properties. The choice of coordinate system represents a mapping between a property and a percept. By changing coordinate systems, a property will be mapped to a different percept and vice versa. *Prāna* represents a coordinate system to map various language models. We saw earlier how the coordinate system represents the choices of consciousness. In the way that algebra and geometry are separate categories but connected by the coordinate system, similarly, the coordinate frame of choices connects various semantic categories.

Concepts in Matter

Our cognition understands sensations in terms of types. These types include the primitive methods of sensing such as hearing, touching, seeing, tasting and smelling. Each primitive method is divided into many facets; for instance, hearing perceives pitch, tone and phase and seeing perceives form, color and brightness. Each such facet of perception creates many types in experience; for instance, 'red' for color, 'round' for shape and 'sweet' for taste, etc. Additionally, each of these properties and sensations can be used to denote meanings or concepts beyond those properties or sensations. For instance, red can symbolize passion while white symbolizes peace. Sounds can symbolize colors while colors can symbolize taste. Concepts denote what we get from a symbol beyond the properties of that symbol itself; we generally call these meanings. In Sāṅkhya, all the senses can perceive meanings. For instance, the sense of sight can intuitively know that red means danger in some contexts. While sensations give us the redness of the object, the eye also perceives it as a sign of danger, under a contextual interpretation. Such perception results in autonomic behavior in animals; for instance, intuitively staying away from dangerous situations.

This may appear to be a well-known aspect of our perception but it is not regarded as real in modern science. Science prefers to describe matter in terms of primary properties such as mass and charge rather than color and taste. Accordingly, the values of physical properties are measured as numbers rather than types. This difference between primary and secondary properties has driven a wedge between scientific and everyday descriptions of reality. We believe that mass and charge are real while color and taste are not and nature should be described in numbers rather than as types. Types, however, create other interesting properties which cannot be accounted for in current science. The main property of interest here is that a type can denote meanings beyond those that can be grasped simply from the sensation. For instance, the color red can denote additional meanings of love, passion, war, danger, etc. While sensations are commonly believed to be due to properties inherent in the objects (although current science doesn't believe that color itself is inherent in an object, science does attribute color to something that is inherent in the object), meanings associated with color are obviously not inherent properties of objects. Rather, these meanings arise contextually, within a collection of objects. Thus, red in the context of green and yellow denotes danger as opposed to safety. In context with white, red denote war as opposed to peace. In context with black, red denotes life as opposed to death. In context with yellow, red denotes passion as opposed to intellect. The same color produces different meanings when distinguished from other colors in a context. This is important for a type-based description of nature because it marks a dramatic break from the idea that all properties of objects are inherent in the object itself. If the inherent properties were also types, it would be far easier to extend this to the idea that contexts bring additional types to an object. It seems much harder in current science because inherent properties are quantities while contextual properties are types. Contexts thus create a need for two types of transitions—(a) quantity to type, and (b) inherent to contextual. The former has made the description of contextual properties nearly impossible within current science.

Red is not alone in depicting meanings. Yellow almost universally indicates intelligence, green denotes prosperity and health, Blue denotes creativity and depression, while pink denotes femininity. Apparently meaningless sounds too have been known to denote meanings. In experiments on the Bouba-Kiki Effect, different individuals almost universally identified the word Bouba with round, bulbous objects while the word Kiki was associated with sharp, angular objects. Sounds of vowels often denote the nature of shapes. The sound 'a' denotes rectangular shapes, 'o' denotes round shapes. The sound 'u' denotes curved lines while 'i' denotes straight lines. The word 'above' or 'high' has semantic connation of being superior, while 'below' or 'low' connotes inferiority. Things in the 'front' are things in the future while things 'behind' us are in the past. 'Left' is an austere, intellectual side, while 'right' is an artistic and gregarious side; left may also denote the collective good vs. the individual good. The sound 'b' appears in words like bulging, bursting, bloated, balloon which create a picture of something round and fat.

Are these merely human associations? Or is there something natural about them? The hurdle in thinking of these as natural phenomena is that current science is based on primary properties, which are measured as quantities, while these meanings are associated with the perception of *types*. For instance, we can associate passion with the concept red, but not with a frequency. To interpret matter contextually, therefore, we must first describe the physical objects themselves in terms of types. We saw earlier that in Vedic philosophy matter is described in terms of types rather than as quantities. This includes not just meanings that the mind discovers but also sensations. Thus, for instance, Earth has smell, Water has taste, Fire has form, Air has touch and Ether has sound. When the mind perceives these sensations, it sees them as types rather than as quantities. Even the properties that are inherent in the objects are therefore described as types rather than as quantities. The perception of additional meanings in these types (e.g., the meaning of red) only requires the transition from inherent to contextual. Current science objectifies these types as quantities by comparing them to other standard objects. By this comparison, both the inherent types as well as the meaning represented by the objects are discarded while only the measurable quantities are retained. Effectively, this is like reducing a book to its weight and length rather than the meanings it conveys.

The distinction between sensations and concepts is seen in the distinction between a letter and a font. The letter represents a *type* with meaning while the fonts denote physical properties. A given squiggle can denote many different letters based on context. For instance, the sensation 'I' can context-sensitively denote the numeral 1, the capital letter I or the small letter l. To know the letter, the reader must contextually contrast a symbol to discover its meaning. This property of meanings leads to new phenomena where the behavior of an object cannot be explained only in terms of their sensations because the same sensation may denote different meanings. To know meanings, we have to see other sensations and assign them a meaning context-sensitively. The collection of such types in a context represents the *vocabulary* of a *domain*.

For instance, the cognition of types amongst squiggles represents the alphabet of a language. Thus, each object must be an *orthogonal* meaning relative to other objects such that collectively all objects form an orthogonal *basis* of meanings. This phenomenon is also seen in everyday collections such as a team, family or organization. When a person joins a team, family or organization, they acquire semantic properties in relation to the other members. In a team, someone leads while others follow. In a family, people are distinguished by types such as father, mother, child, uncle, aunt, niece or nephew. In an organization, members are distinguished by their functions such as marketing, engineering, human resources, finance, marketing, etc. Outside the team, family or organization, the individuals only have physical properties. Within a team, family or organization they have additional semantic properties. These semantic properties exist only as long as the individual belongs to the larger system, and disappear when the individual steps out of the system. This makes the comprehension of semantic properties difficult, so long as we think of object properties as features of those objects independent of the features of everything else in the universe. The comprehension of semantic properties requires us to think of whole systems, and how they condition and create new properties in their parts.

Conceptual properties are associated with locations in closed spaces, such as the space inside a home. In classical physics, all spatial locations within a home are physically identical. Semantically, however, locations in a home are conceptually distinct as kitchen, bedroom, bathroom, study, dining, guest room, etc. These distinct types of locations in a house cannot arise until we demarcate the boundary of the house from the rest of the world. Once the house is demarcated, there are many ways in which the internal space can be divided into different functions, each of which creating a different *type* of house, with different properties of each of its parts. One branch of the Vedas—called *vāstu-shāstra*—is devoted to how properties of space change with changing divisions within any enclosure. In classical physics, space is homogenous and isotropic. With semantics, space is not homogenous or isotropic because locations denote different concepts. For instance, top and bottom are not equal, left and right are not switchable, far and near or high and low are not substitutable. Rather, top, bottom, left, right, far, near, high, low, etc. are conceptually distinct and they denote different meanings.

I will describe in the last chapter how atomic theory can be understood by thinking of objects as meanings beyond physical properties. This thinking requires two kinds of shifts outlined above: (a) from quantity to type, and (b) from inherent to contextual. Atomic theory involves both these transitions. Atomicity pertains to the fact that quantities can be infinitesimal, but types must be discrete. There is a limit to how fine we can divide matter because language consists of atomic ideas, or elementary concepts, which require a finite amount of energy and matter before they can be encoded as symbols of meaning in matter. Atomicity can be interpreted as the need to describe matter in terms of sound, touch, sight, taste and smell or concepts such as redness, passion, etc. This is possible when matter is described as information rather than as physical states. Current atomic theory describes atoms as vibrations. In the Vedic view, these vibrations are *phonemes* which can denote meaning in a collection of particles. Without the collection, the phoneme is just a sound vibration and has no meaning. However, within a collection the phoneme also has a meaning. Current atomic theory reduces contextual properties to possessed properties, but this reduction cannot be done, because the contextual properties indeed do not exist outside of the context. Their effects are seen as different locations and orientations of atomic objects. Similar to how locations in a house are distinct as meanings, distinct locations of quanta can also be understood as meanings that are contextually tied to their physical properties in an ensemble.

Propositions in Matter

The mind creates properties and intelligence combines them into objects. When sensations and properties denote meanings, then objects can be viewed as propositions. To create logically, syntactically and semantically valid propositions, intelligence must adhere to certain rules that determine which forms are logically, syntactically and semantically well-formed. Linguists speak of generative grammars that produce syntactically correct statements. Of course, syntax correctness is inadequate because there can be syntactically correct statements that are logically false and semantically meaningless. To form propositions, language construction must therefore employ rules of logical, syntactical and semantic well-formed-ness. We might say that such well-formed statements are logically not self-contradictory and represent a definite meaning. These meanings may contradict facts out in the world, which makes the propositions empirically or referentially false but semantically meaningful. To form propositions, therefore, the rules that divide an information domain into distinct concepts must be extended to include logic, syntax and semantics.

The meanings of words depend not just on the other words in the vocabulary, but also upon the order of these words in a sentence. Two sentences such as "Have a bath after massage" and "Have a massage after bath" have identical words and identical meanings associated with each word. And yet, the meaning of the proposition depends on the order of words. The meaning of statements such as "Time flies like an arrow" depends on the grammatical structure associated with the sentence. In one structure, the word 'flies' is treated as a verb and in another structure it is treated as a noun. Changing the grammatical structure therefore changes the basic meaning of the word itself. These examples illustrate that grammatical structure creates new meanings by—(a) changing the meanings of words, and (b) changing the order of words, without changing a word's meanings. This property of structures can lead to new properties in matter that combine parts into structures.

This fact has important implications for atomic theory because in the current theory we only measure the word frequencies, not the order in which they are observed. The meaning of a proposition depends not just on the words, but also on the order of the words in a sentence. This order is empirically visible in quantum measurements but cannot be explained by the current theory. The order can, however, be explained if the individual atomic objects are seen as symbols similar to words.

Checks of semantic well-formed-ness can include comparison with statements that are well-formed but may have different meanings. For instance, the same logical system should not produce contradictory statements such as 'the sky is blue' and 'the sky is red'. The comparison may also be done with prior beliefs which are already represented as relations in the observer's memory. Rules of logic, syntax and semantics must ensure that only consistent statements are produced. This goes beyond conventional studies of syntax which permit even false statements to be produced, because they are syntactically correct. Currently, mathematics and logic deal with logical correctness, grammars deal with syntax correctness, and semantic correctness cannot be checked because the alphabets of language themselves don't have meaning. Indeed, logic, mathematics and linguistics are today separate fields of inquiry. And yet, these three checks for well-formedness—namely, logic, syntax and semantics—should constitute a single rule-based system that can check both syntax and semantic correctness of propositions.

Propositions add new meanings to words. For instance, the word 'address' can denote a noun and a verb. In nouns, the word 'scale' has different meaning in relation to a fish and to a measurement, respectively. In verbs, the word 'read' has different meanings in the present tense and the past tense (e.g., "I would like to read the book that you have just read"). Within adjectives, the word 'windy' has a different meaning in relation to a road (a windy road) and a day (a windy day). Language usage changes the meanings of words by associating with them different *categories*—nouns, verbs, adjectives, tense, gender, plurality, etc. These categories are decoded in the context of a complete proposition and the proposition's meaning depends on which words are assigned which categories. If meanings have a representation in matter, then categories must also be represented. This category representation creates new kinds of semantic properties.

The distinction between concept and category is that concepts can be distinguished through distinction in spatial location but categories require a temporal order. I will argue in the last chapter that the semantic effects of categories are relevant to the study of molecules and chemical reactions as a new kind of phenomena not captured by atomic theory. The chemical atoms are meaningful propositions, and the aggregation of atoms into chemical molecules represents the act of structuring concepts to form propositions. This structuring involves *ordering* concepts into a temporal sequence which gives the concepts additional categorical meanings. The meanings (and locations) associated with concepts can change when they are ordered and this can form the basis of a semantic study of isomorphism where the same atoms produce different molecules. The structure of atoms in a molecule has a counterpart in the order of words in a sentence, and the study of molecules therefore cannot be reduced to the study of atoms because these involve different types of meanings. The same set of concepts ordered differently produce different propositions. The temporal ordering of concepts therefore produces new semantic effects. This ordering can be understood as chemical procedures that produce complex molecules by combining individual chemical atoms.

It is possible to create new propositions by merging existing propositions. In classical syllogistic logic, for instance, two propositions (e.g., "All men are mortal" and "Socrates is a man") lead to a third proposition (e.g., "Socrates is mortal"). These forms of semantic deductions are routinely seen as chemical reactions where two chemicals combine to create other chemicals. This insight provides a new way to approach the study of matter, not as an interaction of forces caused by mass and charge, but as semantic processes of logical deduction that involve an understanding of meanings. The dynamics in matter can be seen as the computational processes of finding the most optimal ways of representing consistent information. To achieve this, ideas may be refactored into different propositions. Propositions may themselves be combined or divided. Similar to how mechanics uses the Least Action Principle which minimizes the total action needed to go from point A to B, a semantic science will constitute the search of the most optimal scheme to represent and encode information across a set of possibly diverse propositions.

A collection of consistent propositions represents a body of information. There are many ways in which a set of propositions can be organized. In many cases, the insight gained from a body of knowledge is independent of the order amongst propositions. Such propositions may be called *associative* and *commutative* in a way similar to how natural number addition and multiplication exhibit grouping and reordering properties without changing the outcome. But there are also cases where the knowledge from a set of propositions does not have associated and commutative properties. In other words, the meaning depends on the order of propositions. This is similar to how quaternion algebra is not commutative. Non-associative and non-commutative meanings also represent new properties in matter not described by present atomic theory. They roughly correspond to isomerism in chemistry where a set of particles can be organized in different structures that exhibit different chemical properties. Most biological molecules have a very large number of isomers, and a slight modification in the molecule's structure drastically changes its biological properties. This is a well-known fact in biology but it does not have a good theoretical foundation today. A semantic view of matter can answer questions of isomer properties.

Most scientists today believe that chemistry reduces to physics, although in practice chemists formulate different theories to predict chemical phenomena. From a semantic viewpoint, atomic physics deals with meaning while chemical processes involve proposition reasoning.

Intentionality in Matter

I broadly spoke earlier about the role of intentions in nature as the relation between an observer and the world that is contemplated or used: the role was that the conceptual nature of an object (i.e. whether it is a table or a chair) is underdetermined by the possessed features of that object alone and depends also upon the intentions of the object's user. There is, however, another sense in which philosophers use the term *intentionality* which refers not to our intentions but to the *aboutness* in our knowledge and experience: all knowledge *refers* to something outside itself; knowledge is the description of the properties of things beyond the knowledge itself, although the knowledge also has a material existence. The material properties of knowledge therefore have to be interpreted in two ways: (a) as the possessed properties of a material object, and (b) as the description of the nature of things outside that object. The term *intentionality* refers to the latter interpretation.

The simplest example of this intentionality is the feeling we all have that our experience pertains to the external world; that there is something out there which is represented in my cognition. This representation can be studied as the properties of the brain, although the brain too has to be interpreted in the two ways mentioned above: (a) as the physical and chemical properties of the brain and (b) as a referential description of facts that exist outside the brain. So far science has only done the former. That is, when we see a book, we measure its height, weight, length, speed, etc., not the meaning it might encode. To understand how the brain encodes a description, a symbolic view of nature is necessary in which material objects themselves *point* to other things.

Intentionality is therefore not a unique property of living beings or their brains; it exists in ordinary material objects such as books, art, music, street signs, etc. In the living beings, it exists not just in the brain but also in the DNA which represents the behavior of other biological systems. All representation involves abstracting—i.e. leaving out—many details from the object being represented and then encoding the resultant leftover information into a new object. This latter object must also point to the first, either explicitly through a *name* or implicitly through the morphological similarity between the object and its representation. In modern science, objects cannot denote concepts or names and therefore there cannot be abstraction and naming, and hence knowledge. Therefore, a neuroscientist might say that such and such neural electric pattern corresponds to seeing a red apple, but there can never be a *theoretical explanation* of how an object signifies another, using the kinds of concepts that current scientific theories employ.

In the semantic view described earlier, both the world and the brain are symbolic. Therefore, when we read a book, the material states in the brain point towards the material states of the book while the book itself points towards other things in the world. Clearly, the brain is part of a living being but a book is not. However, both the brain and the book have symbolic or intentional properties by which they refer to other things, which can in themselves be symbolic descriptions. For instance, the book in question might review another book which in turn discusses the information present in the book which in turn describes other things (even perhaps other books). The brain, the book, and the things that the book refers to must therefore be treated as *propositions* rather than things. Intentionality entails that the referring proposition abstracts the information in the referred proposition and represents it through a name, and then could provide additional meanings about it.

Besides this *descriptive* form of intentionality, there is also a *purpose* form of intentionality where one proposition represents the problem while the second represents a solution. This intentionality is seen when solutions are meant to address problems—e.g., as the relation between a mathematical conjecture and its proof—and we connect them by a purpose. Note how the referencing and referred propositions or the conjecture and the proof are complementary opposites; they are, mutually, the reason for the existence of the other. A proposition is called a proof in relation to a conjecture (and vice versa), and a proposition becomes knowledge only in relation to reality (and vice versa).

If we take away the conjecture, then the proof is no longer a proof; it is a set of symbols which logically arrive from premises to conclusions but this sequence of symbols serves no purpose—i.e. the proof of a conjecture. Similarly, without the proof, we cannot say the conjecture is true or false, even though it exists. This is quite like the fact that if our brains did not have intentionality, we could not say if our experiences are true or false, even though the experiences would exist (in common experience, such intentionality is lost during dreams or hallucinations). Concepts and names are therefore indispensable ingredients for forming knowledge because all knowledge employs abstraction (given by concepts) and refers to something outside itself (given by names).

The descriptive and purpose forms of intentionality are often tightly related: e.g., we create knowledge about the world because it solves some problems or meets some purposes. If the problem did not exist, then its solution would be unnecessary, and without such necessity the need for knowledge would itself not arise. Therefore, while an object can be abstracted and represented symbolically in another object, whether or not such symbolic representations are created depends on purposes. While such purposes will exist in the observers, their products—i.e. the intentional connection between knowledge and reality, or that between problems and solutions—exists even outside the observer. The observer may partake in the activity involving representation and problem solving, but the byproducts of this activity can be non-living.

In that specific sense, intentionality requires a fundamental shift in our thinking about matter, both living and non-living. Conventionally, many philosophers have relegated this problem to some special features about the brain, and with the confirmation that experiences are correlated with observations of brain activity this belief seems validated. The problem for science, however, is not just empirical confirmation of such correlations but also *theoretical explanations*. How will we fit the idea of knowledge and purpose within a notion of matter that previously attributed these properties only to observers and considered the mind different from the body? Obviously, the notion of matter has to be revised to accommodate knowledge and purpose—not just in the case of living beings but also for ordinary material objects like books. If all matter is treated as a symbolic representation of ideas, it would allow the fact that both brains and books can be intentional objects. However, it would unseat the current physical notions about material objects.

The basic property of intentionality is that it creates complementary, related opposites. In Vedic philosophy, the element of Ego is divided into two types of triads. The first triad is called *manas*, *prāna* and *vāk* as it represents the aboutness form of intentionality. *Manas* denotes the referencing, *vāk* denotes the referenced and *prāna* denotes the connection between the referencing and referenced. The second triad is called *daivika*, *bhautika* and *ātmika* as it represents intentionality in the purpose form. *Ātmika* represents the problem, *bhautika* represents the solution and *daivika* represents their relation. A problem can be solved in many ways, and the same solution can address many problems. The relation between a problem and a solution is therefore many-to-many, not one-to-one. Similarly, knowledge and objects underdetermine each other. To map knowledge to reality and problem to solution a choice is needed. Intentionality therefore has three parts rather than just two.

The Three Modes of Nature

Concepts have traditionally been very problematic in science because scientists believe in the frugality and parsimony of ideas while the everyday world employs infinitely many concepts. Sāṅkhya philosophy is particularly useful in this regard because it says that all types are built up from three modes of nature—*sattva*, *rajas* and *tamas*. These modes are the most fundamental *types* in nature and they in turn create all other types. All the types that we have discussed thus far, including sensation, properties, objects, intents and morals, are in turn built up from even more fundamental modes of nature. The relative proportion of each mode varies in each type. Since all entities are basically types, Sāṅkhya says that every entity is a combination of three modes.

The notion of three modes considerably simplifies our representation problem within a naturalistic theory because these three modes can be treated as the three axes of ordinary space. The three modes, Sāṅkhya states, are churned by Causal Time, to create their various combinations. All these types and their changes can be denoted as space-time forms. These forms will represent relative proportions of three modes of nature into a type. Three dimensions of space suffice for the purposes of representing forms but not for an *understanding* of the types, because the understanding depends on seeing the dimensions in space themselves as three distinct modes, or as three different types.

The term *tamas* denotes objects, the term *rajas* denotes activity, and the term *sattva* signifies the subject. The term subject here does not mean the soul; it means that observer which is experienced; in every experience, an image of the experiencer is constructed from the experience. For instance, in seeing an apple, there is a 'seer' who is *perceived* to be seeing the apple. The real conscious entity and the entity that is perceived to be conscious are different. In that respect, experience does not just create an image of the world, but also creates the image of the self. *Sattva* refers to the image of the self. The *chitta* which is the moral sense and consciousness of happiness is dominated by the mode of *sattva*. The mind, which creates and perceives concepts, is also said to predominate in *sattva*. Intelligence, the senses of knowledge and action are said to dominate in *rajas* or activity. Intentionality in the ego and the objects perceived by senses of knowledge and activity dominate in *tamas*. These three modes combine to create all the types and these types are encoded in space-time as various kinds of space-time forms.

Consciousness is different from the modes of nature, but it can come under the domination of the modes. It can be under the influence of objectivity (*tamas*), such as when we think that objects are reality and activity and the observer are byproducts of physical properties in objects, much like how science conceives activity and observers today. Consciousness can be under the influence of activity (*rajas*), such as when we think that all objects and subjects are produced by actions; in this case, we attribute causality to choices and activities. Consciousness can also be under influence of subjectivity (*sattva*) if we believe that objects and activities are produced because there is a subject behind them. This last notion comes closest to the overall Vedic view of nature, and therefore the mode of *sattva* is preferred over *rajas* and *tamas*.

Note however that if *sattva* was the only mode of nature, the only type in creation would be the observer; there would not be any objects, nor any activity. This would be an inadequate account of experience because every experience requires the existence of subject, object and activity. The real cause of experiences is not the subjective experiencer produced as part of the experience, but the soul or consciousness. The ultimate Vedic injunction is therefore to transcend the modes and 'see' that the subject, object and activity of experience are all phenomenal products and not reality. The phenomena indicate the existence of a consciousness, which is different from the observer. Thus, all three modes are needed to create experience, but someone who intends to transcend the universe must realize the primacy of the subject relative to activity and objects. There is first a subject, who then engages in sensual activities, which then produce objects. In that respect, the subject is 'superior' to activity and objects, although Sāṅkhya describes that all three modes are needed in creation. Prior to creation, the modes exist in equilibrium. That is, there is consciousness, but there is no experience. To experience, there must be categories to experience, and objects, subjects and activities are the most fundamental categories. Creation therefore springs from the separation of these three fundamental categories. By the separation of the basic categories, consciousness experiences itself as the doer, as the instrument of activity and as the effect.

The Vedas describe that these three fundamental categories are repeatedly split into more categories, each time using the same basic three-way distinction of *sattva, rajas* and *tamas*. First, the subject splits into three states called thinking, feeling and willing. Thinking represents cognition of ideas, such as yellowness. Feeling represents likes and dislikes of ideas, such as that I may like or dislike yellow. Willing represents a desire, such as the idea that I want yellow. Of course, yellowness itself has not appeared as a unique type yet; therefore, thinking, feeling and willing are at this point just basic types which will be refined by subsequent additions of the three modes to these basic types. Together, all these types constitute what is generally known as the mind.

Next, activity splits into judging, knowing and acting, which become the senses of knowing (seeing, tasting, touching, smelling and hearing), acting (walking, holding, evacuation, procreation and speech) and judging (intelligence). Each of these senses further divides into multiple parts. For instance, sight itself can be divided into color, brightness, shape, length and direction. Each such mode of seeing is perceived by the senses; for instance, color is divided into violet, indigo, blue, green, yellow, orange and red. Sensations divide matter into five kinds of elements, which represent properties in sensation. Once the objects have been created, then the thinking, feeling and willing in the mind create an intentional relation between subject and objects and our thoughts and desires are *about* the object. In this and in myriad other ways, the basic categories mutate and combine to create new types in experience.

Sāṅkhya is a theory of how all types are created from very basic and primitive types. As types, they can only be perceived by a consciousness that is purified of these modes of nature and the Vedas describe how an enlightened person is able to see everything in nature as the play of the modes of nature. However, even when we do not perceive these types, we can postulate them as *theoretical* constructs in order to explain the creation of types. These types are represented in matter as space-time forms, and they embody concepts into tokens.

The Paradox of Counting

Sāṅkhya is the theory of counting objects and, to count, it elucidates a theory of types. Why is such a theory of types even needed for counting? Why can't there be a theory that simply counts objects without types? The answer to this quandary lies in a basic problem that arises in the counting of objects. To count objects, there must be some properties *in terms of* which objects can be distinguished (before we can count, we must distinguish them). For instance, there must be properties like sight, taste, smell, sound, and touch to distinguish objects before they can be counted. Counting is therefore an *outcome* of distinguishing, but distinguishing itself requires sensations that can be used to distinguish.

Before we can count objects, therefore, there must be types of sensations that help us distinguish objects. But, of course, a type of sensing is not enough, because there are many outcomes of sensing the object through each type of sensing. The sense of seeing, for instance, comprises of many distinct properties such as form, color, distance, direction, size, luminosity, etc. It is not therefore enough to just see objects but also to distinguish them along these different properties. Therefore, sensations are inadequate to distinguish objects unless we also have properties. A sensation helps us see how something that has taste is different from that which only can be seen. But it doesn't help us distinguish between two things that both can be seen. To distinguish objects within a particular type of sensation (e.g., sight), there must be properties (like color, size, form, luminosity, distance, and direction) that help the observer comprehend and cognize the sensation. The simple act of seeing is then divided by properties such as color and form, and a perception (beyond the sensation) is constructed. While the senses produce sensations, the mind divides these sensations by properties. For instance, the eye can see yellow, but it cannot see color; the eye can sense that something is circular, but it cannot understand that it is form; the eye can see something is large or small, but it doesn't understand size. Properties such as size, color, form, etc. are provided by the mind.

The cognition of the object is however still not complete, because we have only comprehended the properties (e.g., color) and their values (e.g., yellow) but not combined them into *objects*. Of course, it is not necessary that the perceptual field be divided into objects; we might, for instance, think of the entire universe as a single undivided object, and all the perceptions of this universe as its myriad properties. However, commonsense intuition prevents this because we can see that there are parts of the universe that change without necessarily changing the other parts. In fact, if the universe were a single undivided object, then different observers themselves could not change independently, nor could they distinguish themselves from the world they observe. The latter conclusion would in turn entail the impossibility of knowledge: How can one property in an object *know* another property? Isn't the act of knowing hinged upon the fact that the knower and the known are separate objects? These and other similar problems lead to the separation of objects. To separate objects, we must divide the perceptual field again, this time by drawing boundaries that aggregate and separate properties.

In Sāṅkhya, the intelligence draws these boundaries and creates objects from the perceptual field. Once objects have been created, they can also be counted. However, to count objects, we must find a way to *order* them. Note how the use of sensations, properties and objects allows us to *differentiate* objects but they do not enable *counting*. That is, we don't know if object X comes before Y or vice versa. In modern mathematics, object ordering requires an order function, but this function is ultimately defined through a choice, not within mathematics.

Mathematics doesn't delve into the structure of this choice, as the choice depends on many contextual factors. As an example, suppose that I'm asked to sequence a collection of books and label them as first, second, third, etc. If I'm educated in modern science, I may choose "fundamental to less fundamental" as the criteria to order the books. Accordingly, logic will be ahead of number theory, then physics, then chemistry, then biology and, lastly, medicine. I have, in this ordering, used a theory of the universe—namely, the idea that nature is built from smaller atoms, and the most fundamental ways to see the universe is in terms of logic and numbers. The colors, shapes, sizes and fonts of the books have almost no relevance in my act of ordering, although they would have had an impact on the design and production of the books. My method of ordering the books based on a certain philosophy of nature is a choice, and there may as well be other methods of ordering such as one based on book marketing value (e.g., total number of readers, individual book ratings, ease of procuring and selling a book, etc.)

These methods of ordering books are based on different intents, such as to organize books by the knowledge they provide or as business value. Such intentions represent the ego in Sāṅkhya philosophy, which constitutes an observer's material personality and represents a coordinate reference frame to semantically order objects. Even in modern mathematics, object ordering depends upon a coordinate system, although this coordinate frame is described quantitatively rather than qualitatively. Objects too are described in mathematics using numbers, which represent quantities rather than types. Obviously, such ordering functions (coordinate systems) cannot distinguish and order objects when each object represents a different type; all objects being ordered in a physical coordinate system must have the same type, and it is due to their similarity in type they belong to the same physical 'space'. The semantic ordering function therefore becomes necessary when the space comprising the objects contains all possible types of objects. The dimensions of this space are the perceivable properties, and the values of these properties are the qualities experienced during perception. For instance, color, form, size, distances, and directions would constitute the dimensions of the semantic space and red, square, large, far and above will be amongst the possible values of these dimensions. The objects formed through such properties and values would also be types. For instance, objects would now be called tables, houses and cars. Senses, mind, intellect and ego therefore create an ordered space of objects which are described entirely in terms of types instead of quantities.

The ordering of a space, however, depends upon the choice of a coordinate system and this choice in turn rests upon preferring a method of ordering over other such methods. For instance, we might choose an ordering method that orders books by their knowledge rather than their monetary value. Whether knowledge should be preferred above money requires a value judgment, which is performed by the moral sense called *mahattattva*. Each moral position values different kinds of ideas, which can then be used to construct ordering functions, which will then order objects, which are in turn comprised of properties and values.

These facts about ordering objects stretch the problem of counting from a simple numerical computation of distance and direction in space and time to an understanding of how the observer perceives the world, conceives the properties in the world, aggregates these properties into objects, and then sequences the objects into an ordered collection. The problem of counting takes us into deeper recesses of the observer, requiring each time a new kind of sense that perceives sensations, properties, objects, coordinate frames and eventually moral values. Each successive type of sense invokes a different aspect needed for counting.

Sāṅkhya is a complete theory of counting entities because it delineates the stages through which objects must be counted. All these stages are different aspects of the observer. However, since these aspects of the observer are relevant to the problem of counting objects, they can be associated with objects (instead of just being associated with the observer). Now, the properties of the observer are relevant to study of objects. Indeed, they are different stages of counting things that represents a complete theory of counting and therefore a theory of numbers.

Modern mathematics encounters the problem of counting in set theory when it tries to define types as collections of objects. The problem stems from the fact that to distinguish objects, types must exist in the first place. So, how can we reduce types to some basic logical constructs? If there are only objects, how will concepts be formed? The basic idea that set theory uses is that concepts may be formed by aggregating objects into classes. In other words, instead of defining types—which will be used to distinguish and count objects—in a new fundamental way, set theory reduces concepts to objects which are supposed to be counted by the type distinctions. This represents the genesis of a problem that is encountered in many places in mathematics. To understand this problem, let us take an example. A mathematician can define the idea of a car by the set of cars if every member of that set is a car. This definition involves a circular notion of what a car is because we cannot know how to distinguish a car from other objects before we put it inside the set of cars. What is car? It is that which belongs to the set. And what belongs to the set? Everything that can be called a car. The point is that we need to know what we *mean* by a car independent of the objects to which this concept is applied. To give such a definition, we need to understand what we mean by a car prior to individual cars.

Mathematics ignores the fact that when types are created by aggregating objects, the multiplicity of objects in that aggregation is already assumed. How are these objects individuated? That is, how do we know that there are individual objects, if we don't know how to individuate them using some properties? Furthermore, to represent a class of things, objects in the aggregation must also be similar in some sense, which in turn means that the type that denotes that similarity must be present in the objects themselves even before they are aggregated. Like I mentioned before, the problem of counting is that it requires the ability to distinguish objects, which in turn requires types. Types can't be formed only by aggregating objects, because such aggregation assumes distinct objects, and their similarity by types. For instance, to suggest that the idea of a car is delineated by the set of all cars, we are required to form the set first which in turn requires knowing which objects can be called cars, which requires the concept of a car. It has been shown that this notion about concepts leads to paradoxes in certain cases which arise because of category mistakes between types and objects[16].

Science cannot be done in a universe that only has objects but no types because without types objects cannot be distinguished, classified and ordered. If, however, the universe already has some fundamental types which can be used to distinguish and count objects, then new complex types can be created by aggregating simple types. The new types can be used to classify and aggregate objects in new ways. In summary, to form a type, there must already be some types, which can then be used to jumpstart the process of counting and aggregating. A universe without types also cannot have any science because without types, objects in the universe cannot be distinguished and counted.

Modern science assumes that nature has a type, but there is only one type. Or, at least, the diversity of all types can ultimately be reduced to a single type. Descartes, for instance, thought that all matter had a single fundamental property: namely, that it was extended; he called it *res extensa*. This idea has proven immensely powerful as modern science has been able to reduce a variety of physical properties to properties of space-time. This theory is however flawed in one fundamental sense: it builds space-time from infinitesimal points, an idealization that cannot be conceived or created. This idealization violates the idea that objects can encode information in matter, or that there are fundamental limits to dividing things in nature due to the presence of information. If space-time is built of elementary forms which encode the same types as the mind perceives them then a complete theory of counting forms in space will have the same structure as the counting of objects using sensations, properties, objects, intents and morals. Such a theory will also explain how the observer perceives many types: sensations, properties, objects, intents and values, which seem to be very different. To account for the types an observer experiences, a new fundamental theory of types is needed that has more than one type. Sāṅkhya is such a theory where the variety of types in experience is created from three fundamental types. These types can be mapped to dimensions in space, effectively reducing space-time forms to different types of entities.

The two ideas about Sāṅkhya—namely that it is a theory of counting and a theory of types—are closely linked by the problem that objects cannot be counted without types. Objects can be counted if objects are made out of types. To create objects, types must be instantiated and ordered. Sāṅkhya states that all objects are created by combining the three modes of nature. Thus, the fact that the mind sees types in objects is not just a property of the mind. Rather, these types are real properties of objects because the objects are built up from type-instances. A type-instance is distinguished from other instances of the same type by the *order* of that type within the object. This order is another type of meaning. For instance, a sentence uses letters of the same type by instantiating them and these letters can be distinguished by measuring the *position* of the letter in the sentence. But letters can also be characterized by the fact that they participate in sentences at different locations to create different meanings. The instantiation of a type in one sense adds order upon a type. But that order is also another type, a 'deeper' kind of type.

Types can be counted if they are built out of fundamental types, which are also countable. For instance, the fact that we can distinguish different types of colors is based on the fact that we intuitively know how to distinguish between red, blue and yellow as primary colors, which in turn is based on the idea that there are three modes of nature that mutate to form colors. In this case, *rajas* represents red, *sattva* represents yellow and *tamas* represents blue. Sounds, tastes, smells, shapes and touches are cognized in types because they can be reduced to some basic types, which in turn can be reduced to the basic *form* of distinction between the three modes of nature. These distinctions would however still be inadequate if the modes themselves were not fundamentally countable (note that distinguishing and counting are separate notions; we can say that there are three modes without saying which mode is first, second and third). To count objects, the modes themselves need to be counted, and Sāṅkhya counts *sattva* as first, *rajas* as second and *tamas* as third. Even though the meaning of these modes is best understood in relation to the other modes, there still is an order to them.

This order is ultimately based on the idea that consciousness is the most fundamental entity in the universe, and it is represented as the type of subject in experience. Consciousness has capabilities to know and act, perceive sensations, properties, objects, intents and moral values, which are created as the senses of the subject and lead to activity. Objects are produced from the activities of the senses; this is a unique idea in Sāṅkhya, that senses don't just grasp ideas, but they can also create ideas. Thus, obviously, the mind has creative abilities to construct properties, intelligence has the ability to combine properties into objects, the ego can originate intents, etc. But this ability is generally not extended to the senses of hearing, tasting, touching, seeing and smelling. In Sāṅkhya the five senses can also create *tanmātra* which are forms perceived by the senses. Indeed, we can clearly perceive how these forms are created during dreaming. Matter, therefore, is created by the senses and the mind, which were created from conscious abilities.

Sāṅkhya states that the modes of nature cover the native capabilities of consciousness which then produces a 'contaminated consciousness' or the observed person (also called *mahattattva*). The contaminated consciousness then produces the ego, the intelligence, the mind and the senses. Lastly, these in turn combine to produce the material objects. The order in the modes of nature therefore has a basis in the theory of creation, and how objects come out of abilities in consciousness.

The Concept of Self-Regulation

Self-regulation is a concept that has baffled thinkers because the regulation is not conscious and does not seem to involve mental states although regulation is associated with self-preservation, something we would not generally associate with non-living things. The human body for instance controls breathing, digestion, body temperature, circulation and immune response which do not involve mental states, although it seems that these things would not happen if there was no mind with the body. The general idea today about self-regulation is that each organism has an Autonomic Nervous System (ANS) besides the conscious or mental nervous system. The ANS comprises the spinal cord and brain parts such as the hypothalamus and the medulla oblongata. The functions of the ANS include the control of breathing, circulation, digestion, immunity, swallowing, coughing, sneezing, vomiting, evacuating, etc. The ANS is also described as comprised of endocrine glands that release hormones in the bloodstream regulating bodily functions.

The autonomic functions in the body are described in a different way in Sāṅkhya, which attributes them to ten kinds of *prāna*—*prāna* (breathing), *apāna* (evacuating), *udāna* (sleep and mind-body control), *vyāna* (circulation), *samāna* (digestion), *nāga* (eyelid, salivating), *krkara* (hunger, sneezing), *kurma* (burping), *devadatta* (yawning), and *dhananjaya* (immunity). The ANS is said to control the bodily functions through endocrine glands such as pineal, pituitary, thyroid, thymus, pancreas, adrenal, testes, etc. In Yoga philosophy, the locations of these glands are congruous with the locations of the *chakras* along the spinal cord. The *chakras* are seven in number and they are called *muladhāra, swadhisthāna, manipura, anahata, vishuddha, ajna* and *sahasrara*.

Prāna itself is said to flow through the nerves and veins in the body and *ida, pingala* and *sushumna* are said to be three main channels of nerves and veins, which are aligned with the spinal cord. That *prāna* flows through veins closely corresponds to the fact that the endocrine system controls the body by releasing hormones directly into the blood stream. The close correspondence between the *chakras* and the endocrine glands, the ANS and *ida, pingala* and *sushumna*, and the similarity between the functions of ANS and those performed by *prāna* are some of the few areas of similarity between Sāṅkhya and modern science which, by and large, espouse highly divergent views about nature.

However, despite the morphological and conceptual similarities, Vedic philosophy and modern science describe these autonomic functions in quite different ways. The difference is that medical science describes the ANS as comprised of cells, molecules and atoms, while Sāṅkhya describes this control as an outcome of a vital force in the body. The dilemma about the relation between the ANS and the vital force is similar to the one that we earlier saw in the case of mind-body relations. In the mind-body dilemma, the key question was: Does the fact that we can *know* about an observer's mental states from the physical state imply that the physical state is the mental *experience*? In the ANS-*prāna* dilemma, the key question is: Does the fact that we can see an autonomic control in the body imply that this control is due to physical states?

The ANS-*prāna* dichotomy has not received as much attention in the academic world as the mind-body duality. This can obviously be explained by the fact that the mind is conscious and we are much more intimately aware of its workings than those of *prāna* and *chakra* which are not conscious. But there is another reason for this discrepancy: the idea of self-regulation, and indeed of *control* itself, does not seem to be a semantic idea and most scientists would like to think that regulation can be built into physical systems. Indeed, control systems are studied in science as equilibriums of negative and positive feedback loops, which is sometimes called an 'attractor' in complexity theory because any deviation from the equilibrium state brings the system back to equilibrium. Many such systems have been modeled using mathematical theories, and the idea that control systems do not require a type of physical entity separate from matter is more prominent than the idea that the explanation of experience does not require a mind different from the body.

Nevertheless, a physical control mechanism does not adequately explain why mental states have an effect on the ANS. Common examples of the effect of the mind on autonomic functions include changes to breathing patterns during stress, the effect of positive and negative emotions on the release of useful and harmful hormones, and instinctive fight-and-flight reactions during fear. The idea that the ANS is totally autonomic is wrong because conscious mental states do have an effect on the ANS. It is rather more correct to say that the ANS works autonomously unless the mental states intervene in its autonomy. If mental states are volitional, they can influence the ANS. Self-regulation thus creates a problem similar to the mind-body problem, though perhaps not identical to it. This is because when mental states can interact with the body, then the body itself has to be described in a new way. This new description will now alter the nature of the ANS as well. In the mind-body problem, matter works according to natural laws until the mind intervenes. In self-regulation, the ANS works autonomously until the conscious states intervene. The difference between them is primarily that in the mind-body case, we can *intend* a specific type of thought or action and affect it, but in the case of self-regulation, we cannot intend a blood pressure, body temperature or immunity and then affect it.

A fairly common assumption in biology, and indeed in any kind of control system, is that control systems are of the same *type* as the things they control. For instance, the thermostat that controls the working of an air-conditioner works on the same principles as the air-conditioner; both follow the same laws of nature. They are different only in terms of how they have been *structured* or designed to carry out different functions. In the human body, this idea is extended to the ANS, which is supposed to be another chemical control system that manages other chemical systems. Evolutionists claim that these complex systems—and their functions—have evolved over time, and there are persistent debates between evolutionists and creationists on whether evolution indeed suffices to explain the complexity of the biological systems. The creationist, for instance, argues that the design of biological system requires a huge amount of information, which can only be imparted by God and all the species were therefore created by some divine intervention.

There are some important differences between creationism and Vedic philosophy. The main difference is that in Vedic philosophy material objects are inert and they don't move on their own. They are rather changed by an agency called *prāna* which is material and yet distinct from the objects themselves. Contrast this with the notion of causality in modern science where properties in objects themselves cause these objects to change. For instance, the mass in an object is said to exert a gravitational force which causes other objects to move. The Vedic view is that what we currently call gravitational force is not produced by mass, but is rather the effect of *prāna* which causes the objects to move, similar to how a car is driven by a driver. The driver 'behind' the action is consciousness, but the will of consciousness is expressed through *prāna* which is also a material 'force' but different from current scientific forces. However, everything that *prāna* does within the body is not necessarily willed or conscious. The control of bodily functions such as breathing and circulation are part of the activities that *prāna* performs, although *prāna* is also involved in the conscious control of the body. The difference between creationism and Vedic philosophy is therefore that the creationists accept that the scientific laws of nature cause material objects to move naturally whereas Vedic philosophy states that even the motion of objects is under the control of an agency called *prāna*.

To see the relevance of *prāna* in the context of modern science, we first need to understand why material objects in modern science are also, in fact, inert. If the inertness of these objects is understood, then the need for a causal agency different from the objects will also be clearly seen. It would then be easier to understand the role of *prāna*.

Unlike classical physics where objects moved in space-time due to the action of deterministic forces, objects in quantum theory settle into stationary states within an ensemble of particles. While force in classical physics was responsible for motion, the same force in quantum theory is responsible for a *stationary* state. Thus, when an ensemble is formed, quantum theory stipulates a redistribution of matter and energy in the ensemble such that all these particles are in fixed states. The states can change only if the total energy of the system is altered by adding or removing matter and/or energy. This means that closed systems (which do not exchange energy or matter) will always be in stationary states. Such quantum ensembles can change their states in one of two ways. First, two or more ensembles can be 'merged' into a single ensemble, thereby creating a bigger ensemble. An ensemble can also be divided into smaller ensembles, thereby creating multiple ensembles from a single ensemble. Second, matter or energy can 'jump' from one ensemble into another. The *mechanisms* for both of these types of changes are unknown in quantum theory. In quantum theory, the ensemble is a logical construct and not a physical one, and therefore the mechanisms that define how such ensembles can be merged or divided are unknown in the theory. Also, since each quantum ensemble is in a stationary state, there is no causal explanation for why matter or energy will 'jump' from one ensemble to another. Quantum theorists assume that separate quantum ensembles can get entangled causing a redistribution of matter or energy, without offering an explanation of these mechanisms.

In Vedic philosophy, there are three categories that represent the ensemble, the energy in the ensemble, and the flow of energy across ensembles. These are called *kaphā, pittā* and *vāta. Kaphā* represents the structures and boundaries that organize and divide matter. *Pittā* represents the logical distribution of matter and energy in the whole, and roughly corresponds to the idea of energy in quantum theory. *Vāta* represents the causal agency that moves this matter or energy from one ensemble to another. *Vāta* is also sometimes called *prāna* as it is the 'force' that circulates energy.

In the living body, the organization of the body into cells, organs and bones represents *kaphā.* Science does not acknowledge the structure itself because it reduces it to atoms and molecules, which correspond to *pitta* or the energy inside the structure. The reductionist view claims that the whole is built up by combining parts, while the Vedic view is that the whole and the part are separately real. The latter view becomes necessary due to the problems inherent in atomic theory[17]. The notion of *kaphā* corresponds to the logical notion of an ensemble in quantum theory, although this notion is treated materially and not logically in the Vedic view. These wholes are, however, in stationary states and they cannot change on their own. Changes are caused by *vāta* which moves energy and matter from one structure and ensemble to another. *Vāta* is thus responsible for blood circulation (and thereby the transport of food and energy to the other parts of the body) and the transfer of electronic signals from the brain and the ANS to other parts of the body.

The yogic practices of *prāṇayāma* are meant to voluntarily control the flow of *prāna* in the body and this is possible because *prāna* can act under the volition of consciousness. Through this mechanism, consciousness controls the rest of the body by transporting energy and nervous signals to other parts of the body. By the practice of *prāṇayāma* a living being can develop enormous powers of transformation, free the mind of its attachments to material objects, as well as lead a healthy life.

Prāna is considered superior to matter because all matter is inert and it is caused to move by the influence of *prāna*. This idea is also scientifically very useful because it solves the problems of causal incompleteness in current atomic theory. Unlike classical physics where forces caused motion, and were therefore supposed to be agents of causality, these forces only determine the total energy of a system in quantum theory which now rests in a stationary state. To move this energy, forces are not sufficient. A new cause is therefore needed. *Prāna* denotes the power of transformation and different types of *prāna* represent different kinds of transformations. Like Earth, Water, Fire, Air and Ether are described in terms of everyday concepts about material objects, *prāna*, *apāna*, *udāna*, *vyāna* and *samāna* are also described in terms of everyday concepts of transformation, as already mentioned above. However, similar to material elements, these forces are not the ordinary activities of ingesting, digesting, eliminating or breathing. They are rather the *causes* underlying these changes. The causes are visible in the activities but they are not those activities. The notion of *prāna* is therefore a causal construct, and its understanding requires a *type* theory of change. That is, if objects are defined as types rather than as quantities, then changes to these objects must be described as changes to types, and these changes can further be described as change types. We describe everyday changes in terms of such types—walking, talking, breathing, driving, writing, teaching, etc.

Vedic philosophy teaches us that these activities are *possible* in matter but they are not actuated unless some change is caused in matter by the exertion of the causal 'force' of *prāna.*

But why does *prāna* create cycles of change? The reason for this is that all change in nature is cyclic and Time itself moves cyclically. This is indicated in the body by the breathing patterns, by the cycle of consumption and elimination, and by a variety of circadian rhythms. Moreover this cyclicity is also manifested in the passing of days and nights, months, seasons, years and millennia. Cyclic time is also reflected in the rise and fall of civilizations, ideologies, and cultures. *Prāna* follows the rhythms of Time and it is said to be disturbed when the activities of the body are out-of-sync with the rhythms of Time. Aligning the rhythms of the body with the rhythms of nature—such as by adjusting our sleeping and waking patterns or the times for eating, working and recreation —are considered healthy lifestyles. Cyclic time creates *semantic* notions of change rather than physical notions of change which arise with the linear notion of time used in modern science. If time moves cyclically, then it can be described in terms of a finite number of *types* such as day and night, morning and afternoon, summer and winter, age of reason and age of illusion, etc. A type theory of change requires a cyclic notion of time in which activities are described as types rather than motion.

5

Understanding Vedic Cosmology

My soul is the mirror of the universe, and my body is its frame
—Voltaire.

What Is Vedic Cosmology?

In modern cosmology, the universe is uniform at all places and in all directions. This means that matter is the same everywhere in the universe and the same laws of nature apply in faraway galaxies as they apply on Earth. The laws of nature are also not changing with time; that is, the laws of nature at the origin of the universe are the same as the laws today. In Vedic cosmology, however, all locations, directions and times are different. This difference arises because space is closed and time is cyclical. Closed space converts locations and directions into types. For instance, the space inside the house is described in terms of types such as kitchen, bedroom, bathroom, living room, study, guest room, etc. Each direction such as up and down, before and after, to the left and to the right, under and over, etc. has a unique meaning. Cyclical time, similarly, converts instances and durations into types. Within a day, time is divided into morning, noon, evening and night and different meanings are tied to these times. There are divisions such as days in a week, weeks in a month, months in a season, seasons in a year, etc. And there is a type difference between past, present and future. The basic difference between Vedic and modern cosmology is in how they treat space and time. Space and time are described in terms of types in Vedic cosmology while, in modern cosmology, they are described in terms of quantities. A location is position $x=5$ in science, while, in Vedic philosophy, it is a kitchen. A time is $t=15$ in science, while it is morning in Vedic philosophy. This basic difference between types and quantities changes the Vedic scientific outlook about space-time in the universe.

Different locations, directions and times in the universe are not the same; they are of different types. We cannot move an object from one location to another and preserve its properties. For instance, if you move a chair from your study to the kitchen, it becomes a kitchen chair. Similarly, the objects in different parts of the universe are not the same. The laws governing these locations, directions, times and objects are not the same; they are of different types. If a human being were to be transported to a faraway galaxy, he would need to transform his body to live in accordance with the laws and properties of that new location. If you were to travel back into the past or into the future, again, you would need a different body that conforms to the laws and properties of that time.

The laws governing objects are tied to their semantic properties which are tied to their location in space and time. Therefore, when space and time are typed then objects too are described in terms of types. In Vedic philosophy, therefore, the universe is described as the study of various different types of locations, times, durations, directions, objects and laws. This description will be understood in science when notions about space and time are modified from quantities to types.

Difficulties in Vedic Cosmology

The study of Vedic Cosmology is fraught with difficulties. There is a hard to grasp association of cosmological entities with deities and demigods, because the scientific search for life on other planets has failed. There is a geo-centric view of the cosmos that contradicts established scientific notions about the solar system and the universe. And there are similarities between Vedic cosmology and astrology that attribute causal influence to planets and these make the theories difficult to understand.

There are also apparent contradictions in the placement of deities. For example, Lord *Brahma* lives in the *Satya-loka*, he is the principal ruler at the top of *Sumeru* Mountain, and is also worshipped in *Puṣkara-dvīpa*. Where is he really situated? The moon, similarly, is a planet between *bhū-maṇḍala* and 28 constellations (but not a satellite); the moon is on top of *Manasottara Mountain*, the moon is one of the 33 demigods living on the *Sumeru Mountain* and the moon also resides on the *Sālmali-dvīpa*. *Yamarāja* likewise lives in *Pitṛloka* at the bottom of the universe, on the *Sumeru Mountain* and on the *Manasottara Mountain*. Where do we go about placing these luminaries and deities? Do these varied explanations even constitute a consistent system? Without a clarification of these issues it is difficult to understand Vedic cosmology.

Vedic Cosmology and Science

While a good understanding of Vedic cosmology cannot be developed without a new type-based view of space and time, an overall understanding of Vedic cosmology need not wait until the space-time physics is complete. It is possible to identify a broad approach to the study of Vedic cosmology, based upon some preliminary ideas about space, time and matter taken from the Vedic texts. With these ideas in the back of our minds, it would be easier to comprehend and explain the apparent contradictions in the Vedic texts and the obvious differences with respect to modern cosmological theories of the universe. The broad sketch would also motivate an alternate view of the universe. Here, I will attempt to describe the Vedic space and time view that can form the basis of the study of Vedic cosmology. This sketch draws upon Vedic notions of space, time and matter that were described in previous chapters.

To briefly recapitulate that discussion, there are several differences between Vedic and modern science. In modern science, objects are governed by deterministic laws of force and motion. In Vedic science, living beings are governed by moral laws of choices and their consequences. Matter in modern science exists in an open space-time, while matter in Vedic science is divided by boundaries into contexts. In an open space-time, matter has only physical properties, but in a closed space, matter also acquires semantic properties. The universe of modern science is practically of the same type everywhere. In Vedic philosophy, space is hierarchical and time is cyclic and this gives different types of meanings to matter. Matter is therefore not the same everywhere. Rather, different types of matter are found in different parts of the universe. Since the laws of nature depend on the type of the object, the laws are also different in different parts of the universe. In modern science, the universe is the closure[18] on a certain amount of matter. In Vedic philosophy, the universe is a closure on language and experience. The universe is not all that exists or can exist, but all that we can know and communicate via language. In modern science, there is one type of reality—material objects. In Vedic science, matter is not even a reality; it is a phenomenon. Objects, however, are not the only phenomena; phenomena include sensations, concepts, propositions, intents, morals and personalities. These are phenomena because they can be created, destroyed and modified. Reality is that which is not created, destroyed and modified. By that standard, consciousness is reality, because it is never created; it experiences, but experiences don't change consciousness.

Amongst all these differences, one fact stands out for the purpose of a better understanding of Vedic cosmology. This is the idea that physical properties of space can also denote meanings. Space and time in modern science are homogeneous and isotropic[19]. But semantic space-time is neither homogeneous nor isotropic. The directions in a semantic space are not equivalent because there are meanings associated with above and below, left and right, front and behind, forward and backwards, inside and outside, before and after. If directions in space were flipped, this would also invert the meanings of symbols in space. Direction inversion in a semantic space also requires the inversion of sensations in the senses, properties in the mind, objects in the intelligence, intentions in the ego and moral values in the moral sense. Unlike the notions of space in science which are invertible without creating any noticeable difference, directions in a semantic space are not equivalent because the inversion of sensations, properties, objects, intents and morals creates noticeable differences. Similarly, all locations in space are not identical in a semantic space because each location represents a different meaning. Motion in a semantic space represents an evolution of sensations, properties, objects, intents or morals. Two objects in two locations must be different. The cyclic nature of time also creates new meanings, depending on which point in the cycle time is known.

The semantic view of space and time therefore changes the outlook towards the Vedic universe. Now, there is a sense in which parts of the universe are higher and lower; higher representing farther removed from objects, less use of the senses and greater use of consciousness, while lower representing greater involvement with objects, more engrossed with the senses and less with consciousness. There is also a sense in which the universe has a core and a periphery; the core representing the mainstream experiences while the periphery representing fringe experiences. In short, locations in space are not just different places in the universe. Each location also represents a type—such as a type of sensation, property, object, intent, morality and personality. Different parts of the universe are not just physically distinct. They are also different types of places that produce different kinds of experiences. Matter in this space is not just 'stuff' with physical properties. It is rather described *in terms of* sensations like taste, smell, sight, sound and touch, in terms of it being *thinkable* (mind), *judgable* (intelligence), *ownable* (ego) and *enjoyable* (consciousness). Rather than seeing matter as things that exist irrespective of how they are experienced, the Vedic view defines matter in terms of sensual, cognitive, conative, judging, owning and enjoying properties. The Vedic view of space is coupled to a semantic view about matter, and this view should be understood before descriptions of planets, deities and demigods can even be attempted.

The Vedic View of the Universe

In the Vedas, the structure of the universe is isomorphic to the structure of experience, and distinct parts of the universe afford different experiences. The universe as the possibility of experience contains all possible experiences that gross and subtle matter can produce. By this consideration, the edge of the universe affords fringe experiences and the center affords core experiences, and if we can understand what the fringe and core of experience is, we can also understand what the edge and center of the universe is as experience. The universe is not a uniformly extended space. It is instead divided into regions by the kinds of experiences those regions afford. The Vedas describe the universe as a *virāṭa-puruṣa* or a universal being. This universal being is not a single person. However, the universe can be thought of as various types of experiences. The notion of *virāta-puruṣa* gives us valuable clues about how the universe can be studied as the domain of any possible experience with divisions of space in the universe aligned with various divisions of experience.

In the Vedic universe, to experience a different meaning one must be in a different part of the universe. Travel in space requires a semantic evolution of the abilities to experience. Since this ability consists of senses, mind, intelligence ego and consciousness, going to another part of universe implies changes to the cognitive apparatus and abilities of the traveler. When a person has evolved their experiential capabilities, they will automatically be situated in a different part of the universe because locations in space are differences in *types*. Thus, with new abilities in the senses, mind, intelligence, ego and consciousness, a soul naturally transmigrates to a new body in a different location. The Vedas state that by changing the mind and intelligence consciously, a person can take on other kinds of bodies and travel to new locations inhabited by people of a different mentality. The former is the basis of moral laws and the latter of mystic abilities. Transmigration and travel in the universe is thus related to a semantic space wherein a difference in location is also a difference in type of concept, proposition, intent and morality.

The notion of *virāṭa-puruṣa* draws a parallel between the structure of experience and the structure of the cosmos. Since the body and the mind afford a variety of experiences, the structure of the universe must have parallels in the structure of experience. The cosmos can therefore be studied by analyzing all possible experiences. Today, this idea may be discarded as unscientific, not because we can refute it experimentally but because there is no theory about how this is even possible. By contrast, it is perfectly valid science to pursue the detection of atomic particles because there is a theory backing their existence.

This is less a question of ideological superiority of one viewpoint over another and more a question of our scientific sensibilities. A new theory of semantic space coupled with semantic matter would make the Vedic view scientific.

Metaphors in Vedic Cosmology

Vedic cosmological descriptions use many metaphors: (a) conscious experience, (b) a functional society, (b) a geographical division, and (d) a living body, which are derived from the idea that the universe is a *system*. General Systems Theory, which is an approach to studying the material world by dividing it into complete systems, claims that there are general patterns in systems that are common across different types of systems. For instance, most systems are self-regulating and self-preserving. They are organized into functional parts to affect this regulation and control. Systems are goal-oriented and adapt themselves to their environment. These principles were originally intended to lead us to a theory of how systems must organize themselves into distinct parts and functions, but that science of organizing is yet to be developed.

Every system organizes into logically distinct functions. A business is structured into departments such as marketing, finance, engineering, support, sales, human resources, operations, etc. A living being's body is structured into circulatory, respiratory, digestive, excretory, nervous and immune functions. Societies are organized into businesses, governmental, non-governmental, correctional and educational institutions. The universe, similarly, in the Vedic view, is organized into a system, comprising many types of parts that can be understood by comparison to the other systems we are familiar with. This analogy between the universe and other systems is often misunderstood by people who interpret Vedic cosmology as an anthropomorphic view of the universe. They criticize that the ancient Hindus wanted to see the universe in terms of things that they understood, and often drew parallels between the universe and the geography of the land they were living around, between their body and the universe, or between their social system and the universe as a society. This criticism is not invalid, although it misses the deeper point that Vedic cosmology is organized around a systems view of the universe, in which the system is managed and administered like an organization. The principles by which we study organizations, society, and living beings can therefore be applied to the universe as a whole.

Experientially, our body and mind provide a glimpse into the entire universe in miniature form and the universe is an expansion and elaboration of the miniature world of individual experience into infinitely many living beings each focused upon one kind of experience. Socially and culturally, our world holds the universe in miniature form and the universe is a large cultural and social organization. Geographically, just as there are different locations for work, cooking, resting, gathering, worshipping and bathing even within the confines of a house, the universe can be described similarly by geographical differentiation. On the face of it, each of these is a metaphor. But, in reality, it hides a new semantic view about space and matter, with far-reaching consequences.

As our ordinary world is organized into personal, social and physical components—each of which is treated semantically—the universe is, similarly, divided and differentiated. A description of the universe in terms of geographical, personal and social metaphors is not an anthropomorphic imposition of a limited worldview on the wider universe, as critics of Vedic philosophy say. Rather, the description is based on a type-based view of space, time and matter, different from their current quantity based descriptions. The type-based theories of space, time and matter have important scientific and technological consequences. However, these benefits can only be visualized within a new type of theory.

The universe is a society, and like our societies are administered by governments, the universe also has a government. Administrators in this government are empowered individuals who have conceptual powers (recall that all causality in the Vedic view is conceptual) over different *types* of concepts. There are thus demigods for water, fire, health, food, love, health, and innumerable other concepts. Just as ordinary society organizes itself into differentiated roles and functions, the universe is also differentiated to work as a system. When society is divided into different kinds of functions, each location has a functional property. Living beings with different conceptual powers reside in different locations in the universe. These divisions are often mirrored in smaller regions of the universe, and in some parts of the Vedas, the universe is described in analogy to *bhārata-varsa,* which is also a name for the Indian peninsula. Critiques of these descriptions claim that Vedic authors wanted to see the universe in light of the land they were familiar with, or worse, they thought that the land they knew was the whole universe for them. A more thoughtful approach however suggests another possibility, namely that Vedic descriptions are made around systems, and the universe is described in metaphors of *bhārata-varsa* by mapping functionally similar parts in the large and small systems, respectively.

Like an ordinary city is comprised of different places for entertainment, worship, residence, work, correction and education, the universe is also divided into different parts which are conceptually and functionally different. When geography is understood semantically, the universe can be described semantically in analogy to geographical metaphors. This description does not mean we are identifying a geographical location with a piece of the universe in the modern scientific sense of space. It can however mean that we are identifying a part of the universe where work dominates as opposed to entertainment or worship. Thus, jails and correctional institutes in society are compared to hells in the nether world. Places of pleasure and entertainment are compared to *svarga* or heavenly planets. Places of meditation and worship are compared to higher planetary systems like *jana, tapa, mahar* and *satya-loka.* The middle planetary system is identified as the place of work, while the lower planetary systems dominate in pleasure, intoxication and lower forms of morality. The universe in the Vedas is therefore described as a gigantic social system with administrators running the system quite like we organize institutions for a smooth functioning of human society.

The *meru-daṇḍa* or spinal cord in the human body is compared to the *meru-parvata* as the backbone of the universe. Like the spinal cord automatically controls the working of the rest of the body, and the *chakras* in the body are identified with locations of different types of autonomous control, similarly, the planets along the *meru-parvata* are places for residence for different demigods who control various concepts. Thus, *chakras* in the spinal cord are compared to different planetary systems. As *kundalini* in the living being rises through various chakras, elevating the consciousness through various grades of existence, similarly, the consciousness rises through the different planetary systems, providing it with different kinds of powers and grades of existence.

The stark difference between the scientific and the Vedic outlook about the universe will disappear when science evolves to describe matter, space and time *semantically*. The challenge in developing this new science is that current science studies matter in open spaces while semantics deals with closed systems. Current science views time as open-ended, whereas in the Vedic view time it is cyclic. When space and time are closed and cyclic, respectively, then material objects in this space and time will be treated semantically. In current science, physics studies atoms, chemistry studies molecules, biology studies cells and information, physiology studies functions, neuroscience studies the brain, etc. There is no systems science that unifies all these different branches of phenomenal study using a common systems-based model. In the Vedic view, the divisions between sciences as seen in current science don't exist. There are instead sciences of sensations, concepts, propositions, intents and morals. These sciences together constitute a complete theory of a system, which is created for the purposes of consciousness.

The project of scientifically explaining the universe is so complex today because different theories apply to different facets of conscious experience—personal, social and physical. But such a project can be simplified if these domains of experience are seen as different types of meanings being created by consciousness. The approach benefits from a far wider base of forming intuitions than is available within present science. Specifically, if we are thinking of the universe as meaning, society or geography, we can see in its workings many things that we would not see if we treated it as a flat space-time extension containing meaningless objects. Modern science needs a transfusion of semantic ways of thinking about geography, society, human body, systems, organizations and conscious experience paving the way into understanding the universe as a living system. The *virāṭa-puruṣa* can be seen in analogy to a living being whose existence involves social and personal dimensions.

The Economic Control of the Universe

One of the important ways in which we understand the human world today is in terms of its exchange of wealth to create a sustainable economic system. The primary aim of a government is to control and manage the flow of wealth so as to maximize the well-being of its citizens. The Vedic universe is governed by the same type of principle. Specifically, the universe as a whole forms a tightly coupled economic system. Individual planets in the universe are smaller, local economies but they are not independent of the universal economic system. To properly understand this aspect of the Vedas, we need to better understand the nature of economic systems themselves. The essence of any economic system is an *economic cycle* which transforms raw materials into products, and products back into raw materials. Products are produced, transported and distributed to their consumers, who then transform them into waste. To continue the economic cycle, waste must be transformed back into raw materials. Modern economic theory studies the demand-supply cycle, processes of efficient production and distribution, and the effects of information on economic systems. However, they do not consider the origin of raw materials themselves. Economic theory assumes that nature has provided us with a finite amount of raw materials, but how this material came into existence is outside economic theory.

Since the raw materials are in short supply, modern economic theory claims that living beings must compete for them, and this lies at the root of Darwinian evolution where survival involves a struggle for acquiring food, shelter, sex and survival. But what if the production of raw materials itself were part of the economic cycle? What if there are methods by which waste is naturally transformed into useful matter?

As environmentalists realize, we don't have an unlimited supply of air, water, minerals, soil, energy, fuel, etc. If the supply of raw materials ceases, the entire economic cycle will come to an abrupt standstill. Current economic theories do not see beyond the point when scarce resources like oil, minerals, water, soil and air will be exhausted. An evolutionist will only say that in an environment of scarce resources, living beings must evolve to survive even in the bleak circumstances.

The Vedic view discusses the origin of raw materials. The Vedas state that raw materials are controlled by living beings in other planets. They can supply air, water, minerals, energy, fuel, etc. in exchange for other kinds of raw materials from Earth. In the symbolic view of nature, the causality is in concepts and not in the matter that embodies the concept. Therefore, to exchange these raw materials, it is not necessary to transfer the air, water, minerals or fuel from one planet to another. It suffices to transfer the meanings, which can be encoded in various physical properties, including sound. Ordinary objects like grains, water and fire can also be used to symbolize complex meanings. In such cases, the transfer of meaning (when meaning and physical properties are different) has the same effect as transfer of matter (when meaning and physical properties are identical). The Vedic process of transfer of meanings is thus based on the performance of *yajña* which offers sophisticated meanings to demigods through the chanting of *mantras*, elaborate rituals and fire sacrifices. The sounds, oblations and activities offered during rituals are symbols, whose meanings are fixed by the context of the sacrifice. Vedic rituals were designed to fulfill needs in other living beings, especially those beings that could fulfill needs on Earth. By executing their obligations, various living beings can live together in peace.

The Vedic economic theory is not based upon hard work, industrialization and the optimization of scarce resources to increase production. It is rather based on satisfying the source from which all necessities of life can be obtained through a semantic exchange. Thus, human life is expected to be lived on the supply of grains, milk, clothes and shelter. Opulence and luxuries are in the form of domestic animals, gold, jewels, cultivable land, etc. None of these is achieved by industrialization. They depend upon an abundant supply of raw materials in nature, which can be obtained by the performance of *yajña* which satisfies demigods and obliges them to provide the necessities of human life, in turn. The scientific basis of *yajña* is a semantic view of matter where sound, water, fire and grains are converted into symbols of meanings and given to the demigods as an offering. Each demigod is a master of a particular kind of meaning and capable of controlling the world according to that concept. Thus demigods can supply many kinds of desired objects.

The important role played by demigods in economic cycles means that the universe does not function automatically. The universe is regulated by controlling the supply of raw materials. Modern consumerist society survives on the exploitation of raw materials available in nature, until the supply of raw materials ends. The consumerist society must then undergo turmoil, strife, war, disease and famine. The long list of problems that arise without clean water and air are well-known to environmentalists and ecologists. But the science by which nature can provide all the necessities automatically is unknown to scientists today.

The Role of Universal Time

In Vedic philosophy, every living being has a limited amount of freedom to make choices. This freedom exists as (a) the type of senses, mind, intelligence, ego and consciousness—since a different type of body produces different types of sensations, concepts, proposition, intents and morals, and (b) the context or environment in which the living being exists—since the environment constrains choices. Through the performance of prescribed duties, *yajña* and mystical practices, a living being can change their senses, mind, intelligence, ego and consciousness, allowing them to enter new types of contexts. However, ordinary beings are not powerful enough to create contexts. Contexts are produced by Time which is a form of universal consciousness, different from the consciousness of individual living beings. The individual consciousness chooses alternatives within a context while Time creates and destroys the contexts themselves. The significance of this idea is that contexts are created, destroyed and maintained by Time and not by individual choices. These include one's body, organizations, societies, cultures and nations in which individuals are able to exercise their free will (the body of an individual is also a context to exercise the free will of the soul).

The universe in Vedic philosophy is what-deterministic but who-indeterministic. That is, *what* will happen in the universe is fixed by the influence of Time, but *who* will do it is not fixed until the individual living being chooses. All the events in the universe are pre-determined, but the actors of those events are not. We might foresee what is going to happen and choose to participate in those events. We might also not see the future, or see the future but choose not to participate in it. Our choices will not change the actual occurrence of events, because someone else will make the very same choices that we choose to evade. They do however change the outcomes for us and for other living beings.

According to Vedic philosophy, the universe is controlled by Time and all events are already ordained by Time. Individuals can participate in contexts created by Time according to their abilities and desires. But, if one capable individual does not desire, the opportunity will attract another individual. If there are no capable individuals to fulfill tasks in Time's ritual, God advents into those roles performing tasks that could have been done by other capable living beings. Individual living beings, however powerful and capable they may be, must still obey the flow of time. Time undergoes cycles of creation and destruction, rise and fall, increase and decrease. The amount of water and heat rises and falls according to periodic cycles across ages, years, seasons, months, days and nights. The universe follows ritual patterns bringing different quantities and qualities of raw materials that control life. The universe undergoes eras of peace and prosperity or decline and decay, governed by Time's control. Behind these events there are obviously individual living beings and demigods but the ritual is under the control of Time. The Vedas describe how the universe undergoes destruction by water, fire and air, which is possible simply by Time causing an increase in a particular type of raw material which would otherwise be beneficial and useful. Time coordinates the increase and the decrease in the modes of nature, thereby affecting the tendencies and thinking patterns in beings.

This is a highly deterministic view of the universe, similar to the view adopted in scientific cosmology, except for some important differences: (a) while classical scientific determinism is incompatible with the existence of meaning and choices, the Vedic determinism is, and (b) time in modern science is linear, but in the Vedic view it is cyclical. When things do not go as we planned or intended, people demur philosophically: "maybe the time is not right". According to the Vedic view, they are right. However, this view of the role of time in causing events in the universe does not exist in current science where causality is in objects, not in time. This role for time exists in Vedic philosophy because choices are enacted within limited contexts, and there must be a causal agency that enacts contexts for choices to act within them. The role for Time is also necessary to control the universe according to God's will. The creation and destruction of the universe, rise and fall of cultures, societies, empires and civilizations, are thus all controlled by Time.

The ritual structure of this universal Time is effected by setting up luminaries and deities into specific kinds of routines, called their orbits. The periodic motion and rituals of these deities result in a complex ritual for the universe. The periods and orbits of luminaries are meant to achieve a pre-determined ritual cycle that the universe must undergo. Luminaries and deities cannot deviate from these predetermined paths of the ritual cycle. Thus, these orbits are a consequence of the ritual of Time and given a description of the ritual, the paths and orbits of the luminaries can be determined by understanding the effect into the causes.

The ritual structure of the universe connects events in the universe to astrological predictions. Today, the motion of planets is described by the force of gravity. The explanation in the Vedas for this motion is Time, and the universal system is designed to go through a ritual under the influence of Time. The motion of luminaries causes changes in the universe because these luminaries are conceptually different and hence connected to different instances of conceptually similar objects elsewhere in the universe. An increase or decrease in a particular concept resonates with instances of these concepts and causes them to increase or decline. Deities residing in luminaries are living beings who have mastered control of specific meanings or pleasures, and their specific trajectory is tantamount to controlling a particular meaning or pleasure. Their different paths cause changes to certain meanings and pleasures in the universe causing them to become prominent or to decline.

Vedic Cosmology and Astronomy

The Vedic conceptual view of matter explains how planetary motions are connected to the needs in everyday life. But, to understand this view, we need to view the universe through mind, intelligence, ego and consciousness, which produce different results than perception through the senses. It is not sufficient to observe how something looks; it is more important to know what that thing *means*. Perception through the senses is, of course, not denied in Vedic philosophy although in ancient Vedic times, sensory perception wasn't given much importance. Attempts to map Vedic cosmological elements to astronomical objects are quite recent, because this mapping corresponds to seeing the universe in terms of our gross senses—e.g., eyes. The mapping was done during the times of *Āryabhāṭa* and *Varahāmihir* or perhaps originated sometime before their tenure as a means to establish astrology as an empirical science by providing methods to measure planetary motions. The attempt serves to provide some empirical confirmation of Vedic ideas and facilitates its practices for the common population by making its ideas accessible in terms of ordinary experience. The additional reason to assume that this mapping is recent is because the Vedic texts themselves do not have an astronomical description of the Vedic cosmology. Rather, latter day texts such as *sūrya-siddhānta* provide a partial mapping of the Vedic cosmological descriptions into observable astronomical objects.

The original descriptions of Vedic cosmology are in terms of how the universe is seen through the mind, intelligence, ego or consciousness. In many cases, these descriptions introduce things into cosmology that we might not, for instance, find in the astronomy. One example of this fact is planets *rāhu-ketu* that cannot be observed astronomically. These planets play a very important role in Vedic astrology, along with other luminaries like the Sun, Moon, Jupiter, etc. It should be understood that the astrological description of the solar system is a description based on the mind and not based on the senses. The properties that astrology assigns to planets, constellations and phases of the Sun and Moon cannot be understood from astronomy, and critiques of astrology therefore ridicule it as not being a 'science'. The fact is that astrology rests upon a mental rather than a sensual view of the universe. A horoscope with 'houses' that 'see' each other, with each house representing a different facet of our life, inhabited by planets with different concepts bring into the description aspects that we cannot observe.

Similarly, Vedic descriptions of seven higher and lower planetary systems, the divisions of the *jambu-dvipa* into nine *varṣas*, the six other *dvīpas* interspersed with seven kinds of oceans, various kinds of hells, domains of light and non-light have no known astronomical counterpart. While we might admire the fact that astronomy was advanced in Vedic society, it is hard to ignore the gap between the overall Vedic description of the cosmos and the limited portions of that cosmos that have an astronomical counterpart. When we approach Vedic cosmology as an extension of astronomy to map out the missing luminaries in the observable sky into a cosmological theory of the universe, we forget the larger philosophical view of the Vedic universe, and how it is organized not as bodies of inert matter but as domains of experience, as divisions in a functional society, as parts of a large economic system and as semantic partitions of geography into places for different activities.

Perhaps the greatest conflict between the astronomical and cosmological viewpoints exists with regard to the excursions to the Moon. Cosmological and astronomical distances do not match. Fantastic descriptions in the Vedas about the Moon being a heavenly planet do not align with deserted craters easily seen on the moon's surface through a telescope. In light of these conflicts, the mapping between the cosmological and astronomical bodies needs to be re-examined. The reassessment can begin if we treat Vedic cosmology as a cognitive view of the universe while astronomy as a sensual description. Like squiggles on paper can denote meanings, and decoding word-meaning relation requires knowing a language, the universe too has to be understood not in terms of the physical properties that we can sense, but as meanings *represented* by objects. There are infinitely many mind-matter mapping schemes, and in each scheme the meaning is mapped to matter differently. Therefore, the assumption that the meaning derived from an object is equal to the physical properties of the objects is incorrect. The mapping between mind and body is subject to choices of language, and the selection of language is dictated by the context of the observers. For the mind-body mapping to be different on the Moon, for instance, living beings on the Moon only need to use a different type of language.

In the Lunar language, for example, hot and cold could be represented by musical notes rather than high and low temperatures. Living beings on this planet will then experience heat by experiencing different notes in the sounds, even when the climate (from a physical perspective) isn't hot. Languages may represent meanings through the colors of light, in which case beings who think differently will have different colored bodies, enabling others to ascertain what they are thinking. In another language that represents happiness or distress by the size of a living being's body, the observation of the body's size will suffice to know if the person is happy or distressed and the emotion they feel. Countless other mind-matter mapping schemes can be conceived and these mappings allow living beings to experience the same mental state while communicating that state to others in widely different ways.

The reality underlying the universe is consciousness, which manifests the phenomena of personality, morality, intent, proposition, concept, sensation and object. Objects are symbols of the mind, and the symbols are created for communicating the meaning to others. To decode the meanings, one must know the language being used to encode the meanings. The universe as seen in astronomy is communicating to us, but the meaning underlying that phenomenon cannot be understood without knowing the language that maps mind to matter. Since each context creates a different mind-matter mapping, all planets or luminaries cannot be 'read' by the same language. We first need to know the language before we can interpret their physical states into meanings.

The Technology of Mantras

The success of any science depends upon the technology that can be built using the principles of that science. Modern science has given us a number of technologies, and the Vedic science too gives us technologies. Modern scientific technology is based on the idea that the world is built up of objects that follow universal laws of motion, and these objects are perceived through senses. We manipulate matter by adding or removing energy from material objects, which changes their dynamics. Vedic technology is based on the idea that the world is comprised of symbols which have physical properties, but whose causality depends on their meanings. The Vedic technology therefore manipulates matter by adding or removing information. If we are reading a book, the shapes, color and size of the symbols in the book are secondary to its information content. The explanation of symbols in a book rests on meanings rather than on physical properties. The sensual perception of the world can in fact be misleading, unless we are well-versed in the language that converts meanings into sensations. Interpreting symbols that were encoded in one language in terms of another leads to an incorrect cognition.

In Vedic philosophy, mind converts meanings into matter using a language. By learning to see the world as symbolic meaning rather than sensations of taste, touch, smell, sight and sound, we can understand how to manipulate it in a new way. The Vedas prescribe a technology based upon a science of conceptual manipulation. By this science, a desired object need not be created in a factory by industrialization. It can also be manifested by directly applying information to matter. Just as a building is created by applying a construction plan to material ingredients, similarly by applying information directly to matter, a living being can produce the desired kinds of objects. In the Vedic view, this information is transferred by the chanting of *mantras* which are very specific sound vibrations that can be used to encode information in objects.

Although a technologist who understands the science of conceptual manipulation can directly manipulate matter, the Vedas prescribe that this manipulation be directed via demigods who are the administrators of the universe. Every aspect of nature is controlled and ruled by a specific demigod, and manipulating matter without permission of that controller is forbidden, because that aspect of matter is the 'property' of that demigod whose permission must be sought before manipulating it. The Vedas thus describe that there are three aspects to technology, called *ātmika*, *bhautika* and *daivika*. The *ātmika* denotes meaning in the mind that can be transferred into *bhautika* or the external world. But this transfer is mediated by the demigods, who are also called *daivika*.

The deeper point in Vedic philosophy is that matter is not our property; it is rather the property of a Supreme Lord who delegates this authority to administrative demigods. Before enjoying matter, therefore, we must seek permission from the demigod, and rituals are performed with the chanting of *mantras* to seek that approval. These rituals reinforce the idea in the performer that he does not own matter, and that his enjoyment of matter is a facility granted to him by the grace of the demigods, and ultimately the grace of God. The Vedas therefore prescribe many rituals and *mantras* seeking the approval of demigods before starting any activity. This includes commonplace activities such as eating food, taking a journey, or conceiving a child, and offerings are made to the demigods to seek their blessings and benediction so that these actions are not performed in contradiction to their wishes.

A demigod can manifest the desired object upon request, if he has been appropriately satisfied. Each demigod holds mastery over some concepts and he is the 'ruler' of that concept. To obtain objects of a certain conceptual variety, one can please the demigod who holds mastery over that concept. Demigods rule the knowledge concept, the family concept, the sex concept, the love concept, the child concept, the power concept, the beauty concept and these demigods can empower others with the enjoyment of this concept, provided they are pleased.

Since every cycle of consumption ends in waste, to unlimitedly continue the process of consumption there must be a way for the waste to be transformed back into useful raw materials. Thus, soil must convert into fruits and grains, fodder into livelihood for animals, which supply us with milk and labor. Rain, sunshine and air must be present for these purposes and if these are absent the economic system collapses. The cosmic system has touch-points where demigods can easily control the universe. Modern civilization does not understand these touch-points. We suppose that clouds naturally rain, air naturally blows and soil is naturally productive. In the Vedic view, however, demigods and human beings are part of a larger economic cycle and demigods control the supply of raw materials. If there is no *yajña*, demigods do not deliver the basic necessities of life. Thus when *yajña* is not performed, the universe goes through starvation and famine, or excess rain, wind and heat. These are symptoms of the demigods losing their prowess due to lack of *yajña* and therefore unable to control the administration of universe.

A few millennia ago the philosophical content and spiritual intent behind the various Vedic rituals was lost. Rituals instead became a means to satisfy the greed of performers rather than reinforcing the idea that only God is the ultimate enjoyer of matter, and that we must seek His permission before using His property. Priests would perform these rituals for anyone who would offer them some money or gifts, and with time the real scientific understanding underlying these rituals was lost. By becoming entangled into sensual pleasures, the priests themselves lost the ability to perform these sacrifices correctly. The sacrifices and chanting of *mantras* lost efficacy and came to be seen as mumbo-jumbo.

Understanding the Vedic science requires grounding oneself into the spiritual principles underlying the rituals, beginning with the idea that God creates and owns the universe. The living entities can enjoy matter, but with His permission. God is kind enough to grant the living being permission to enjoy, and the living being is expected to gradually purify itself of these desires, giving in to these desires just enough to maintain a healthy body and mind. Thus, the ultimate spiritual principle underlying Vedic sacrifices is transcending the material universe, by practicing detachment from matter and devotion to God, and using matter under the permission and guidance of the enlightened priest.

Vedic science is based on a different view of matter, which can create a much more powerful and sophisticated technology than imagined in current science. In this science, concepts are mapped to matter after the experimenter has prepared himself through a purification process. The mapping of the concept to matter is done by the chanting of *mantras*, while the preparatory process involves supporting rituals and mystical practices used to advance the senses and mind of the practitioner to perceive and manipulate matter in a new way. Like a computer programmer defines the behavior of a machine by adding programming instructions, the chanter of *mantras* instructs matter and programs its states. The Vedic technology of *mantras* can be understood when matter is viewed as a symbol of mind, intelligence, ego and consciousness.

The Scientific Basis of Rituals

Worship through *mantras* can be compared to pouring water from a river back into the river itself. The basic idea is that if God owns everything in the universe, then He owns even the materials by which we worship Him. We cannot offer to God anything that He does not already own. This principle is exemplified in the worship of demi-gods who are offered specific kinds of meanings. Basically, we feed the universal instance of a concept by providing it with more of that same concept. However, since God is the source of every meaning, He can be worshipped by any kind of meaningful object. This forms the philosophical basis of *bhakti-yoga* in which the Supreme Lord is wor-shipped through any form or activity because everything is created out of meanings in God. In the case of demigods, by offering a spe-cific type of object or activity back into that demigod, we worship the demigod by putting back into him an instance of the same meaning from which the offering originated.

The Vedic process of *yajña* transforms a combination of *soma*, *agni* and *vayu* into a physical instance of a concept by the use of *mantras*. In effect, *yajña* pours the water of a river back into the river using *man-tras* thereby rejuvenating the river. Note that the power of the *yajña* is not in the pouring of water but in the *mantra* that accompanies the act of pouring and makes the instance a conceptual object. The act alone looks like a meaningless ritual, but the *mantra* makes it a symbol. In this sense, the basis of the science is not in the gross material act of pouring water but making that act meaningful in a specific way by the chanting of a *mantra*. The basic action in all *yajña* is offering oblations into the fire. But this basic act can be given a variety of meanings by the chanting of *mantras*. Effectively, we impute a new kind of meaning into a physical object. The physical object should in general support the possibility of being the symbol of that meaning, and basic material objects of water, fire and air are used for creating a suitable vehicle to carry the concept.

The Vedic universe is Platonic in a very specific sense. There is a higher realm of existence in which demigods embody pure ideas. For instance, the demigod Sun embodies the idea of health and energy, the demigod Moon the idea of nourishment, the demigod Venus the idea of love and creativity, Jupiter the idea of knowledge, Saturn the idea of detachment and suffering, etc. The world of forms is therefore not a metaphysical world of ideas outside the universe as Plato thought, but actually different locations within the universe that host specific kinds of memes. These memes are found all over the universe but are concentrated in specific locations where the demigod as the owner of that concept lives. The demigods who control these memes control not just the locations where these memes abound but also the specific facets of other objects in which those memes are found. For that matter, our bodies possess those memes as well and the Vedas state that the demigods also reside in every living being. This is because different parts of our body express different memes which are controlled by different demigods.

To understand this idea consider how ordinary physical properties like length or mass are defined in relation to standard objects such as a *kilogram* or *meter* placed at specific locations[20]. These standard objects exemplify the ideas of length and mass, as the perfect instances of these ideas. The perfect instance of the idea is however not outside the universe as Plato believed. It rather exists within the universe. The demigods are the standards for each type of concept similar to how the perfect kilogram and meter as stored as perfect instances of mass and length. The universe is comprised of ideas, and demigods are standard references against which these ideas are defined. Each demigod 'embodies' an idea, and their bodies and powers predominate in that meaning.

Imperfect instances of concepts are created as emanations from the perfect instance. When a demigod is pleased, he donates a part of the information for the creation of an object of that conceptual variety. By means of a ritual, the demigod appears before the worshipper. Since the demigod's body is not imperishable, he needs to be fed back the concept. The science of *mantras* gives a demigod an instance of concepts through sound, and the demigod returns the concept in touch, sight, taste and smell. It is easier for us to speak about a 'table' than go about constructing a table using material ingredients. It is, however, easy for the demigod to create a physical instance of the same concept. Thus, we supply the demigod with the conceptual table and the demigod supplies us with the physical table. This is the great Vedic science of *mantras*.

Unlike the Platonic world in which there are no objects, only pure ideas, in the Vedic view, the demigods and their planets are perfect embodiments of specific ideas. They are the sources of a specific type of information in the universe. If a specific demigod is weakened, then that specific kind of information controlled by that demigod is also depleted. The demigod must therefore be replenished by *yajña*. The key idea here is that information is not conserved. Information can be created by any living being, provided they have been endowed with the power of that type of information. Demigods are empowered but their powers may be depleted unless replenished. The original source of information is God who gives knowledge to *Brahma*, the universal architect who imparts instructions to other demigods, thereby disseminating information all over the universe. This information is often destroyed by Time, which is another form of God, also called by the name *Saṅkarṣaṇa* in Vedic philosophy. God's creator form is called *Pradyumna*. Between the creator and the destroyer forms is another form of God who maintains or sustains information and this form is called *Aniruddha*. The information exists so long as *Aniruddha* observes it, similar to how an idea exists in the mind as long as we remain aware of it. When the mind is withdrawn, the idea disappears. Similarly, *Aniruddha* maintains information by observing it. Besides the creator, maintainer and destroyer forms, there is also a supervisor form called *Vāsudeva* who oversees the acts of creation, maintenance and destruction, but is not involved in these acts.

The Vedic view runs contrary to the deterministic law-based control of material nature, where there is no scope for miracles. In Vedic science, demigods are empowered living beings who can grant benedictions by agreeing to be conceptually present in some location and time. Thus *Kubera* as the demigod of wealth can be conceptually present making someone very rich. This richness is defined not in terms of gross machinery as we do in the modern materialistic civilization. Rather, richness is defined conceptually and this concept is manifest in abundant grains, milk, jewels, gold, livestock, fertile land, minerals, etc.

As representatives of a particular concept, demigods have mastered that meaning. Their bodies, minds, intelligences and egos are suited to deal with that meaning. They eat, think, will and enjoy a specific concept and they are satisfied by that concept. The bodies of living beings on the Moon are thus different from the bodies on the Sun, as they predominate in different meanings. Each planet is organized using a typology similar to the one by which the entire universe is organized, although in miniature form. The 'Moon' within the 'Moon' planet is the demigod *Chandra* who embodies the essence of being on the Moon planet. He controls activities on the Moon planet and is the master of the planet by virtue of mastery of the Moon concept. Ultimately Lord *Viṣṇu* is the "supreme soul" who resides in everything including all atoms because He represents the origin of every type of concept in matter.

The threefold distinction between *daivika, ātmika* and *bhautika* in the case of the Moon, corresponds to the demigod *Chandra*, the planet Moon and instances of the Moon concept manifested in other objects. Each of these constitutes a successively refined level of knowing the concept. First we comprehend the Moon concept by looking at many objects that conform to that concept. This involves distinguishing the concept from other concepts and seeing the conditions in which one applies as opposed to the other. As the conceptual knowledge develops, we can identify instances of a concept concentrated in a particular location in the universe—the planet Moon. The singular object now represents the place of concentration of the concept within the universe. As we enter this planet, we come face-to-face with the embodiment of that concept in its purest and strongest form—the demigod ruling the Moon planet—called *Chandra.* If we look even closer, we will find that *Chandra*'s power of the concept comes from Lord *Viṣṇu*, and that power is a fraction of all meanings that reside in Lord *Viṣṇu*. In different contexts, the demigod ruling the Moon, the planet Moon and different objects of the type Moon are all designated by the same word—i.e. the Moon.

The strongest and purest representation of a concept is not a static form as Plato thought but a living person. More specifically, the purest representation of a concept is a living body. The *form* of the concept is the *form* of the demigod. To know a concept is to be acquainted with a demigod and to be that concept is to acquire his body. Various parts of a demigod's body represent the various facets of a concept. When a concept has many distinct understandable meanings, the demigod's body will have many heads, each of which representing a different way of comprehending that concept. When a concept can be used in various ways, the demigod's body will have many hands and legs, each corresponding to a different type of use for the concept. Depending upon how the concept is visualized, the demigod's body will have a different color. The demigod will carry with him typical signs and symbols by which the concept he represents is easily identified. In short, the demigod's body is a personification of a particular concept in its full resplendence.

Deities of demigods formed out of material elements represent the form of a concept symbolically, just as we might express the meaning of 'table' by creating a physical 'table'. Such embodiment of the concept becomes essential for those who cannot understand the meaning of 'table' as a concept without seeing a table. By meditating on the form of the demigod a worshipper understands the various facets of a concept.

Accompanying each demigod is a female *śakti* through which the demigod propagates his existence by creating other instances of his personality. This *śakti* is his power of communicating information from the source into other instantiations of that specific information. Such instantiations are 'children' of the concept which represent partial manifestations of his persona. The creation of multiple partial representations is done by the *śakti*. The Vedas are replete with stories of how demigods created children that rule over the universe. Dynasties of the Sun and the Moon are common in the Vedic texts and these correspond to how a demigod creates a partial manifestation of his personality via his *śakti* or consort and the offspring predominate in the characteristics of their parents. Many people scoff at such ideas wondering how a planet could have children. The planet as a physical entity does not create a dynasty but the ruler of the planet diversifies himself into many instances of a concept. This is like saying that many chairs are manifested from a pure form of chair. The process of this manifesting needs a new science that explains how conceptual matter expands into instances.

6

Applying Vedic Ideas

It from bit.

　　　　　　　—John Wheeler

It from qubit.

　　　　　　　—Paola Zizzi

Can the Twain Meet?

Today, there is considerable interest in Vedic ideas. The scientific view of matter as things that can be sensed lacks even an understanding of sensation, let alone mind, intelligence, emotion and consciousness. Vedic philosophy describes matter consistent with the existence of mind, intelligence and consciousness. But Vedic ideas are so different, and often couched in such a different terminology, that it has become difficult to have a dialogue between modern ideas and Vedic philosophy. As a result, Vedic science and technology are generally pursued as parallel or alternative paradigms. For instance, Yoga and Ayurveda are practiced as an alternative health and healing approach. The chanting of *mantras* and meditation is treated as alternatives to conventional religion. Vedic astrology is an alternative to Western astrology. Vedic notions of music, art and architecture are alternatives to Western ideas on the same subjects. People interested in Vedic philosophy often encounter it through cultural practices, but given the differences between modern and Vedic outlooks, they may not fully grasp the ideas behind these practices. A deeper understanding of the scientific and philosophical core underlying these practices is needed which can also help relate this core set of ideas to the scientific and philosophical environment prevailing today. I have already illustrated a number of areas where Vedic and modern scientific views are different and the reasons why they are different. This chapter will focus upon how these differences can be bridged.

I envision the bridging between modern and Vedic science in the specific sense of identifying problems in current science and then using Vedic ideas to develop new theories free of these problems. As long as the new theory works, it should not matter where the ideas are coming from. Furthermore, as long as the theory improves our understanding of nature, it should not matter if reality points more towards the observer than towards matter. So long as these are good assumptions, the path to reconciliation is peppered with very interesting discoveries.

While it is generally desirable to discuss problems in current science using concepts within science, in some cases it becomes necessary to step outside of the scientific vocabulary to see why ideas in current science are insufficient. In case of the problems associated with information, incompleteness, indeterminism, uncertainty, inconsistency and incomputability, we have already reached the limits of scientific language. We must either stay with the language and live with the problems, or step out of the language and see how the problem can be solved. To that extent, the discussion here will use intuitions drawn from everyday experience, because experience is always the intuitive bedrock for new discoveries and it helps us find new ways when logic is not fully developed. The development of theories about matter that incorporate properties from mind, intelligence, ego and consciousness obviously requires a deeper understanding of what goes on inside our heads. In other words, the development of this science depends as much on our personal abilities of perception as on conceptual and theoretical advances. The training needed for practicing these new forms of sciences will be different from the training required for doing current science.

In the following sections, I will try to sketch a high-level bridge between modern science and Vedic ideas. In all these cases, the attempt is *not* to see parallels between these two worldviews, theories and ideas, because parallelism essentially reinterprets the known facts in a new way, making no dent in the actual science or in the interpreting philosophy. Once the task is complete, both sides go home thinking that they were always right; indeed, both sides feel vindicated that the other side now sees how they were always right. While I will explicitly avoid attempts to draw parallels between theories, there will be attempts to reinterpret *problems*. To solve a problem, we need to see what a theory indicates is missing. By reinterpreting problems of physical sciences as problems of meaning, I hope to show the relevance of Vedic ideas to science.

Atomic Theory

The problems of atomic theory have spawned a variety of interpretations, none too satisfactory. One fundamental difference between atomic theory and classical physics is that classical physics is capable of describing an individual particle while atomic theory only describes an ensemble of such particles. Einstein considered this the most important problem of atomic theory. He envisioned that one day physics will be able to formulate a description of the individual particle rather than the ensemble. This view was justified because what an experiment actually detects is individual particles. Since the theory is incapable of describing the individual apart from the ensemble, Einstein thought the theory was incomplete. The reason that the theory is still unable to deal with individuals is because the individuals in quantum theory do not behave like classical particles, although they are particles in some sense. To solve the quantum problem, we need to conceive of a particle that does not behave like the classical particle. This particle must change state discretely, should have two complementary state descriptions (position and momentum), explain observer-dependent outcomes of experiments, and must have the ability to get entangled with other particles.

The idea of symbols meets the above criteria. A symbol is a particle but not a classical particle. A classical particle only represents its own state, while a symbol has its own state and the state of another object. Classical physics can deal only with objects that describe themselves, not symbols that describe other objects. Attempts to describe symbols in terms of classical physics will always be incomplete. A symbol changes state discretely because all concepts are discrete. To change state, a symbol must stop being a symbol of one concept and represent another one, which requires a discrete change. Every symbol has a dual meaning in terms of knowledge and its effects; these are not two separate states, but two different ways to describe that state. Finally, symbols get meanings collectively, not individually. For a symbol to be meaningful, there must be at least one other symbol in an ensemble that is collectively given a meaning. This is different from physical particles whose properties don't depend on the properties of other objects. Of course, a symbol also has objective properties. In fact, its semantic properties are reinterpretations of physical properties, just like the shape of a squiggle is a physical property but can also be used to denote a meaning, if you happen to know the language of shapes that is used to encode meanings.

The mystery of atomic theory is simply that physical properties in an ensemble are redistributed amongst various particles such that the properties of one particle are orthogonal to those of the others. This redistribution means that properties of *individual* objects inside and outside the ensemble are different although the properties of the *collection* as a whole remain unchanged. After matter and energy have been redistributed in an ensemble, the contextual properties are also *inherent* in the individual objects, but those properties would not exist outside of the context. Therefore, within the ensemble, an object has new properties that did not exist outside. Current atomic theory is empirically complete but causally incomplete. This means that we will not find any additional observations that can tell us more about the individual quantum. But what we require is an explanation of why a quantum gets some additional properties in an ensemble than outside of it. To provide that explanation, we may claim that an individual quantum denotes types rather than quantities. In a collection, the type of a quantum is different than outside of it. Thus, within a collection, the quantum denotes new meanings. But these meanings are simply reinterpretations of its physical properties, although the properties themselves are altered by the ensemble, since properties are redistributed within an ensemble.

The property of position for example is not just a location in space,

it also denotes a meaning. However, both the position and its meaning are tied to the ensemble of particles as a whole. If some particles
are added or removed from the ensemble, both physical properties
and meanings will change. Within an ensemble, particles at two different positions are different *types* of particles. A change in a particle's
position is therefore a change in its *type*. Once different locations in
space are different types of locations, space is no longer homogeneous
and isotropic. If an object goes from A to B, it has new properties and
therefore a new type. This implies that change in location is a change
in type, and dynamics too must now be described as an evolution of
types, not quantities. Dynamics is an evolution of knowledge rather
than motion. By thinking of dynamics as motion, we disregard the
meanings involved.

To fix the matter-meaning relation, three things are needed: (a)
the boundary of the ensemble must identify the conceptual 'domain'
being mapped, (b) there should be a coordinate system that distinguishes physical properties, and (c) there should be a representation
scheme that converts meanings into ordered physical properties. As
an illustration, consider the mapping of a color palette to points in
space. First, the space being used to represent the color palette must
be interpreted as a color-axis. Second, there must be a way to order
and distinguish points within the space—e.g., from left to right on a
straight line. Third, colors should be given a numerical representation in terms of RGB color codes using, for instance, a hexadecimal
scheme, which maps points in space to color types. Generally, if physical properties make objects distinct, then the second requirement
from the above three requirements is easily given. Only the first and
third requirements are additionally needed.

To apply these ideas to the quantum slit experiment[21], the ensemble as a whole must be given a semantic interpretation, identifying
it as a physical domain of information. Objects in the ensemble are
already distinct due to their physical properties—e.g., locations on
a battery of detectors—but a coordinate system must be chosen to
enumerate these points. The number of slits in the experiment identifies an encoding scheme by which meaning is digitized and mapped
to detectors—this is observed in the slit-experiment although it is not
understood. To give the quanta arrival a semantic interpretation, the

ensemble must be seen as a semantic domain—e.g., that the particles in the ensemble represent shades of color. State preparation requires that a macro system be given a semantic interpretation as a whole rather than as individual particles.

This semantic view of atomic theory hinges on seeing macroscopic systems as *domains* of meaning. Matter is like a book in which meanings are encoded by mapping them to words, and since this mapping varies between domains (physics and business will give different meanings to the same words), the domain must be specified before meanings can be attached to words. To map meanings to objects, there must also be a representation scheme that converts meanings in the symbols into properties such as a location in space. Note that numbers used in a coordinate system and in a representation scheme are derived from two different sources—namely physical properties versus concepts. The numbers are therefore not strictly identical. But in the specific context, the number denoting meaning *is* the number denoting the object.

Understanding quantum theory requires one new concept from Vedic philosophy which is that the mind divides the world into smaller chunks and draws boundaries around them. These boundaries have *forms* which give the parts within those boundaries a type of meaning. The boundary is not a physical construct, but a semantic one. It represents a *domain* of concepts, such as physics or chemistry, which are themselves built up of several individual concepts. To create a knowledge representation, mind maps a domain into matter. Objects in the domain seem to only have physical properties. But their causality (why they have certain physical properties) is due to their meaning.

Looking at objects as symbols of meaning overcomes the interpretive difficulties in understanding current experiments. This view can also bring the same kind of rigor in chemistry and biology, which do not have clear laws but only a set of heuristic rules that change from situation to situation. Laws stem out of the fact that if quanta represent meanings, then complex combinations of quanta represent propositions. The meaning of the proposition depends on the constituent concepts, but is not determined by the concepts because the same concepts can give rise to a different proposition depending on concept ordering and structure. Even when the order of words is fixed, a proposition can have many meanings, and it can be true in some cases and false in others[22].

Now, the laws of chemical combination are similar to the laws of grammar. Unlike first-order logic that produces one interpretation for a sentence, context-sensitive meanings require context-dependent laws. If the meaning of symbols is changed (by changing the domain) then the laws must also change. This implies a new type of universal law that maps types of concepts to the types of laws. Nature only binds us by defining a law against every conceptual worldview. Nature, however, does not dictate the worldview. By choosing different views about the world, we will live under different laws and consequences of actions. The law and consequence can help us decide our conceptual assumptions but nature, but these still remain a choice. By changing our conceptual assumptions, the same reality will be seen as a symbol of a different kind of meaning. Matter does not change its physical properties, although it is now governed by different kinds of laws. Current science is based on a certain type of outlook about nature and the laws it discovers are a subset of all possible laws. The mapping between concepts and laws generalizes the current laws of science to an arbitrary way of thinking about reality. One implication of this idea is that nature is not necessarily described only by the concepts of modern physics. Science can also be conceived in a new way using new concepts and laws. The preference between multiple possible sciences is a choice, with consequences.

In classical physics, every object describes itself and there cannot be knowledge of the world within the world, because to describe another object, the description will have to be identical to its object, which happens to be another object. Quantum theory brings up the possibility that descriptions of matter can exist in matter. This is made possible by reinterpreting the physical states as semantic states. A semantic object has physical properties that in a specific context also denote meanings. In a sense, the semantic property is a reinterpretation of physical properties. But that reinterpretation is based on something that exists objectively but can't be sensed. This is evidenced by the fact that the same color red will be interpreted in different ways in different contexts. The context is objective and yet it cannot be sensed. However, it does have effects, which can be sensed.

For instance, atomic objects arrive at different locations in space due to their different meanings, not due to their mass or charge. The location is the observable effect but it is not due to physical properties in the object. We can sense the effects, but we can't attribute the effects to anything that we can sense *and* call it *real*.

The first major challenge in solving the quantum problem is defining the notion of an ensemble. We have an intuitive notion about an ensemble, but not a physical theory of ensembles. An ensemble in physics is an imaginary boundary that separates one system from another. There is nothing real corresponding to an ensemble in modern physics, since only atoms are real, while boundaries are not. In classical physics every particle behaves independently and the collection of particles behaves only as the sum of independent parts. An ensemble isolates some such particles from other particles, but there is nothing in physics that *physically* defines what we mean by this isolation. For instance, particles in an ensemble will continue to interact with particles outside the ensemble, although we consider the ensemble some sort of physical isolation due to which particles inside the ensemble do not interact with particles outside, or interact so weakly that we can neglect the interaction. The problem of ensembles goes to the root of physics in our ability to identify *macroscopic* objects. For instance, the table in front of me is a macroscopic object, which in atomic theory we will call an ensemble of atomic objects. We intuitively believe that there is something 'really' called a table out there, with well-specified boundaries. But there is nothing in quantum theory per se corresponding to that boundary. This is a great problem because the behavior of atoms inside the boundary depends on how the boundary is drawn. So, unless I can assert that there really is a boundary, I cannot talk about what happens inside that boundary. The problem can be stated quite simply: What corresponds—in physics—to macroscopic objects? Note that this problem did not exist in classical physics because we reduced a macroscopic object to a point particle. The problem manifests when that point has a sub-structure.

Atomic theory exhibits this property of collections, which we see in everyday collections, although our classical physical thinking has biased us into believing that each material particle is an independent object. To alter this view about atoms, the boundary that demarcates different systems needs to have a physical role. In other words, macroscopic objects—which we treat as ensembles—should have a real physical counterpart within the theory. Macroscopic objects are more real than the atoms that constitute these objects because the formation of the macroscopic object decides the nature of the atoms within that ensemble.

The modern theories of cognition do not believe that there is anything real 'out there' in the world that corresponds to a system boundary. In Vedic philosophy, the mind creates and cognizes these boundaries. We cannot, see, taste, touch or smell these boundaries, but they are real. In that respect, a semantic theory requires injecting into science concepts that are understood by the mind but cannot be sensed. An ensemble partitions matter into *logically* orthogonal parts. These parts become symbols of meaning. When these atoms are combined into propositions, new complex meanings are also created. Experiments in current science don't perceive meanings because they are preoccupied with objectivizing the sensations rather than conceptualizing these sensations. Objectification and conceptualization therefore lead to different results.

The Nature of Chemical Law

An area of intense debate amongst those trying to understand the scientific status of chemistry is: Does chemistry reduce to physics? If yes, then why haven't chemists been able to find predictive laws that come close to the accuracy and predictive power of physics—for example, why aren't there any mathematical laws that predict chemical reactions? If no, then what is the unique thing that chemistry is studying, that is still not studied by physics—i.e. what unique concepts does chemistry employ that are fundamentally not dealt with by physics?

This question is very hard to solve in current approaches to chemistry. In the current view, molecules are formed from atoms through orbital sharing; atoms are built up of sub-atomic particles, which are studied by physics. In principle, therefore, quantum theory should be able to make all chemical predictions. The only difficulty is that the mathematics of quantum theory allows us to solve only a few-body problem. As the number of quantum objects increases, mathematical equations have hundreds (if not thousands of variables) and such large equations cannot be accurately solved. The approximations developed by Born-Oppenheimer and Hartree-Fock (and named after them) have been used to simplify the *computation* of the many-body problem. These approaches suggest that the problem of chemistry reduces to the problem of computing the many-body problem using the laws discovered by atomic theory. Is chemistry then a subject different from physics?

Current quantum chemistry reduces structure to bonds, bonds to atomic or molecular orbitals, orbitals to eigenfunction states, and eigenfunction states to the Hamiltonian function which is constructed assuming that quantum objects have mass and charge. It is believed that all the properties of molecules can be understood on the basis of particles with mass and charge, which were known even during classical physics. Approximate orbital calculations leave out many important developments in physics in the last several decades—relativity, weak and strong nuclear forces, electron correlation are primary examples—because even without these effects the computational problem is overwhelming. Probability and uncertainty are hugely important in physics, but they are irrelevant to current chemistry. Chemists thus don't face the problems of quantum theory because they draw ball-and-stick models of molecules, in which each ball has some mass and some charge. Typically, the atom with a bigger mass and charge can be represented by a bigger ball. The result of various approximations in chemistry is that a molecule is converted to a ball-and-stick model, like a classical object.

Prior to the application of quantum theory to molecules, chemists were studying molecular *structure* as envisioned through ball-and-stick models. Developments in physics have assisted in determining the molecular structure using mathematical and spectroscopic techniques, but the key object of study in chemistry—which used to be molecular structure prior to the advent of quantum theory—has now reduced to mass and charge together with the laws of quantum theory. In what way, therefore, is structure a new property that can't be reduced to atoms? This question has a meaningful answer when atoms themselves have semantic properties because structures formed out of semantic units have properties that cannot be reduced to the properties of atoms.

In analogy to an English sentence, the meaning of the sentence depends on the order of words; two sentences with the same words but with a different order amongst words can have different meanings. A sentence is a visible string of words but has an invisible grammatical structure. Grammar classifies words into *types* that are not percepts and concepts but *figures of speech*. The figures of speech vary from language to language, but generally all languages have nouns, verbs and adjectives. A word like 'fly' can contextually denote a noun (the housefly), a verb (soaring in the sky) and an adjective (a flying balloon). When used in the sentence "Time flies like an arrow", the meaning of the sentence depends on whether the word is used as a noun or as a verb. Thus a meme is contextually modified by a structure to denote different figures of speech, which change the meaning of a sentence. The meaning depends on which word is mapped to which figure of speech. In short, grammar creates new meanings beyond the meanings of the words themselves.

If atoms are concepts, then the structure that connects these concepts also has semantic properties. A physical structure can be reduced to its parts, whereas a semantic structure cannot. In that sense, the study of semantic structures involves a different type of science. It depends on the science of concepts, but it represents a newer class of meanings and properties. Thus, under a semantic view, chemistry is a different science than physics. The semantic view also helps us understand the nature of chemical caws. Unlike the laws of physics which define how a collection of objects become concepts, the laws of chemistry will define how combinations of concepts create *propositions*. The chemical laws will describe how the meaning of a proposition is created from the meanings of concepts by adding a structure to the concepts. The result of the law is also a computation of meaning, but the meaning falls into a different category. In that respect, chemical laws will also be deterministic and accurate just as physical laws. This is obviously a huge progress over the current state of laws and thinking in chemistry.

With the ability to formulate chemical laws, a new view of chemical reaction emerges: a reaction is a *deduction* that takes two or more propositions as input and creates a new proposition as output. Since Greek times, a variety of deductive schemes (or 'logics') have been created (for example, Syllogisms, Propositional logic, Predicate logic, Boolean logic, etc.). Logic, however, has not been seen as the interplay of structures in linguistics. In modern linguistics, grammar decides meanings while logic decides truth. Since the domains of logic and grammar have been different (computing vs. linguistics), there has been no need to bridge this gap. In fact, the gap between grammar and logic was reinforced by Gödel who postulated the equivalence of meaning and truth, and then arrived at a contradiction because of not distinguishing between two different models of meaning—things and concepts. We know that these are not the only possible models; there can also be models of meaning involving sensations, propositions, intents and morals. With the ability to distinguish between different models, Gödel's incompleteness will not exist, but the equivalence between logic and grammar needs structural additions. This change can be seen in chemical reactions where molecules may be combined in many ways, and via different structural interactions. In a chemical reaction, for example, a large molecule may be broken into smaller parts before the parts are combined. The manner in which the molecule is broken into parts and how these parts react to form newer wholes requires context-sensitive laws of reactions.

The semantic view redefines the nature of chemical laws. These laws depend on the meaning of the combining molecules which, in turn, depend on the structure of meme combining. The laws combine structures and there are multiple ways in which the molecules can be combined. The resulting science is a science of structures and structural laws. The subject is different from that of physics, because it pertains to a different aspect of ordinary language—concepts versus grammar.

The DNA Phenomenon

Science studies phenomena and then provides causal explanations for them. In the case of biology, the diversity of species is the main phenomenon to be explained. Biology explains this by attributing diversity to a common ancestry which was subsequently diversified by climate, natural resources and the survival of the fittest, as Darwin first described it. At first sight, Darwin's theory seems to be an intentional theory because the survival of the fittest implies desires to survive—i.e. the intent to live, propagate and create more of one's own type. This in turn implies the existence of a mind that can distinguish between friend and foe, has the ability to perceive danger and feel fear, is capable of thinking and planning, and is smart enough to execute those plans. Thus, if the living being is 'trying' to survive, then the living being is already quite well-developed. But Darwin did not mean 'survival of the fittest' in the sense of wishing to survive and fearing extinction. He meant it in the sense that changes randomly occur and some of these changes make an animal fit to survive. The animal does not know which change will improve its chances of survival, but once the change has taken place, some animals will survive, creating more of their kind, while others die.

Darwin's theory uses two key ideas only one of which is generally given a great deal of attention. The more popular idea says that an animal randomly acquires new traits which improve its chances of survival. The idea that is generally ignored says that these changes can now be *passed* on to their offspring. Evolution will not work if an animal can acquire random traits but is unable to pass them. Of course, all the species that Darwin studied were already reproducing, so this did not seem like a serious problem. But there are two key phenomena that the theory of evolution must explain—(a) random mutations and (b) passing the acquired traits to the offspring. If a longer neck in the giraffe helps it survive better, then the giraffe cannot suddenly acquire a very long neck. Some predecessor of the giraffe must first get a slightly longer neck, and pass this trait to its children, who get an even longer neck, and pass it to their children. Giraffes therefore get long necks over time.

For this scheme to work, the acquisition of traits must have its roots in something that is being passed from parent to child. Mendel's work in genetics proved useful at this point. It showed that to change the physical traits of a plant, you had only to change the gene. Therefore, a species passes its changes (as Darwin claimed) if the gene undergoes random changes. The gene is a set of molecules, and all molecules are chemical structures. The question of evolution now hinges on the idea of random mutation in the genes. If genes can change randomly, then new traits can be acquired and passed on to the offspring. Gene mutations are known to occur, and gene modification is the basis of modified life forms. It thus seems that genetics and molecular chemistry have solved the key problem of diversity by associating it with genetic mutation.

A closer look however shows that both genetic mutation and gene replication are *phenomena* that haven't yet been properly explained. Of these, the mutation problem is easier to address by supposing that radiation or exposure to other chemicals causes changes to DNA constitution, because the DNA is, after all, just another molecule. But the mutation only creates evolution if there is replication. Why does a molecule replicate itself? Why don't we see salt, sugar and water replicating, as they too are chemical molecules? Everything we know about chemical laws tells us molecules undergo reactions to create molecules different from the ones that went into the reaction. So the idea that a molecule creates its own copies in what we call reproduction is still a mystery.

The primary problem in biology is not that there are many species that need to be explained on the basis of an original species. The primary problem is why there is even one species that is capable of reproducing, and passing its traits to its offspring. The question of the diversification of the species arises after there is at least one species that can mutate and pass its traits to offspring. Indeed, the notion of a species is not that there are many individuals of the same type, but that they can replicate and create more of that type (the problem of reproduction). Before biology can address the problem of many species, it should address the problem of a single species, no matter how primordial or primitive that species may be. Again, the first problem of biology is not the diversification of the species but the very appearance of a single species. The existence of species may be a fact, but it is on par with any other fact that science is trying to explain—namely that we must find *causes* responsible for making phenomena happen. Unfortunately, there is no good causal theory today that explains reproduction within a species. Without reproduction, there is no species, and hence the question of the diversification of species does not even arise. So, before we focus on issues of species diversification, we should focus on a single species.

Reproduction within a species is supposed to happen on the basis of gene replication, which is supposedly caused by chemical reactions. But there is nothing in the theory of chemical reactions that explains how a molecule can create its own replicas. If chemicals are explained by atomic theory, then atomic theory must itself explain replication. However, there is nothing in today's physics that explains replication.

The DNA-RNA-protein transcription and translation sequence itself represents a new type of phenomena that cannot be explained by known physical-chemical theories. The supposition that DNA, RNA and proteins are 'just' molecules is false; they are molecules, but they have additional properties that cannot be reduced to concept and structure. Biologists see DNA replication but they do not have a causal explanation of this fundamental biological phenomenon. And because of the reductionist tendency to reduce biology to chemistry, chemistry to physics and physics to classical properties, the biologist does not see that the properties in DNA are also present in idea evolution, mob psychology, social trend creation and in science itself as a phenomenon. Rather than model these similar phenomena in a new way, the biologist capitulates to the physical view, which is causally inadequate to explain replication.

In the semantic view, molecules are propositions and their replication requires an intentional relation between propositions such that one proposition becomes the meaning of the other. In this case, one DNA is the 'original' DNA that creates a 'clone', just like a reality creates its knowledge in the brain, or a problem creates a solution. The phenomena of reproduction and DNA replication represent intentional properties in matter. Through this representation, matter is copied and combined into intentional copies—e.g., there is an aboutness relationship. DNA replication cannot be explained based on atomic theory or on structural laws of molecular combination, although DNA replication depends on a semantic understanding of atoms and molecules. Replication represents a deeper physical phenomenon that *connects* propositions, and propositions are created because of this connection.

Thus, there is already a chemical intentional system in place in all living cells, where information in the DNA is *about* other molecules and chemical reactions. This intentional system is however today seen as a physical system, because DNA is viewed as a molecule, which is described by quantum theory, which treats matter as things rather than symbols. The semantic approach changes this view of matter, because atoms are concepts and molecules are propositions. A proposition however does not *refer* to another proposition automatically unless we *connect* these propositions through an intentional relation. When two propositions are connected, one proposition becomes the *cause* of another and information in one proposition *refers* to facts in another proposition.

A proposition creates another proposition like reality creates its knowledge or problems create solutions. In the biological case, the DNA creates RNA which creates enzymes which catalyze reactions. There is nothing in chemistry that can explain how one molecule can create its replicas, transcribes its information into chunks and then translates the design into catalyzing agents which will then control chemical reactions.

A causal theory of gene replication requires a semantic entity that exhibits the properties of replication and intent, which can explain the behavior of DNA molecules. DNA molecules replicate, transcribe and translate because these processes are caused by an intentional cause, not just by physical properties. Of course, from an observational standpoint, the measured properties of atoms and molecules are sufficient. But the explanation of these properties requires new semantic mechanisms.

Biology is empirically complete but causally incomplete. Causal completeness requires reinterpreting physical states as intentional states, besides conceptual and propositional states. Reproduction is therefore an intentional phenomena not a physical one. Even though every aspect of biology can be reduced to observation, that observation does not reduce to physical properties. Evolutionary theory views the DNA-RNA-Protein-Catalysis path deterministically although there is no *causal* explanation for the replicating, the transcribing and the translating. Note that causal *explanations* are different from the *descriptions* of phenomena—a description of the phenomena of replication,

transcription and translation is not an explanation. A causal explanation must account for *why* that change takes place. Indeed, the idea
that a DNA molecule holds information *about* a living being is itself
foreign to all physics and chemistry because salt and water in chemistry or particles and waves in physics are not about anything. In what
way is the DNA about another molecule? The novelty of DNA is that it
has introduced aboutness in biology when aboutness did not exist in
chemistry and physics. An atom or molecule describes itself, not other
objects. The ability in matter to represent information about other
objects is novel

Evolution vs. Ecology

The evolutionary approach to the diversification of the species maintains that DNA molecules mutate randomly, and these mutations are
passed on to offspring, and some of these random mutations help an
organism fare better in its environment. The tricky part here is what
we mean by the environment. The assumption in evolution is that the
environment is static, and its changes are irreversible. The organism
therefore has no choice but to react and adapt to that change. However, if we take a closer look, the environment is itself comprised of
other organisms, which may belong to other species. Typically, in an
ecosystem, a number of diverse species are interlocked in exchanges
of give and take. Each species in the ecosystem is equally likely to
undergo mutations, but no species has a better chance of that mutation surviving. If species A mutates unilaterally, thereby impacting
species B, we can never predict whether B will mutate in turn to adapt
to A, or whether A will be eliminated because B retaliates to A instead
of adapting to its changes. For example, if giraffes have longer necks
to eat the leaves on tree tops shouldn't the trees become even taller
to retaliate in competition with giraffes? Thus, even if we assume
that there is random DNA mutation, it is not clear which competing
mutations will succeed. Regardless of the physical differences a species may have from other species, those physical characteristics don't
make DNA mutation more effective in one case than in the other. Mutation depends on DNA and the DNA in one species is not more likely to

mutate as compared to the DNA in another species.

If every species is equally likely to mutate for its own benefit, then there is literally zero chance for a mutation to be successful, because a mutation that puts one species in advantage may be nullified by the mutations in another species that retaliates against these advantages.

The only exception to this cancellation is if there is a *set* of mutations that collectively benefit the ecosystem as a whole, or at least the majority of the ecosystem at once, thereby creating a win-win situation for most species. For instance, suppose that there is a mutation in trees that dramatically increases the number of leaves on trees, making the branches on the trees unable to manage their own weight, accompanied by another mutation in giraffes that dramatically increases their sexual activity creating more giraffe offspring, who now need more leaves. These two mutations will mutually benefit giraffes and trees because trees are better off losing their leaves and giraffes are better off eating those leaves. In this case, more leaves are a problem while more giraffes are a solution to that problem (we could inversely claim that more giraffes are a problem and more leaves are a solution to that problem).

The above mentioned pairing is only illustrative of what is needed, but hardly a complete alteration in itself. In reality, more leaves on trees requires more water and soil nutrients for the trees, which require more rains and a faster recycling of waste produced from giraffes into soil. The problem isn't therefore completely solved without a concerted modification of trees, giraffe, soil, water and climate. The story doesn't end here because there are factors that control soil and water, which should change before a mutually beneficial mutation between giraffes and trees can randomly take place. The point is that evolution cannot effect unilateral changes in a single species because species are closely connected in an ecosystem. For a change to be permanent, it must ripple through the entire ecosystem, and there are many hurdles in that process. If all species are equally likely to mutate, and there is no direction in evolution, then two species in an ecosystem can mutate in opposite ways, forcing each other to adapt in contradictory ways. Neither species is better off in this competition in the longer run, although until the other species has reacted to that change, it might seem that one species has a better payoff than the other in the shorter run. For example, if I unilaterally stop paying taxes to the government, it might seem that I'm better off for the time being as I have more money, until the government finds out. The only way lesser taxes can work is if there is lesser crime, lesser disease, lesser geo-political uncertainty, and lesser natural calamities. The lessening of these factors puts a lot of people employed as military, police, doctors and emergency response departments out of their current jobs, and they must now be employed in newer ways. My unilateral reduction in taxes can work only if there is also a huge systemic change accompanying it. The larger and more interconnected the ecosystem, the more resilient it becomes to any kind of change, because there are so many more vested interests holding it back to the status quo.

The question of the diversification of the species is not about evolution in the classic sense of mutate-and-survive. It is rather a question of how many different types of living beings exist in a system and must co-evolve to make any small change in the system benefit every member in the system as a whole. Without a concerted evolution of various stakeholders in an ecosystem, unilateral changes will only be detrimental to the evolving species, because other species that do not benefit from such unilateral changes will evolve in ways opposite to the unilateral change, to nullify the advantages to the benefitting species. To know how a system can co-evolve collectively, we must know how many types of species exist within a system. This in turn implies knowing all the DNA types in an ecosystem to make the ecosystem as a whole a viable system for all the players. An ecosystem circulates meanings (e.g., useful things) like an economy circulates products and services. The survival of a species depends on how well it fits vis-à-vis other members of the ecosystem. In a stable ecosystem, no species can change unilaterally and expect to have a better chance of survival because changes to the consumption patterns of a species will affect other species and these effects can ripple back to the original species, as a retaliation to change.

The only way a large ecosystem can evolve is if all the stakeholders (or at least the majority of them) are collectively benefitted by the transition. Now, evolution is not about the usefulness of a single mutation to that individual. Rather, the ecosystem should evolve as a whole. This puts the evolutionary and ecological approaches to diversification at odds. In evolution, many species are created from a single species because they mutate and diversify, and are selected by the environment. In an ecosystem, all species must *co-evolve* as no individual has a better chance of surviving unless other species are also going to cooperate.

The ecosystem view shifts the perspective considerably. The problem of many species is not about how they emerged from a single species, but about knowing how an ecosystem can be *logically* built from different species. There should be only those species as the ecosystem currently needs. Inserting or removing a single species has drastic consequences that cannot be reconciled unless the ecosystem as a whole changes. For example, if giraffes eat many leaves, and the trees run out of leaves at some height, the problem isn't solved by giraffes growing longer necks, because they will now eat the leaves at even higher levels, causing those leaves to be finished, just as leaves at a lower height were finished earlier. If giraffes continue to consume the leaves, they will wipe out the trees and then will be wiped out themselves. But, before that can happen, the ecosystem can also find a balance by reducing the number of eating giraffes, which will happen if the giraffes simply *don't* evolve to have longer necks. In other words, longer necked giraffes are not necessarily better even for giraffes, let alone for the whole system.

To understand ecosystems, a new approach is required in which a system as a whole is controlled as a whole rather than by its parts individually. In Vedic philosophy, the universal ecosystem is controlled by Time, which affects every individual at a very subtle, unconscious level simultaneously. Time affects the personalities of individuals by which they become more cooperative or more competitive. Subtle changes in the unconscious cause bigger changes in the conscious experiences and material bodies. The Vedas state that personality changes are not permanent and may eventually be reversed at a later time, causing the universe to undergo cycles of change. This cycle may create and destroy species, change the relative numbers of different species, and also alter the behaviors within each individual species. But these changes are not attributed to environmental factors, or even to random mutations in individual members of the species. The changes cut across the entire system and cause the entire system to *collectively* evolve. The collective evolution of the universe, of which the evolution of the species is but a smaller part, is the actual phenomenon that needs to be understood.

In the collective evolution of species, the causality is not in any individual or species. The causality is rather in the Time that causes all parts of a system to evolve simultaneously. The evolutionary model extends the causal model of individual change into a change to the ecosystem. Its predictions are flawed because random mutations cannot succeed unless the ecosystem as a whole changes for the better. If an ecosystem eliminates one species and creates a new one, should we say that environmental changes prompted the elimination of a species or was it the extinction of that species that caused a change in the environment, creating a new species? In classical notions of causality, there is a unique choice that alters the individual form, concept, proposition or intent. This change affects other entities logically, structurally, intentionally and morally related to it. There is, however, a point at which the entire universe is interconnected as a single ecosystem which cannot be modified as a result of some change 'outside' of it. Rather, all (or at least most) parts of the ecosystem must change collectively at once.

The scientific component of this ideology is that evolution is not linear but cyclic. An ecosystem oscillates through a fixed set of states. The oscillation at the systemic level can be modeled as a redistribution of matter into different contexts; both contexts and matter have to be seen semantically. Intentional semantics divides matter into pairs of problem-solution and referenced-referencing entities. An ecosystem is built up of many intentional pairs, which together form a cycle of meaning. In this cycle, a change ripples through a system and returns with a delay. Studies of non-linear systems (systems that send the effect back to the cause) that have a built-in delay are known to oscillate. The canonical example of such an oscillating system is the shower faucet that controls the relative amounts of hot and cold water. The user who is trying to get to an optimal water temperature in the shower adjusts the relative amounts of hot and cold but their effects show up after a delay. As a result, the water out of the faucet is either too hot or too cold. Users of showers, of course, learn to *dampen* these changes by not responding too quickly until a desired temperature is attained. This is because there is a single intent controlling that oscillation. In the case of the universe, oscillations are never dampened because there is no final state of the universe. The universe is thus perpetually in a state of oscillation.

The biological theory of the evolution of species, in this view, is inextricable from the universe's cosmological oscillation under the control of Causal Time. This type of evolution is more deterministic than current evolution, and a theory of this evolution will have more predictive consequences. The collective evolution also has direction even though there is no *intention* behind the ecosystem as a whole because there is no final state (even a perpetually moving clock has a direction but no intention). An oscillatory ecosystem similarly represents a perpetually oscillating system that doesn't have a final state and hence no intent. The only purpose (intent and purpose are different—e.g., a clock doesn't have an intended state, but it has a purpose) for the universe is that living beings can use it as a source of knowledge about consciousness.

Game Theory and Altruism

Morality was foreseen as a problem in evolution early on. Evolutionists saw that many animal species are altruistic even to their own detriment. If the intent of the gene is selfish then how does the altruistic behavior come about? The behaviors of collections of rational individuals are often modeled using Game Theory (GT) and this has been brought to bear on the evolutionary genesis of altruism as well. A fundamental premise in GT is that every individual acts for maximizing their payoff, and so evolutionary game theorists attempt to see if sometimes the payoff for even a selfishly acting individual may be maximized by acting altruistically. In general, if each player knows the alternatives of its opponents, GT shows that every game settles into one of two main possibilities. Either the population is stabilized at the Nash Equilibrium where no player in a group is benefitted by changing their strategy unilaterally. Or, if the game has not settled into a Nash Equilibrium, then the evolutionary process actually favors the selfish.

Therefore, if actors are rational there is no incentive to be altruistic in games with full information available.

However, it can also be shown that altruistic behavior dominates in a group if the majority of the group is altruistic to begin with. The payoffs for the majority are higher by being altruistic and the minority also sees that being altruistic increases their payoffs. This is because even an altruistic group will settle down into a Tit-for-Tat (TFT) strategy and reward the altruist and punish the selfish. In other words, if there is a negative consequence for a selfish act, then over a period of time altruistic actions are preferred. If the majority is altruistic, therefore, the entire group tends towards virtuousness. But, for this to work, the majority in a group must be altruistic to begin with, for which there is really no explanation. Assume for the moment that each member in a group is punishing the other members for their past selfish acts. How will any member ever act altruistic in this scenario? To act altruistically, the player must see an example which shows that being altruistic gets you better payoffs. But if everyone is acting selfishly, then no one is going to set a good example for the others. Indeed, any altruistic actions in a selfish group will look silly because altruists will be exploited by other selfish members. An altruist can only be rewarded by other altruists. So, for any altruism to exist at all, multiple such altruists must emerge at once.

Evolutionists claim that natural selection must act on groups that are altruistic versus groups that are selfish. But how can an altruistic group emerge when the payoffs to an altruist within a group of selfish players are always negative? If nature begins in selfishness, then a single random mutation of altruism will be eliminated quickly. A number of altruistic players must emerge at once, which is very unlikely. For such a group to survive, they must be altruistic to each other but selfish to others. A random mutation that will create a large group that can survive based on altruistic support from other altruists looks highly unlikely.

GT assumes that every individual acts selfishly and it thus fails to explain altruism. We have to assume that in any altruistic society most players will be altruistic. The altruistic can then use TFT to keep the selfish at bay. But as the selfish players increase altruism rapidly declines. Everyone now acts selfishly and everyone is worse off as a consequence. GT has the potential to explain how a group—in the case of a majority—tends as a whole either towards altruism or self-ishness, improving everyone's life or worsening everyone's life. But GT cannot explain how these trends are reversed—e.g., why a selfish group will become altruistic or why an altruistic group will become selfish, if everyone in that group has the same basic choices, strategies and payoffs.

GT is a theory of choices, but it does not take into account individual *personalities* which will act altruistically or selfishly even if the payoffs are bad. Personalities don't change quickly—i.e. over a couple of bad payoffs. People with altruistic tendencies think that they may have had a few bad payoffs, but there is still merit in continuing on that path. The selfish too rely on the fact that they would not be caught in the selfish act and that they can cloak it long enough to fool others. GT is inadequate in the sense that it takes individuals to be rational agents who will compute their payoffs at every move. But living beings are not always rational in that sense. Most living beings have more or less fixed strategies about dealings in life. A lion will not stop hunting even if the rest of the animals decided to periodically sacrifice one from their group to feed him. Note how both the lion and the rest of the animals are better off in this case: the lion doesn't have to hunt and the other animals don't have to live in fear. But this doesn't really happen because lions will hunt; it is part of what it *means* to be a lion—aggressive, not nonviolent.

In GT, a player is rational but doesn't have a personality; the player is not *a priori* predisposed to act in a certain ways. The truth is that we all have predispositions to behaviors which determine whether we will be altruistic or selfish. These predispositions make a player belong to a specific species. Different personalities can be connected in an ecosystem that is designed to accommodate such variety. The player doesn't have to act more altruistically or more selfishly than what its personality dictates. The ecosystem as a whole works not because a species is particularly altruistic or selfish, but because it has the right intentional relations of give and take with other species. Evolution theory and Game theory therefore lead us to similar conclusions. Evolution theory cannot explain evolution unless cooperative effects happen in different species simultaneously. Game theory also doesn't explain altruism unless we start out with a large altruistic population. The ecosystem model replaces these approaches with a new type of cause that controls the whole universe as an ecosystem. This cause is counterintuitive in current science, but has more predictive capabilities than current theories.

Every living being has a moral compass by which he or she evaluates desires before acting upon them. This moral compass varies from being to being, and is therefore a contextual property. The morality of a tiger, for instance, can be different from that of a cow, which will again be different from that of the human being. But all species have a moral compass by which they will control their actions. For instance, most animals have the moral sense to nurture and feed their children before they eat. Many animals have a sense of loyalty and commitment to other members of their species, and in the case of domesticated animals such as dogs or horses, to their masters. In the human species, this sense is generally more advanced as compared to animals. Thus, we think that being polite, kind and considerate to other people is morally right. Supporting those who cannot support themselves is the duty of the mighty. That every human being has basic rights to education, job, marriage, etc.

In Vedic philosophy, a person's moral compass is tied to the meanings that make that person's life worthwhile. These meanings determine what makes us happy and sad, and therefore they guide our choices. Morality sets bounds on acceptable forms of happiness. In different contexts, different types of pleasures and actions may be acceptable and the definition of morality changes based on circumstances. Vedas call this moral compass one's *dharma* or *rta*; in some places this is called *mahattattva* and in others it is equated with consciousness due to moral choices. It should, however, be noted that this consciousness is not the soul's pure consciousness. It is rather a 'contaminated' consciousness that creates a subtle meaning of life; we might also call it the living being's persona. This persona is also a material element which represents our beliefs and understanding of what is morally right. Since this definition is contextual and changes with time, it is a phenomenon, not reality.

The *mahattattva* is the most subtle material element in the conscious experience, which include *vaikhari* and *madhyamā* (waking and dreaming states of experience). There are, in Vedic philosophy, causes which are even more subtle than the *mahattattva*. These causes shape our personality and they correspond to an individual's unconscious (deep-sleep state of experience), also called *paśyanti*. I will not try to describe them here[23]. The key takeaway from this aspect of Vedic philosophy is that living beings are not just freely choosing individuals. Rather, each individual has a moral compass, no matter how depraved that compass may be. The moral compass is the fundamental cause of intents in this world. Therefore, even if we understand someone's intentions, we incompletely understand causality unless we also know the moral person underneath who is the foundation from which intentions spring.

A physical counterpart of morality is seen in ecosystems where living beings are organized into species with different moral values. These living beings are connected in the ecosystem such that they can execute their choices even when their morals conflict with the morals of others. This connection in an ecosystem is based on the moral consequences of actions performed in prior lives. Each species and personality has a specific role in an ecosystem, and the Vedas state that living beings are transported into an appropriate body and part of the ecosystem based on their work. The diversity of species is not defined through the evolution of a few initial species. It is rather defined by a consideration of all personality types that *can* exist and how species must fit together to form an ecosystem. The Vedas thus define that there are 8,400,000 possible species of life, which together form the universe's ecosystem.

A semantic study of moral types, and how these types combine to create an ecosystem, is needed to show why only certain types of beings exist. Arbitrary types cannot exist because the addition or removal of a single type changes the entire ecosystem. The evolutionary idea that molecules combine to form living beings through random chance mutations is therefore not accepted in Vedic philosophy. The Vedic view starts from the premise that a number of species have to collectively exist in an ecosystem, and the ecosystem is sensitive to the presence of every species. The emergence or extinction of a species can only be understood in relation to its effects on the whole ecosystem. In the last chapter, I will relate the consequences of this idea to problems in evolutionary biology and evolutionary discussions based on game-theory.

Choices in Relativity

Relativity theory was formulated as a description of gravity from an accelerating frame of reference viewpoint (the acceleration could be zero). The theory suggests that there are many equivalent descriptions of the universe, from the viewpoint of different accelerating observers. However, since acceleration can be substituted by gravity, relativity permits multiple matter distributions for the same events. This possibility suggests that the theory is indeterministic in connecting material objects to experiences. Critics of indeterminism however argue that the empirical content of the theory is exhausted by events and not by matter distributions. The inability to distinguish between matter distributions does not have empirical consequences, because the space-time event-set is fixed. The problem thus hinges on the ability to distinguish particles. If these particles can be distinguished, then there is indeterminism. If they cannot be, then the symmetry is an artifact of theory not of experience.

All particles in classical physics are indistinguishable. We can swap two particles with identical mass without affecting predictions. The only reason this doesn't happen in classical physics is because of continuous trajectories. Objects cannot 'jump' and 'swap' states in classical physics because trajectories are continuous; a particle is identified by its trajectory. If, however, matter does not have continuous motion—as in atomic theory—then object swapping is possible and now this fact has real empirical implications. Imagine that the two objects that are being swapped are *observers*. From a nowhere-nowhen standpoint, the universe is comprised of identical events with or without the object swap. However, from the standpoint of observers who are being swapped, they now participate in different events, when the swap takes place versus when it does not. The total energy and mass are still conserved, but the *identity* of the particles with that mass and energy has changed.

This scenario indicates the existence of a new kind of indeterminism in which events are fixed, but the participants in the events are not. If observers X and Y swap events M and N between them, without changing the total mass and energy, the empirical difference cannot be known by someone who is not X or Y. But, for X and Y, the events they experience are different. Thus, from a third-person perspective there is no empirical difference due to the swap. But from a first-person perspective, there is a great difference. Relativity indicates that events in the universe are fixed, but who participates in these events is not.

Since the events and matter are both fixed, the only thing that differentiates these alternatives is the possibility that the observers themselves are unique and while material object swaps cannot be known *or* experienced, the swaps of observers cannot be known but they can be experienced (by those observers). The unified theory of matter (that incorporates gravity and other types of physical forces) will therefore still leave a room for choices. These choices cannot be studied in a third-person manner but will nevertheless be real in the first-person manner.

This indeterminism in a unified theory of matter is closely related to the viewpoint about Causal Time in Vedic philosophy because Time determines the events, without determining which individuals participate in those events. This participation, instead, depends on the abilities and powers in the participating individuals, as well as on their choices to participate. Furthermore, if the events in the universe are fixed, my participating in some events precludes others from taking my place. In that sense, the total energy in the universe can be constant, but the experiences of each observer are not fixed *a priori*. If two persons swap events, the difference can and will be known at least to those persons.

Numbers and Types

Philosophers have debated what mathematics is about, and, so far, three dominant approaches to this question have emerged. Platonism claims that mathematics is about another world of ideas, of which the present world is a poor imitation. Thus, everything in mathematics is real, although the notion of reality pertains to another world of ideas and not the present world of things. Platonism creates the problem of how we get to *know* this pure world of ideas, and why that pure world of ideas is reflected in matter. This question has never been answered satisfactorily. Intuitionists now claim that mathematics is not about another world of ideas, but about the minds of mathematicians. In this respect, mathematics is not timeless and independent of the human mind. Only things that the human mind can think and execute constitute the domain of mathematics; for instance, infinite sets cannot be understood by the human mind, and proofs pertaining to these hypothetical objects are not part of mathematics because the mind only deals with the finite. Intuitionism however still does not explain how mathematics interacts with the world, and why mathematical theories are useful to the world, although moral and ethical intuitionists argue that truths are discovered by our intuitions about the everyday world. Formalists now claim that if we have to rely on the external world, then why not reduce mathematics to demonstrable proofs? In this view, mathematics is not at all about ideas—in the mathematician's mind or in another world of pure ideas. Rather, mathematics is about *proofs*. It is pure symbol manipulation, which can be executed in an automated fashion even within computers. This view however leaves us with the problem of how we *understand* mathematics or why some people find it meaningful and beautiful.

The main application of Vedic ideas to mathematics is that mathematics is a language that has many models, and these models must be described in the same theory as the language. Language consists of symbols, which exist as objects. But these objects are also perceived by the mind, intelligence, ego and consciousness, producing different kinds of meanings. Within mathematics, this perception results in several different *models* of the mathematical theories. For instance, a number can denote a concept, a name, an order and a vector. Generally, mathematicians separate the theory of numbers from its various models. This is because we suppose that models are only specific realizations of the theory and the theory will be true in each of these realizations. This assumption is false, because in the everyday experience, we simultaneously have symbols, names, concepts, names, order and vectors in the same world. Within mathematics, this corresponds to the fact that a number can be alternately used as a sign, a concept, a name, an order, etc.

The mathematical separation of theories and their models represents a mind-body problem within mathematics. The theory is the 'body' and its models are the 'mind'. Cartesian dualism separates the material world from its meanings. But reality includes both things and meanings. The mathematical counterpart of this problem is that a number can alternately denote a concept (e.g., twoness), an order (e.g., the second object) and a name (e.g., Employee Number 2). The current theory of numbers applies indiscriminately to each of these notions about numbers, but these notions are distinct. The distinction, however, cannot be maintained in current mathematics, and this leads to category mistakes when a concept is equated with a name, or a name is equated with an order. These category mistakes lead to mathematical paradoxes and contradictions. Many such paradoxes have already been found in mathematics. These include Gödel's Incompleteness Theorem[24], Turing's Halting Problem[25], and the Barber's Paradox[26], just to name a few.

Solving these paradoxes requires a solution to the mind-body problem within mathematics. The solution should allow a theory and its models to exist in the same space. Since there can be many different types of models of a theory, it should also be possible to distinguish between the various models, without detaching them from the theory.

Such a foundation of mathematics is not possible in the current formulation of number theory because of the fundamental divide between quantities and types. The theory of numbers treats numbers as a study of *quantities* because operations such as addition, multiplication, division, etc. operate upon quantities. The meanings attached to these numbers are, however, viewed as *types*. So long as we treat numbers as quantities but their meanings as types, numbers and their meanings cannot exist in the same space. To solve this problem, we have to treat numbers themselves as types. Their meaning interpretations can then be viewed as additional types. Numbers and meanings can exist in the same space if the space itself is construed as a space of types rather than a space of quantities. One might argue that mathematics already deals in types by formulating the idea of *sets* which is a representation of a concept. A set, however, is defined as a collection of objects. To form a collection of objects, we must first have individual objects and their individuality itself implies that they can be ordered and hence counted. It is therefore true that mathematics describes types as sets, but these sets are in turn derived from objects which in turn are known as quantities. The mathematical notion of a set is therefore derived from quantities and thus does not truly capture the ordinary notion of types.

When we reduce a type to a set, this leads to many problems. These problems all arise from the fact that a set that conveys the idea of 'shoes' must include all possible shoes, which may include shoes that no one has ever seen, built, worn or even thought of. To make a set a reasonable substitute for the everyday notion of types, we have to allow a set to have infinitely many objects. Furthermore, sets themselves can be made members of other sets, thereby becoming objects. This is a source of great confusion if you remember that the original intent of sets was to denote concepts, not objects. By including sets as members of other sets, a set is both an object and a concept. Philosophers would have called this a 'category mistake', since until the time of Descartes, objects were physical and concepts were in the mind. By converting concepts to sets, and then sets to objects, we blurred the mind-matter divide under which rational thinking was supposed to be done. This blurring represents the germ of a problem, which, in the hands of an able manipulator can lead to infinitely many paradoxes. The lesson from these paradoxes is that mind and matter are not identical, even though you can use the same language to describe both. Thus, a thing 'shoe' and a concept 'shoe' are both called 'shoe' but the words do not have the same meaning in the two cases. To keep the mind-matter difference, but also create a similarity between them, a new way of representing types is needed.

The central problem in mathematics is that there are two ways of thinking about numbers—quantity and type. The quantity notion of numbers is derived from a collection of objects which requires individual objects to exist prior, and if they are already individual then they can be counted. The deeper question is also how these objects are distinct. To distinguish objects we need to have types such as color, taste, smell, sound or touch together with concepts like yellow or sweet or bitter. Before we can form collections, we must have distinct objects. And before we can have distinct objects, there must be types in terms of which they can be distinguished. Mathematics assumes distinct objects, then forms collections using these objects, and then attributes types to collections. Now, there are two contradictory notions about a type. First, a type is that which distinguishes objects into individuals that can be counted. Second, the type is the outcome of forming a collection. In the first case types are the basis of distinguishing things and in the second case they are the outcomes of distinguishing. In the first case, the type is embedded in the object itself and in the second case the type is only present in the object collection but does not exist in individual objects.

The paradoxes in mathematics arise from this inconsistent notion about types. We need types to form objects, but we derive types from collections. Types must be inherent in the individual object for it to be countable but they are associated with collections of such objects. In the case of numbers, for instance, a collection of three objects requires the ability to distinguish three things using some types before they can be collected into a set. The distinction is the cause and counting is the effect. But if we *define* a number from the collection then the collection is the cause and the individuals are the effect. However, we already assumed distinct objects before we formed the collection, and therefore the idea that the type must be defined from the collection is false.

There are several reasons why the type mode is more fundamental than the quantity mode. First, to even arrive at the quantity mode, we need to *distinguish* objects and order them. The quantity mode represents the highest order object in a collection, and the quantity therefore depends on the order. Second, if there is a limit to the smallest and largest things in the universe, then the type notion becomes more fundamental because the quantities now need to be comprehended in terms of these types. In the case of letters in a language, a letter is a type of object or a collection of pixels that together make up the type. In other words, a letter can be seen as a type or a collection. Learners of the language see it as a collection while experts see it as a type. In mathematics, and science in general, there has been a trend to *reduce* types to collections. Philosophically, this started as the need to reduce the variety of types to a few fundamentals. But at what point do we stop the reduction and assume that we reached fundamental types? Logicians claimed that there is no such logical limit to reduction. Logically speaking, we can postulate objects and collections, without actually defining what we mean by an object. This is a mistake because the notion of an object is vacuous unless we define how an object is distinguished from other objects. To define these distinctions, we must know how to distinguish and count. To distinguish objects, we need to use types. So, if in fact there are objects, then they must be distinct. And if they are distinct then their distinctness has to be based upon some type distinctions.

The mistake in mathematics is in assuming the idea of an object, without defining what it means. Is an object a fundamental idea? In Vedic philosophy, objects are not fundamental because objects are created by applying ideas to space-time. Space-time is *a priori* undifferentiated. When types are applied to space-time, then objects are differentiated. Therefore, objects should be derived from types, rather than deriving types from objects. Current mathematics derives types from objects while in Vedic viewpoint the objects are derived from basic types.

Type Number Theory (TNT)

Mathematical foundations today start with the notions of logic, objects and set theory and attempt to construct number theory. This construction is known to be incomplete (Gödel's Incompleteness) and riddled with logical paradoxes. These problems, as shown above, arise from deriving numbers from classes, which are in turn derived from objects. Since object distinctness assumes the ability to distinguish and count objects, number theory today does not stand on sound foundations. To fix these problems, we need to realize that counting is an outcome of object distinctness and this distinctness itself needs to be explained.

In the everyday world, distinctness between objects is known by their unique location in space and time. Objects that exist at distinct locations in space can be *distinguished*. To count these objects, we must also *order* them. If objects can be distinguished, they can also be counted, although counting also requires the choice of an ordering procedure. Numbers are outcomes of distinguishing and ordering and mathematics needs to formulate the principles on which objects can be distinguished and ordered. Such a theory of numbers is also a theory of space and time, because if we can distinguish and order objects then that distinction and order is identical to location in space and time. In Vedic philosophy, objects are created when distinctions from the mind and order from the intelligence is applied to an undifferentiated Ether. All distinctions exist as oppositions between ideas; for instance, the meaning of hot is always defined in opposition to cold, and the meaning of yellow is defined in opposition to red, green, blue, etc. Order, similarly, requires the distinction of before and after. Once distinctions and order have been applied to create objects from space and time, a separate counting procedure to map these objects to numbers is unnecessary. The distinction of object itself is that it has a unique space-time location. The identity of the object is that it can be associated with a unique number.

Both objects and numbers therefore emerge simultaneously from the ability to distinguish and order. Since distinguishing and ordering are an outcome of applying type distinctions to space and time, these type distinctions are more fundamental than both objects and numbers. The foundation of mathematics is therefore in the fundamental type distinctions. A complete catalogue of the most basic distinctions can help us understand how objects are created from space-time when these distinctions are applied to distinguish a symmetric and undifferentiated space-time into unique events. This catalogue will include the basic modes of sensation such as taste, touch, smell, sound and sight, because objects can be distinguished based on their sensations. It will include the fundamental properties that divide each sensation into further distinct types; for example, form, color, size, brightness, distance and direction can divide the sensation of sight. The collection of all sensation-types and property-types will comprise all the ways in which we can *distinguish* things in space. These sensations and concepts must also be *ordered* in various ways before they are counted. The types of ordering include basic figures of speech such as nouns, verbs, adjectives, etc. Concepts and activities are also ordered by the time of day such as morning, afternoon, evening and night. These and many other distinctions are commonly used to distinguish and order events in the everyday world. The Vedic view is that there aren't individual objects which are given space and time locations. Rather, the space and time location itself defines object identity and uniqueness.

The foundation of counting is thus in object distinguishability, which arises from type distinctions. These types themselves are products of three modes of nature called *sattva, rajas* and *tamas*. All distinctions are mutual oppositions, as are the three modes themselves. All types can therefore be produced from three modes because the modes are the most fundamental types in nature from which all other types are created. When these modes act on space-time, the world of events is created. The cause of an event is therefore a unique type. And these unique types are produced from the combination of three basic modes. Each object's identity is the unique type that causes it. This identity is expressed in mathematics as a number. The cause of an object and that of a number is therefore a product of some combination of the modes of nature. We can say that each object and number is a product of the three modes. The foundation of mathematics must also be in the three basic types together with space-time. Such a foundation will not only explain how various events are created from space-time, but also why some of these events encode meanings beyond their physical properties.

The radical perspective from Vedic philosophy is that each object is a unique type because it is a unique combination of the three modes of nature. Each number—which essentially counts these objects—is also therefore a unique type. Now, we can derive the idea of number not from the notion of set which collects a finite number of objects, but from combining basic types. Arithmetical operations—such as addition, multiplication, division and subtraction—are now operations on types rather than on quantities! For instance, when we write 2+3=5, we are adding two different types to arrive at a new type. Similarly, when we write 5-3=2 we are subtracting two types to arrive at a new type. Every number is a type and arithmetic operations are defined over types. If you move an object from position 2 to position 5, you have performed a type operation not a quantity operation. That is, the object at position 5 is not the same object that earlier existed at position 2. Both the object and the numerical labels that describe that object denote different types.

The difference this idea brings to science is that we don't have to know many properties about an object besides their position in space and time. Rather, the position itself is a complete catalogue of all the object's properties. For instance, now, we don't have to measure momentum, energy, mass, charge, temperature, etc. in addition to position, before we uniquely identify an object. We only have to know the position in space-time and we will know everything that needs to be known about the object. This, of course, is already intuitively obvious to us: we know that if an event exists at a unique space-time location then it can be counted. In current science, the space-time location is determined by other properties like mass, charge, energy, momentum, etc. In the Vedic view, the space-time location is determined by types in the senses, mind and intellect. Physical properties in science are measured against material objects, but they assume that the object already exists. Cognitive properties on the other hand measure the object, but they are the causes of the object. The manner in which we observe the object should be the manner in which it was originally distinguished from space-time.

When objects and numbers are types then locations in space and time must also be types. Indeed, the type of the object is the number, which is the space-time location. Now we need to think of space-time as a domain of typed-things rather than a domain of things that are typeless. This requires a radically new way of conceiving space-time. For instance, a position in space-time cannot be not defined in a linear fashion as coordinate frames in current geometry depict. Rather, this position must be defined by *nesting* spatial locations inside spatial extensions and temporal instances inside temporal durations. Each space-time event is embedded inside 'larger' space-time contexts and it must therefore be defined *relative* to the locations and times that embed the event. This is similar to how we define postal addresses but different from how geometry defines position. In geometry, there are some coordinate axes and an origin relative to which an object's position is described. In the postal address scheme, the world is divided into countries, cities, streets and buildings. The number of a building is not globally unique. Rather it has a number relative to the street name, which is relative to the city, country, etc. In geometry, we assume a flat naming convention. In postal addresses, we assume hierarchical naming.

In Vedic philosophy, space and time are not 'open'. Rather, space is closed and time is cyclic. The space inside my house is enclosed in the space of the city, which is enclosed in the space of the country, planet, solar system and so forth. Time, similarly, is not linear. Time flows in cycles. The moment of now is embedded in a minute, hour, day, week, month, year and so forth. Closed spaces and cyclic times make space and time semantic, which must now be described in terms of types. These types are associated with hierarchies of space-time division. To go from one point to another we must cross the boundaries of the hierarchy. The properties in an object are not its possessed properties. Rather, the property of an object is relative to the hierarchy it is embedded in. The number of the building therefore does not have a meaning by itself. Rather, it acquires meaning in relation to the street address, which acquires a meaning in relation to the city name, country name, and so forth. In current thinking, hierarchies are man-made constructs. In Vedic philosophy, these hierarchies are the *cause* of objects. When these hierarchies are applied to space-time, then objects are created. The conceptual hierarchy is produced from some combination of the three modes of nature and their mutual opposition. And this hierarchy exists in a subtle material form even before it is manifest within the objects.

Objects, numbers and space-time events are therefore byproducts of the three modes of nature. These modes combine and divide to produce innumerable distinctions, by nesting within each other. An infinite variety is created through this combination and nesting of modes. When these modes apply to an undifferentiated material reality—which can be equated with an undifferentiated space-time—objects are created.

Objects inside closed space and cyclic time must be described in terms of types because the location and time itself is described in terms of types. Both space and time need to be described in terms of the three modes of nature, which are the original types. Objects in this space-time are typed events. The number that identifies these objects is also a type. And arithmetic operations on these numbers are also operations on types. All of mathematics therefore has to be developed from fundamental types, and this includes space, time, objects and numbers. This needs a new mathematical foundation, which we can call a *Type Number Theory* or TNT. The typed nature of numbers is a consequence of the typed nature of objects, which in turn is a consequence of the typed nature of space and time, which is a byproduct of the three modes of nature.

Paradoxes in mathematics which arise because of the separation between the theory and the models of that theory will not arise in a typed number theory because meanings are already types. If we can also define the individuality of an object as a type, then the basic contradiction between a type and an instance of that type will disappear. The fundamental notion of number is *counting* and not *quantity*. If we can count, then we can also come up with quantities. But quantities cannot be defined without counting. The notion that a number denotes a quantity is therefore a fundamental flaw in modern mathematics. It creates logical paradoxes because types cannot be derived from quantities. Quantities can however be derived from types and the incompleteness in mathematics can be solved if we can develop a Type Number Theory.

The Foundation of Nature

The dynamics of the three modes of nature constitute the *algebra of types* because these basic types combine to produce all numbers. By forming that algebra we can know how all types are created. When these types act on the empty space-time, then the geometric world is created. The empty space-time is an absolute coordinate frame and is called *pradhāna* in Sāṅkhya. The three modes of nature are called *prakṛti*. The manifest world is called *mahattattva*. This manifest world is like space-time in which unique locations or events have been defined but objects in those events still don't exist. The *mahattattva* therefore represents the domain of all *possible* events. We can compare it with the set of all possible numbers. These three ideas—namely, *pradhāna*, *prakṛti* and *mahattattva*—are very similar to the ideas of manifold, algebra and geometry in modern mathematics. Like algebra when applied to a manifold produces geometry, similarly, the three modes of nature in *prakṛti* act upon *pradhāna* to produce *mahattattva*. Of course, in Sāṅkhya these three are not separate things, but rather the development of a single entity. That is, the three modes of nature are not outside *pradhāna*. They exist within *pradhāna* but are not manifest due to what Sāṅkhya calls the equilibrium of modes. When this equilibrium is disturbed, then first *prakṛti* and then *mahat-tattva* are created. The key import of this thinking in Sāṅkhya is that the universe is produced from emptiness by applying an *algebra of types* to that emptiness. The algebra of types is also material, but is not objective. Rather, this algebra produces numbers and distinct space-time locations.

The number that denotes the space-time location in *mahattattva* is information about the world, but it exists in a very abstract form. Further steps of manifestation expand and decode this number into observable and sensible types. For instance, if we call something "Object #55" you would not immediately know the properties of that object from its number. The properties are embedded in that number and yet they are not immediately knowable. The successive development of the universe expands this number into various kinds of sensible properties.

The foundation of the physical world is the foundation of the mathematical world, in Sāṅkhya. Recall that the word Sāṅkhya means the theory of counting. The view that science has discovered a mathematical description of reality while the ancients relied on unsound and irrational thinking is incorrect. In Sāṅkhya, the universe of objects is manifest through the same steps that numbers are created from the algebra of types and an empty manifold. The foundation of the physical world and the foundation of the mathematical world are identical. By knowing the foundation of mathematics, we can know the foundation of physical reality. The theory of reality is therefore called Sāṅkhya which is also the theory of numbers. In a way, this is similar to the Pythagorean insight that the universe is comprised only of numbers. But, in another sense, the Greek notion of numbers as quantities is flawed and it has led to paradoxes in mathematics, and the inability to describe the mind in terms of matter in other physical, chemical and biological sciences.

It is therefore fascinating and remarkable that a subtle shift in the nature of numbers from quantities to types changes not only the foundation of mathematics and of the physical world, but also reintroduces a role for senses, mind, intelligence, ego and consciousness back into the world. When numbers are types, then we can talk about many different types within mathematics. There have been a slew of philosophers and spiritualists in recent times who have believed that the mind and conscious experience cannot be described by mathematics. I believe that they would greatly benefit from a study and understanding of Sāṅkhya.

Epilogue

The central goal of this book was to illustrate the idea that matter can be described in terms of properties of the observer, different from current science which describes matter in relation to the properties of other objects. Current science takes sensations—which are properties of the observer—and objectifies them into physical properties. This objectification converts a typed view of nature into a quantity view of nature. The Vedic approach employs a typed description of reality, rather than a quantity view. It extends types into the deeper recesses of the observer. Thus, properties in the mind, objects in the intelligence, intentions in the ego and morals in consciousness are objectified into matter to create new types of phenomena. I have, in this book, tried to illustrate how material phenomena—already known in science but either not adequately understood or misunderstood in many cases—can be clarified through the Vedic theories on senses, mind, intelligence ego and consciousness. The Vedic ideas are both contemporary and relevant in this regard, if the linguistic and conceptual barriers are overcome.

But there is another sense in which Vedic philosophy is quite different and, indeed, opposed to the ideology of modern science. The main opposition between the two is that matter in science is reality whereas matter in Vedic philosophy is a phenomenon. Space-time forms, sensations, properties, objects, intents and morals are all temporary; they are created and they will be destroyed. Only three things are eternal and real—(a) consciousness, (b) the abilities of consciousness as expressed in language and its various interpretations, and (c) a primordial undifferentiated matter. Thus, while individual space-time forms, sensations, properties, objects, intentions and morals are all temporary, the ability in consciousness to have these kinds of experiences and to describe them to others in language is eternal. Science and Vedic philosophy therefore deeply differ in what they consider reality. Reality is the most objectivized, abstracted, mathematical entity in science. Reality is the most subjective, contingent and personal entity in the Vedas.

Vedic philosophy and modern science do, however, have a meeting point in the study of natural phenomena. From a Vedic standpoint, all aspects of the observer are reflected into matter, and this reflection creates different observable phenomena. Science looks at these phenomena and says—there must be a reality 'behind' each phenomenon. The Vedic view instead says—there must be a reality 'before' each phenomenon. Like we might see our image in a mirror and interpret the reflection of nose, eyes, ears, lips and hair as indications of a real nose, eyes, ears, lips and hair on our faces, similarly, the Vedic view treats material phenomena as giving us information about the real nature of the observer seeing the phenomena. Reality in Vedic philosophy is not something that existed prior to consciousness. Reality is that which is created due to conscious choices (they may be the choices of different individuals).

Current science has been founded on the basis of an analysis of phenomena. However, in analyzing these phenomena, science has also developed a bias for objectivity: scientists believe that all phenomena should be modeled in terms of *things*. Early physicists postulated particles and fields as simple object-types to which every other type could be reduced. But these concepts are no longer useful even in physics, which has replaced particles and waves either with probability or with space-time. Nevertheless, the theories are still incomplete and uncertain. The current bias towards objectivity completely fails when it comes to dealing with experiences of the observer, although experimental studies show that there is a relation between the brain and the mind. The way out of this quagmire is to recognize that matter is a symbol of the mind; it reflects properties of the observer as phenomena. If we are looking for reality 'behind' the phenomena we can only search for objects. However, if we are looking for reality 'before' the phenomena then sensations, properties, objects, intents and morals are all useful constructs in modeling natural phenomena. Vedic science therefore leads to a methodological shift in how we approach the study of phenomena in science. In this new way of looking at reality, we should model phenomena after the properties of the observer rather than on the properties of things.

Endnotes

INTRODUCTION

1 This point is further elaborated in later sections and chapters. By 'representation' of sensation I mean the objective representation of the information that describes the sensations. For instance, if the observer perceives the color 'red' then the representation of that sensation is the information about redness.

2 In current science, the practical experience of reality is called experiment, which is how we manipulate matter through the senses. As science deepens to study ever more subtle forms of reality, the theoretical and practical aspects of science must involve subtle senses.

A DIFFERENT KIND OF SCIENCE

3 Whether induction solves the problem of illusion is however an issue of much debate. For instance, the sun and moon always appear small to us although they aren't small. Repeated observations of sun or moon will not change the perceived size and therefore induction does not change the fact that we might be under illusion every time we observe something.

4 A thorough examination of this issue has been done in my book *Gödel's Mistake: The Role of Meaning in Mathematics.*

5 For a detailed discussion of the problems of indeterminism and its relation to meaning please refer to my book *Quantum Meaning: A Semantic Interpretation of Quantum Theory.*

FOUNDATIONS OF VEDIC SCIENCE

6 The creation of a table is a general point about the objectification of

meanings into matter. In Vedic view, however, even our bodies are created by objectifying meanings in our minds. Thus, while there is no 'creator' involved in the creation of plants and animals, their minds are the creators of their bodies. Even things that we generally consider inanimate—such as mountains or rivers—are animate in Vedic philosophy; i.e. they too are bodies created by some mind.

7   The term sound in Vedic philosophy refers to information which is present objectively as a vibration. Thus, physical objects are vibrations in space-time, and this idea is well-known in modern science which describes sub-atomic particles as vibrations. Further, each location and direction in space-time is also a vibration, and they can be distinguished as different locations because they produce a different sound. These sounds represent different types, and both objects and space-time locations and directions are typed.

8   The living being and God are however quantitatively different. A detailed discussion of the similarity and differences between living beings and God can be found in my book *Six Causes: The Vedic Theory of Creation.*

9   It is said that the living being falls from the spiritual world due to jealousy, which arises only when one compares oneself to others. The genesis of comparison is in the ability for measurements which requires a standard. If a living being thinks he is the standard and then compares himself to other living beings, this naturally leads to notions of higher and lower, greater and smaller, and this is the beginning of dualistic logic.

10 Many Eastern philosophies such as Zen claim that truth cannot be captured in language because language uses duality and distinctions and reality is, ultimately, non-dual. The idea of complementarity has emerged from this inability to capture reality into words and reality must be described by opposing words to describe its nature. These words are only vehicles to the nature of reality and must be discarded once the truth has been grasped. This viewpoint is not accepted in Vedic philosophy. All reality is a manifestation of sound, and can therefore be encoded in language. These sounds may not be the sounds that currently exist in an ordinary language. But reality is language and every experience can be encoded in language.

11 Manus, Margaret (1999), Gods of the Word: Archetypes in the Consonants, Truman State University Press.

12 An important point in Vedic philosophy is that consciousness too is created although the soul which is the reality behind that consciousness is eternal. Consciousness is a symbol of the soul, and we infer the presence of the soul by the existence of consciousness. Consciousness is the individuated ability to experience and this individuation may not always exist. In certain cases, the individuality is lost and therefore the experience ceases although the soul remains an individual. This point is important because impersonal interpretations of Vedic philosophy incorrectly equate the soul with consciousness. The experience of individuality is different from the individuation itself, and the soul sometimes experiences itself as individual and sometimes not. The soul is however at all times individual although it sometimes loses its experience of individuality.

13 This has direct implications in how the mind is modeled in science; for instance connectionist models of the mind are not supported but models of semantic computation where the symbols hold meaning will be very useful.

14 This consistency however does not entail *completeness*. There can be several interpretations of the world that are consistent with the world although these interpretations only describe selected parts of the world. Many previous theories of science have, for instance, have been consistent with selected parts of the world; they fail when other parts are added. All such theories are consistent although they are only partial and therefore incomplete descriptions of nature.

15 For instance, the responsibilities of a fireman and a bystander are not the same in the event of a fire and their reaction to the fire (helping or fleeing) will be judged differently, according to their freely chosen role. In the same way, according to the Vedas, we have our own nature, called *svadharma*, and acting in congruence or in contradiction to that nature has different karmic consequences.

THE VEDIC THEORY OF MATTER

16 Russell's Paradox is an example of such a paradox. The paradox shows

that the idea of a "set of all sets that do not include themselves" is logically contradictory. The paradox arises if we ask: Does such a set belong to itself? If it does, then it should not belong to itself, because the set is only supposed to contain those sets that do not include themselves. If, however, the set does not include itself, then it should belong to the set. Either way, the set represents a logical contradiction.

17 The reality of the whole apart from the reality of the parts becomes useful if the whole can be described in many different ways, each time using a different set of parts. In atomic theory, an ensemble of particles can be described using several different eigenfunction bases, each of which represents a different energy distribution. These bases are a matter of 'choice' in quantum theory, which means that the same whole can be described in many different ways. The whole is the same, but the parts are different in each case. To reconcile this problem with the issue of realism in science, science needs to recognize the reality of the wholes and parts separately. That way, we can claim that the reality being described is the same whole, but it can be divided into different parts by different observers. Without such a hypothesis, the observer dependent observations imply that there is in fact no reality apart from the observations.

UNDERSTANDING VEDIC COSMOLOGY

18 The term 'closure' is often used in mathematics to denote the idea of a set such that operations on the members of the set produce another member of the set. The idea that the material universe is closed means that operations on matter will produce another material object in the universe. Similarly, language is closed implies that a combination of words will produce a statement which is possible in language.

19 Homogeneous means all distances are equal and isotropic means that all directions are equivalent. Homogeneity of space is responsible for the conservation of momentum and isotropicity of space is needed for the conservation of angular momentum.

20 The standard kilogram and the standard meter are made out of a platinum-iridium alloy and these standards are kept near Paris.

APPLYING VEDIC IDEAS

21 The quantum slit experiment is a standard textbook experiment used to teach quantum ideas. The experimental set up consists of a hot radiating body that emits quantum objects (e.g., electrons or photons) which are passed through a screen with two or more slits before they hit a photographic plate that detects the quantum particles. The mystery of the slit experiment is that with one slit the particles are seen everywhere on the photographic plate but with two or more slits, they are not found at many locations. The locations of detection depend on the number of slits used in the experiment.

22 A classic textbook example of such a proposition widely used in describing the problems of Artificial Intelligence is "I saw a man on the hill with a telescope." The proposition has many meanings, depending on whether you interpret "I saw" as applying to the noun-phrase "a man" or "a man on the hill" or "a man on the hill with a telescope." The meanings of propositions depend on the meanings of the words, in addition to the laws of grammar that make the sentence meaningful.

23 The book *Six Causes: The Vedic Theory of Creation* discusses the unconscious at great lengths.

24 Gödel's Incompleteness Theorem is a foundational result in mathematics that proves that any theory of numbers must be either inconsistent or incomplete. The proof depends on using numbers in three different ways as things, names and concepts. The reader is referred to my other work entitled *Gödel's Mistake* for a detailed analysis of this theorem and its real meaning.

25 In computing theory, it is desirable to know if a program will halt. Programs that do not halt will run forever and their results will never be known. A program that never halts is like a conjecture that can never be proved. On the other hand, a program that halts is a conjecture that can be proved. Alan Turing proved that there is no automated procedure that can determine whether a program will halt or not. This proof implies that the meanings of programs cannot be measured by any automated procedure. For a detailed discussion of this problem, the reader is referred to my other

book entitled *Gödel's Mistake*. That book analyzes the genesis of this and other paradoxes, and problems in mathematics and computing theory.

26 The Barber's Paradox arises from the following innocuous statement: "A barber shaves all those who do not shave themselves". The paradox is that if we ask "Does the barber shave himself?" there is no clear answer. If the barber shaves himself, then according to the above claim he should shave himself since barbers are supposed to only shave those who do not shave themselves. If, on the other hand, we suppose that the barber does not shave himself then he must shave himself because the barber is supposed to shave all those who do not shave themselves. This paradox is the outcome of the inability to distinguish between two meanings of barber—a person and a class of persons. A person is in the class of persons sometimes but not at all times. The person and the class therefore cannot be equated. They are two different *models* of the same word—barber.

Acknowledgements

The inspiration behind this book lies in the writings of His Divine Grace A.C. Bhaktivedanta Swami Prabhupāda. He spoke about matter and science with as much ease as he did about soul and God. From his work I first came to believe that there is indeed an alternative way of looking at the material world, different from how it is described in modern science. I am deeply indebted to him in more ways than I can express here in a few words.

The book in the current form would have been impossible without the tireless efforts of Ciprian Begu. He has been my friend and partner in bringing this to life. He read through drafts, edited, did the layout and helped with the cover design. He has tried to teach me the nuances of English grammar, although I haven't been a good student. He figured out all the nits on publishing—something that I did not have the time, energy or the inclination for.

I would like to thank my long-time friend Rukesh Patel. His exuberance, encouragement, patient hearing and drive have helped me in innumerable ways. We have laughed so much together—often at our own stupidity and ignorance— that simply thinking of him makes me smile.

I would like to thank Prof. Pinaki Gupta-Bhaya, my professor and supervisor at IIT Kanpur, who showed me the beauty and excitement of science. From him I learnt that it was not important to know everything, as long as you know where to find it. Looking at his breadth and depth, I came to believe it was possible to step out of the parochial boundaries in science.

My immense gratitude also goes to my parents, who taught me honesty, hard work and simplicity. They gave me the values and upbringing for which I am deeply indebted. My heart also reaches out to my daughter, whose affection and kindness inspires me everyday to become a better person. My wife has been the leveling force in my life. She keeps me grounded to reality, distills complex problems into a succinct bottom-line, and manages the relationships that I would not.

And finally a big thank you to all my readers who have, over the years, written (and continue to write) showing a deep sense of excitement about these books. Their encouragement continues to instill confidence in me that there is a need for these types of books.

My Story

I have always had a great curiosity for the inner workings of nature, the mysteries of the human mind and the origins of the universe. This naturally drew me towards pure sciences. My father, a more practical man, saw this interest as pointless; he was upset when I chose a 5-year program in Chemistry at IIT Kanpur rather than one of the engineering programs, which stood to offer me a better career.

When I started at IIT Kanpur, I believed that my long-held curiosities about the inner workings of nature would be satisfied by an understanding of science. But as I scraped through the coursework and scoured through nearly every section of IIT's extensive library looking for answers, I found that, contrary to my belief, many fundamental and important questions in science remained unanswered. That prompted me to turn towards other departments—since chemistry pointed towards physics which in turn pointed towards mathematics, it seemed that the answers lay elsewhere. However, as I sat through courses offered by other departments—mathematics, physics and philosophy—my worst fears began to materialize: I realized that the problems required discarding many fundamental assumptions in science.

That started me on a journey into the search for alternatives, which has now been spanning 20 years. It was not uncommon in India for students in elite institutions to spend a lot of time discussing philosophy, although often in a tongue-in-cheek manner. My intentions were more serious.

I studied Western philosophy—both classical and modern—as well as Eastern ideas (such as Zen and Taoism) before turning towards Vedic philosophy. I was primarily interested in the nature of matter, the mind and the universe and only Vedic philosophy seemed to offer the kind of synthetic detail I was looking for. I suspected that if the

ideas of reincarnation, soul and God in Vedic philosophy were connected to a different view of matter, mind and the universe, then I
might actually find an alternative view that could solve the problems
in modern science.

At the end of my 5 years at IIT Kanpur, I knew I wanted to pursue
the alternative, but I wasn't quite clear how that could work.

I anticipated the pursuit of an alternative in mainstream academia
to be very hard. The development of the alternative would frequently
run into opposition, and would not fit into the publish-and-tenure
practices. A reasonable understanding of ideas often requires longer
discussions which may not fit into 3000-word papers. Alternatives
often require stepping outside the parochial boundaries of a single
field and the journals that accepted such multi-disciplinary articles
did not exist at that time—they are more common now.

I therefore faced a difficult choice—pursue a mainstream academic
career and defer the search for alternatives until I had established a
reputation through conventional means, or pursue a non-academic
career to finance my interest in academic alternatives. I chose to separate academics from profession. It was a risky proposition when I
started, but in hindsight I think it has worked better than I initially
imagined. This and my other books are byproducts of my search for
answers to the problems in science, outside mainstream academia.

My career is that of a computer engineer and I have worked for over
17 years in multi-national corporations on telecommunications, wireless and networking technologies. I have co-authored 10 patents and
presented at many conferences. I live in Bangalore, India, with my wife
and 10-year old daughter.

Connect with Me

Has this book raised your interest? You can connect to my blog or get
involved in discussions on www.ashishdalela.com. For any questions
or comments please e-mail me at adalela@shabdapress.net.

Other Books by Ashish Dalela

Is the Apple Really Red?

10 Essays on Science and Religion

Conventional wisdom on science and religion says the former is based on experiment and reason, while the latter is based on faith and belief. Is the Apple Really Red? discusses how the notions of soul, morality and afterlife in religion can be scientific. But for this to be possible, a new science that studies meanings instead of objects is needed.

The clash of ideologies between science and religion—this book argues—is based on an incorrect understanding of matter, disconnected from consciousness, and an incorrect notion of God, disconnected from matter, space and time.

A revision of the current views on religion and science is needed, not only to settle the conflict but also to deepen our understanding of matter (and its relation to consciousness) and God (and His relation to matter, space and time)

Written for the layperson, in 10 essays, the book delineates the Vedic view of matter, God, soul, morality, space and time. The author shows how the existence of the soul and God implies a new view of matter, space and time which is empirical and can be used to form new scientific theories.

Such theories will not only change our understanding of matter but will also change our outlook on religion. Readers interested in the science and religion debate will benefit significantly from the viewpoint described in Is the Apple Really Red?

Six Causes
The Vedic Theory of Creation

In Vedic philosophy, creation is modeled as the creative activity of consciousness. Six Causes shows us how the universe's creation can be understood based on insights about our own everyday creative activities.

The nature of material objects when they are created by consciousness is different than when they are independent of consciousness. Six Causes discusses this difference. Essentially, objects in the Vedic view are symbols of meaning originating in consciousness rather than meaningless things.

Different aspects of conscious experience—and the different roles they play in the creation—are called the six causes.

Presented in lay person's language, and written for those who don't have any background in Vedic philosophy, this book will allow you to truly understand the intricacies in Vedic texts.

In the process, you will also see many common misconceptions about Vedic philosophy being overturned through a deeper understanding of not just soul, God, reincarnation and karma but also matter, senses, mind, intelligence, ego and the unconscious.

Quantum Meaning
A Semantic Interpretation of Quantum Theory

The problems of indeterminism, uncertainty and statistics in quantum theory are legend and have spawned a wide-variety of interpretations none too satisfactory. The key issue of dissatisfaction is the conflict between the microscopic and macroscopic worlds: How does a classically certain world emerge from a world of uncertainty and probability?

This book presents a Semantic Interpretation of Quantum Theory in which atomic objects are treated as symbols of meaning. The book shows that quantum problems of uncertainty, indeterminism and statistics arise when we try to describe meaningful symbols as objects without meaning.

A symbol is also an object, although an object is not necessarily a symbol. The same object can denote many meanings in different contexts, and if we reduce symbols to objects, it naturally results in incompleteness.

This book argues that the current quantum theory is not a final theory of reality. Rather, the theory can be replaced by a better theory in which objects are treated as symbols, because this approach is free of indeterminism and statistics.

The Semantic Interpretation makes it possible to formulate new laws of nature, which can be empirically confirmed. These laws will predict the order amongst symbols, similar to the notes in a musical composition or words in a book.

Gödel's Mistake
The Role of Meaning in Mathematics

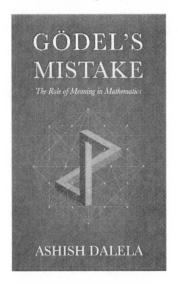

Mathematics is the queen of sciences but problems of incompleteness and incomputability in mathematics have raised serious questions about whether it can indeed be used to describe nature's entire splendor. Proofs that demonstrate the incompleteness and incomputability are respectively called Gödel's Incompleteness and Turing's Halting Problem.

This book connects Gödel's and Turing's theorems to the question of meaning and shows that these proofs rest on what philosophers call category mistakes. Ordinary language contains many categories - such as names, concepts, things, programs, algorithms, problems, etc. but mathematics and computing theory do not. A thing can denote many concepts and vice versa. Similarly, a program can solve many problems, and vice versa. A category mistake arises when we reduce one category to another, and this leads to logical paradoxes because these categories are not mutually reducible.

The book shows that the solution to category mistakes requires a new approach in which numbers are treated as types rather than quantities. This is called Type Number Theory (TNT) in the book. TNT requires a hierarchical theory of space and time, because it is through a hierarchical embedding that objects become symbols of meanings.

Hierarchical notions of space and time are well-known; for instance postal addresses and clock times are hierarchical. A formal theory of hierarchical space-time will also be a theory of symbols and will address problems of incomputability in computing and incompleteness in mathematics.

Signs of Life
A Semantic Critique of Evolutionary Theory

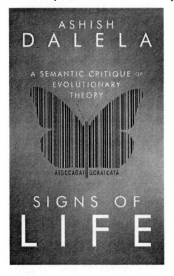

This book challenges the fundamental ideas in the Neo-Darwinian theory of evolution from the perspective of mathematics, physics, computing, game theory, and non-linear dynamics.

It argues that the key ideas underlying evolution—random mutation and natural selection—are based on notions about matter, causality, space-time, and lawfulness, which were supposed true in Darwin's time, but have been unseated through 20th century developments in physics, mathematics, computing, game theory, and complex system theory. Evolution, however, continues in a relative time-warp, disregarding these developments, which, if considered, would alter our view of evolution.

The book illustrates why natural selection and random mutation are logically inconsistent together. Separately, they are incomplete to account for biological complexity. In other words, the theory of evolution is either inconsistent or incomplete.

The book, however, does not deny evolution. It presents a new theory of evolution that is modeled after the evolution of cultures, ideologies, societies, and civilizations. This is called *Semantic Evolution* and the book illustrates how this new model of evolution will emerge from the resolution of fundamental unsolved problems of meaning in mathematics, physics, and computing theory.

Moral Materialism

A Semantic Theory of Ethical Naturalism

Modern science describes the physical effects of material causes, but not the moral consequences of conscious choices. Is nature merely a rational place, or is it also a moral place? The question of morality has always been important for economists, sociologists, political theorists, and lawmakers. However, it has had almost no impact on the understanding of material nature in science.

This book argues that the questions of morality can be connected to natural law in science when science is revised to describe nature as meaningful symbols rather than as meaningless things. The revision, of course, is entailed not just by issues of morality but also due to profound unsolved problems of incompleteness, indeterminism, irreversibility and incomputability in physics, mathematics, and computing theory. This book shows how the two kinds of problems are deeply connected.

The book argues that the lawfulness in nature is different from that presented in current science. Nature comprises not just *things* but also our *theories* about those things. The world of things is determined but the world of theories is not—our theories represent our free will, and the interaction between free will and matter now has a causal consequence in the evolution of scientific theories.

The moral consequences of free will represent the ideological evolution of the observer, and the correct theory represents the freedom from this evolution. Free will is therefore not the choice of arbitrary and false theories; free will is the choice of the correct theory. Once the correct theory is chosen, the observer is free of natural laws, since all phenomena are consistent with the correct theory.

Uncommon Wisdom
Fault Lines in the Foundations of Atheism

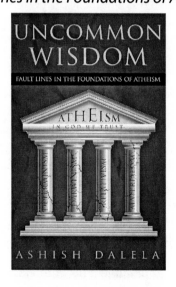

The rise of militant atheism has brought to fore some fundamental issues in our conventional understanding of religion. However, because it offers science as an alternative to religion, militant atheism also exposes to scrutiny the fundamental problems of incompleteness in current science.

The book traces the problem of incompleteness in current science to the problem of universals that began in Greek philosophy and despite many attempts to reduce ideas to matter, the problem remains unsolved. The book shows how the problem of meaning appears over and over in all of modern science, rendering all current fields—physics, mathematics, computing, and biology included—incomplete. The book also presents a solution to this problem describing why nature is not just material objects that we can perceive, but also a hierarchy of abstract ideas that can only be conceived. These hierarchically 'deeper' ideas necessitate deeper forms of perception, even to complete material knowledge.

The book uses this background to critique the foundations of atheism and shows why many of its current ideas—reductionism, materialism, determinism, evolutionism, and relativism—are simply false. It presents a radical understanding of religion, borrowing from Vedic philosophy, in which God is the most primordial idea from which all other ideas are produced through refinement. The key ideological shift necessary for this view of religion is the notion that material objects, too, are ideas. However, that shift does not depend on religion, since its implications can be known scientifically.

The conflict between religion and science, in this view, is based on a flawed understanding of how reason and experiment are used to acquire knowledge. The book describes how reason and experiment can be used in two ways—discovery and verification—and while the nature of truth can never be *discovered* by reason and experiment, it can be *verified* in this way. This results in an epistemology in which truth is discovered via faith, but it is verified by reason and experiment.

Did You Like Sāṅkhya and Science?

If you enjoyed this book or found it insightful I would be grateful if you would post a short review on Amazon. Your feedback will allow other readers to discover the book, and can help me improve the future editions. If you'd like to leave a review then go to the website below, click on the customer reviews and then write your own.

http://www.ashishdalela.com/review-ss

Find Out in Advance When My Next Book Is Out

I'm always working on the next book. Currently, I'm writing *Signs of Life*, which is a semantic critique of evolutionary theory and *Moral Materialism*, a book about the Vedic science of choices and their consequences, both to be released in 2015. You can get a publication alert by signing up to my mailing list on www.ashishdalela.com. Moreover, If you want to receive advance copies of my upcoming books for review, please let me know at adalela@shabdapress.net.

CPSIA information can be obtained
at www.ICGtesting.com
Printed in the USA
LVOW12s0554110716

495771LV00005B/363/P